on track ...

Iggy Pop

1977-1999

every album, every song

Hans Meertens

sonicbondpublishing.com

Sonicbond Publishing Limited
www.sonicbondpublishing.co.uk
Email: info@sonicbondpublishing.co.uk

First Published in the United Kingdom 2026
First Published in the United States 2026

British Library Cataloguing in Publication Data:
A Catalogue record for this book is available from the British Library

ISBN 978-1-78952-446-8

Typeset in ITC Garamond Std & ITC Avant Garde Gothic
Printed and bound in England

Graphic design and typesetting: Full Moon Media

on track ...

Iggy Pop

1977-1999

every album, every song

Hans Meertens

sonicbondpublishing.com

Acknowledgements

This book is an exploration of the art behind the myth, the sound and words beyond the legend. It was born of dedication and passion, written in the hope that it does justice to Iggy Pop and the countless hours of thrill and transcendence he has brought to music fans over the decades.

I would like to thank the outstanding photographers Rob Gander, Bob Gruen, Jilles van Houten, Bruce Jarvis, Paul Natkin and Rob Verhorst for their generous permission, as well as Dorothé Schellekens for kindly allowing me to include images from the archive of Frans Schellekens. My gratitude also goes to Phil Palmer and Eric Schermerhorn for their insights and kindness, to Stephen Lambe for making this book possible through Sonicbond Publishing and to Joyce Vos for her loving support.

I dedicate this book to my daughter, Robin, to whom I passed on my love of music and who, in return, has enriched my life in ways beyond measure.

on track ...

Iggy Pop 1977-1999

Contents

Introduction

Yes, Iggy Pop the stage persona rolled in broken glass, cut himself with knives, carved his chest open with a drumstick, spattered blood on the crowd, smeared peanut butter across his torso and flung it into the pit, leapt headfirst into the masses, goaded spectators to stab him, taunted bikers into brawls, hurled microphones like weapons, took a shit behind the speakers, howled insults at the audience, scaled lighting rigs, let himself be whipped, gifted a fan a watermelon concussion, incited riots, nearly speared his drummer with a mic stand, snorted coke off amplifiers, vomited mid-show, performed butt naked, received fellatio from audience members, got electrocuted, overdosed in real time and was pelted with grapefruit, eggs, beer cans, spit, bras, cigarettes, Quaaludes, fish, stones, light bulbs, a full bottle of vodka and the occasional fist. He walked on the hands of his believers. Unstoppable, reckless. A spectacle no stage could contain.

But Iggy is also the man who posed nude for art classes at 68, practises Qigong for clarity, dines in a smoking jacket and slippers, reads news and classics alike, enjoys C-SPAN and the Discovery Channel, published an essay in a journal of classical scholarship, served as guest lecturer at Midwestern universities, hosted a BBC documentary on William Burroughs and co-produced the Epix docuseries *PUNK*. He recorded Whitman's poetry and Poe's 'The Tell-Tale Heart', delivered the John Peel Lecture, acted in avant-garde films, released a jazz-inspired album influenced by Michel Houellebecq, hosts an eclectic BBC radio show, was named a Commander of the Ordre des Arts et des Lettres, received a Grammy Lifetime Achievement Award, champions animal rights with PETA, adores his plants and shares a quiet life near Miami Beach with his wife Nina and their Instagram-famous cockatoo, Biggy Pop.

He is Dr Jekyll and Mr Hyde, Dionysus and Apollo, reason and chaos, intellect and instinct. Jim Osterberg and Iggy Pop: fused and fractured, forever feeding off each other. Sometimes, the lines blurred. Sometimes, Iggy consumed Jim, hollowed him out, left nothing but a flickering wick. But Iggy also gave him everything: fame, money, immortality. And sometimes, Jim had to seize control, drag Iggy back from the edge before they both went down in flames.

Iggy transcends genre, era and expectation. He has been stolen from, imitated, feared, worshipped, dismissed, resurrected, yet he remains untamed. His fingerprints stain punk, grunge, speed metal and whatever bastard child post-punk spawned. For over half a century, he has been rock 'n' roll's most relentless force: feral yet sharp, raw yet deliberate, a hurricane and an aftershock. Rock 'n' roll doesn't owe Iggy a debt. It inhales his chaos and spits it back out. He has been the rupture, the surge, the blaze. Through every transformation, excess and reinvention, the music remained the pulse of his defiance.

Chaos, Carnage, Collapse: The Story So Far

Iggy Pop didn't just front The Stooges. He was their detonation. A sinewy, bare-chested pharaoh action figure of chaos, unhinged and electrified, leading the filthiest, loudest, wildest rock 'n' roll into the gutter – and changing it forever.

He was born James Newell Osterberg Jr. on 21 April 1947, in Muskegon, Michigan, and raised as an only child in a Ypsilanti trailer park, about 40 miles west of Detroit. His father, James Sr., taught English at Fordson High School in Dearborn; his mother, Louella, worked for Bendix, a manufacturer of car and aeroplane parts. Their world was modest, part of Michigan's industrial sprawl, where factories once built B-24 bombers but now churned out transmissions. Jim had bigger ambitions. He started out banging on pots and pans until his parents crammed a drum kit into the trailer's master bedroom. At Pioneer High in Ann Arbor, he stood out at talent shows with a comedy routine and played in local bands, most notably The Iguanas, sparking a name that stuck: Iggy. After high school, he briefly enrolled at the University of Michigan, then dropped out to head for Chicago, playing gigs, diving into the blues scene and learning from seasoned players.

Back in Ann Arbor, local garage rockers MC5 pushed Iggy's sense of what rock could be, but seeing Jim Morrison live was revelatory; more than performance, it was provocation. He absorbed that energy and would take it even further. After a stint with The Prime Movers, he set his sights on forming his own band. The only ones willing to follow were brothers Ron and Scott Asheton, high school dropouts with no discipline, no father and no real direction except music. In 1967, they formed The Psychedelic Stooges, bringing in friend Dave Alexander on bass. Iggy took the vocals when they debuted on Halloween night at a house party in Ann Arbor. From the start, they pushed boundaries, gaining a reputation for their avant-garde approach. Iggy disrupted the set with unexpected sounds, running a vacuum cleaner and blender through the amps, blurring the line between music and noise. Word spread. Their heavy, feedback-drenched performances and Iggy's unpredictable stage presence quickly drew a small but dedicated local following. By 1968, they trimmed their name to The Stooges and landed a record deal when an Elektra scout, intending to sign The MC5, signed them, too.

At the same time, Iggy's personal life was shifting. He married 19-year-old Wendy Weissberg, to his bandmates' disbelief, but the union was annulled within weeks. More lasting was his son Eric, born in February 1969 from a fling with Paulette Benson. She moved to California with him, and contact remained minimal throughout the early 1970s.

The Stooges' debut, released in 1969 and produced by John Cale, hit like a sonic grenade: distorted riffs, guttural howls and rock stripped to its raw core. It had no interest in peace and love. Bleak, bored, stoned and pissed off, the album stood as a manifesto for the disillusioned. Critics baulked and sales flopped, but something was stirring. Their second album, *Fun House* (1970), sharpened the attack without losing its savagery. Produced by Don Gallucci, it was tighter, nastier and wired with feverish energy. A sweaty, primal scream recorded live in the studio, capturing the band at their most feral, bolstered by Steve Mackay's skronking sax. But heroin loomed. By the time the album was ready for release, they were sinking into addiction. Everyone except Ron Asheton, who watched in frustration as instruments vanished into pawn shops. *Fun House* didn't chart, but onstage, The Stooges were apocalyptic. Iggy was writing the future punk playbook, writhing half-naked in a narcotic haze, transforming rock shows into blood-soaked rituals of excess, violence, sex and danger. Acclaimed in underground circles, awash in cheap heroin, the band collapsed under its own excess. With no sales to justify their chaos, Elektra cut them loose.

With the band in ruins, Iggy met rising star David Bowie in 1971 at Max's Kansas City in New York. The two quickly struck up a friendship, and Bowie secured him a record deal with Columbia. Iggy relocated to London to write and record with James Williamson, The Stooges' second guitarist since 1970. When they failed to find a suitable English rhythm section, they brought back the Asheton brothers, reforming as Iggy And The Stooges. With Bowie at the mixing desk, they unleashed *Raw Power* (1973), a ferocious, metallic snarl of an album: pure high-voltage chainsaw assaults and commercial suicide. By the time it hit the shelves, The Stooges were unravelling, again. Iggy's heroin addiction spiralled. Erratic behaviour and onstage fights turned shows into public meltdowns. By February 1974, it was over. The Stooges imploded.

For Iggy, the aftermath was a waking nightmare. Homeless and strung out, he drifted between New York and LA, a shadow of his former self. Friends found him delirious, volatile, dangerously close to vanishing. By 1975, his self-destruction hit a breaking point. The LAPD gave him a choice: jail or rehab. He opted for UCLA's Neuropsychiatric Institute. Bowie was one of the few who visited, offering support, even bringing a bag of cocaine, more out of habit than help. On weekends, Iggy was allowed out and reunited with Williamson, picking up recording again. The result was *Kill City*, a jagged reflection of his fractured mind and broken body. A record of contradictions, desolate yet defiant, it captured the wreckage of an artist clawing his way out. But Iggy's reputation was in ruins. Labels weren't interested; he was written off as a lost cause.

Bowie refused to let him disappear. He had arranged sessions in LA to jumpstart Iggy's solo career, but Iggy wasn't ready, still erratic and still hooked. Bowie didn't give up. Months later, after being caught shoplifting apples and cheese in Beverly Hills, their mutual dealer bailed Iggy out and passed on the message that Bowie wanted to reconnect. The link was re-established, and Bowie soon invited him as a travel companion on his *Station To Station Tour*. Iggy hesitated. He was proud, wary of being Bowie's pet project. But he had no better option. After four days of thought, he packed his bag and stepped aboard. It was a pivotal moment, a last chance to crawl out of the rubble. The journey gave Iggy structure, a creative spark and a friend who refused to let him go under. Bowie had his own reckoning to face. Drowning in coke, paranoia and the Thin White Duke's occult delusions, he knew LA would kill him if he stayed. As the tour wrapped up in Paris in May 1976, the two men had made a pact: they would not go back; they had to get out. They decided to stay in France. And that's where this story takes off.

The Idiot (1977)

Personnel:
Iggy Pop: vocals
David Bowie: keyboards, synthesiser, guitar, piano, saxophone, backing vocals
Phil Palmer: guitar
Carlos Alomar: guitar
Laurent Thibault: bass
George Murray: bass
Michel Santangeli: drums
Dennis Davis: drums
Recorded at Château d'Hérouville, Hérouville; Musicland, Munich; Hansa Studios, Berlin, between June and August 1976
Producer: David Bowie
Release date: March 1977
Label: RCA
Chart places: US: 72, UK: 30, Aus: 88
Running time: 38:49

In the summer of 1976, Iggy Pop and David Bowie retreated to the 18th-century Château d'Hérouville just outside Paris, a haunted mansion turned recording studio. Its isolated, decadent setting provided the backdrop for an album that predicted the sound of post-punk, when punk had barely put on its pins.

In April, Iggy had celebrated his 29th birthday at Basel railway station, where Bowie gifted him a Polaroid camera to chronicle their European travels. Their journey included a detour to Moscow via Warsaw, during which the KGB detained them at the Polish-Soviet border near Brest and subjected Bowie and Iggy to strip-searches. Among Bowie's belongings were books that included works on Goebbels and Speer, which he explained were research for a film project. Bowie's preoccupation with Germany's past and the Cold War climate foreshadowed a broader fascination – one that would soon pull them both towards Berlin and seep into the music they were about to create. At the afterparty of Bowie's penultimate Paris show, Iggy and Bowie met Kraftwerk's Ralf Hütter and Florian Schneider. Their presence left Iggy transfixed, watching them with unmistakable awe. *Radio-Activity* had been a constant throughout Iggy and Bowie's travels. After Bowie's tour concluded on 18 May, they left Paris for the Château. Initially there for a break, he bonded with the studio's manager and engineer, Laurent Thibault, a former bassist of French progressive rock band Magma. Bowie booked the studio for June and July, setting the stage for what would become *The Idiot*.

Bowie started the recordings with foundational tracks on his Baldwin electric piano. Initially a two-man project, it quickly expanded. He requested a drummer, and Thibault brought in Michel Santangeli, who recorded what he assumed were demos. Unaware that many first takes would remain, he left after the second day, thinking his performance wasn't up to par. While Bowie experimented with a new sound – later teasingly calling Iggy 'a guinea pig' in the 1989 *Sound+Vision* liner notes – Iggy drew on their time on the road for lyrical ideas, often improvising at the microphone. The method fascinated Bowie: 'I thought he was the funniest, darkest lyricist of the time', he told *Seconds* in 1995. Iggy's vocal delivery was instinctive, shifting between detachment and intensity, sometimes pushing the limits of the recording equipment. Bowie layered the tracks with guitar, synthesiser, saxophone and backing vocals, while Thibault handled the bass. The studio buzzed with creative energy, Iggy's handwritten lyrics scattered across the floor. One afternoon, an unexpected muse arrived in the form of Kuelan Nguyen, the Vietnamese girlfriend of French actor and singer Jacques Higelin. 'Higelin was never around, so biff-bam-boom', Iggy told *The Times* in 2023. The couple had been invited to the Château by its owner, and despite language barriers and Nguyen's existing relationship, their brief, intense affair sparked the lyrics to one of the album's standout tracks.

As August approached, the Château was no longer available, and the sessions moved to Giorgio Moroder's Musicland Studios in Munich for additional recordings, including vocals. Working nocturnally beneath the Sheraton Hotel, the atmosphere was both surreal and invigorating. Guitarist Phil Palmer, recommended by Bowie's producer Tony Visconti, was brought in at short notice. He recalled for this book: 'Working on *The Idiot* was a blur. I never saw David or Jimmy in daylight, and their exchanges were often explosive and confusing.' With recording almost complete, Bowie and Iggy travelled to Berlin to finish the record at Hansa Studio 1. Visconti was brought in to salvage the over-modulated tapes in post-production. The disorder of overdubs, some of them by bassist George Murray and drummer Dennis Davis from Bowie's band, and, by some accounts, Château d'Hérouville studio assistant Michel Marie, likely contributed to the missing, sparse or incomplete musician credits on the final album and subsequent rereleases.

In Berlin, Bowie and Iggy settled into a seven-room flat above a car parts shop at Hauptstraße 155 in Schöneberg, a district of low rents, immigrant households and a trace of old bohemia. Iggy, still largely unknown in Europe, could move through the city unnoticed. He explored the neighbourhoods alone on foot or by train, or with German photographer Esther Friedman, whom he had started seeing; their relationship would last seven years. The group became regulars at the Brücke Museum, home to Erich Heckel's *Roquairol*, whose contorted pose – modelled after fellow Brücke artist Ernst Ludwig Kirchner, plagued by addiction and breakdowns – inspired Iggy's angular stance on the muted black-and-white album cover. The same painting would also influence Bowie's posture on *"Heroes"*. Wearing Esther's tight jacket, Iggy was photographed as rain streaked the frame – officially credited to Andrew Kent, though in 2016, Esther reignited the recurring rumour in *Humo* that it was actually Bowie who took the photo and had suggested that Iggy wear her jacket. The album's title, another suggestion by Bowie, directly referenced Dostoevsky's novel, in which the tragic Prince Myshkin becomes ensnared in a web of moral corruption – a subtle jest at Iggy's expense.

The Idiot was completed in August 1976, but its release was strategically delayed. Bowie embarked on recording *Low*, which echoed *The Idiot*'s experimental essence and featured Iggy on backing vocals for 'What In The World', a song first conceived for Iggy's album. To avoid any impression of derivation, *Low* was released first, in January 1977, with *The Idiot* following two months later, to largely positive reviews. While some found it unrepresentative of Iggy's earlier work, most praised its innovation. *Rolling Stone* called it 'a necrophiliac's delight'; *Melody Maker* found it 'disturbingly pertinent'. *Circus* noted that 'Iggy's got the tainted charisma of a dead poet', while *Zigzag* described it as 'strange, morbid, obscure and unsettling'. *The New York Times* simply deemed it 'a powerful record'. The album charted in both the US and UK, reaching number 72 on the *Billboard* album chart and number 30 in the UK – Iggy's first top 40 appearance. *The Idiot* is now recognised as a landmark, shaping post-punk, industrial and gothic rock. Siouxsie Sioux called it proof of Iggy's genius. Its influence runs deep, echoing in the work of Bauhaus, Gary Numan, The Human League, Killing Joke, The Sisters Of Mercy, Depeche Mode, Duran Duran and Nine Inch Nails. Joy Division, too, absorbed its industrial soundscapes. *The Idiot* was famously the last record Ian Curtis played before he hanged himself.

Musically, the album marked a turning point. Though spiky, metallic guitars are present, it is grounded in the avant-garde spirit of German groups like Kraftwerk, CAN, Faust and Neu!. In *NME* in 1977, Iggy described it as 'a cross between James Brown and Kraftwerk', calling it his 'album of freedom'. Its murky, mordant sound and discordant synthesisers conjure a dystopian world where Detroit's industrial churn collides with echoes of Cold War Berlin's decaying grandeur. Lurking in the chemical shadows are nightclub vampires and the spectre of Nazi zombiism. Despite the darkness, flashes of decadent humour pierce the gloom. This is not just Iggy Pop's comeback but his full-scale reincarnation: refined, restrained, yet still deeply unhinged. After years of chaos, the record stands as a stark testament to artistic reinvention – a bleak masterpiece whose shadow remains impossible to shake.

'Sister Midnight' (Pop, Bowie, Alomar)

First step, firm footing. The opener emerged during rehearsals in Jamaica for Bowie's *Station To Station Tour*, sparked by a jam session. Alomar laid down a taut, funk-infused riff; Bowie added some skeletal lyrics and soon slipped the track into his live set. When discussing recording plans, he passed it to Iggy, suggesting he would make it his own. Iggy did just that, injecting it with a Freudian nightmare of Oedipal transgression:

Calling Sister Midnight
You know I had a dream last night
Mother was in my bed
And I made love to her
Father he gunned for me
Hunted me with his six gun
Calling Sister Midnight
What can I do about my dreams?

The version on *The Idiot*, with the album title namechecked in the line 'Well, I'm an idiot for you', blends proto-punk and kraut-funk into an austere, nocturnal soundscape. Davis' drum patterns lock into a bedrock bassline, a drum part Iggy later praised to *Mojo* in 2006: 'Damn, listen to what he's playing, it's a triple-time on the cymbal and a half-time on the 'wack', it's insane!' Alomar's gripping minor-pentatonic riff, possibly overdubbed by Palmer using an earlier take, cycles with hypnotic insistence, winding the tension ever tighter. Iggy's sepulchral performance, coupled with Bowie's falsetto backing, intensifies the narcotic unease, with an incidental studio beep at 1:05 adding a fleeting, robotic quirk to the mix. The lyrics spiral through delusion, submission and dread, casting Sister Midnight as both obsession and fate. Iggy veers from blame ('You've put a beggar in my heart') to desperation: 'Can you hear me at all?', a line that echoes 'Beyond The Law', from *Kill City*. His escalating delivery, paired with the unyielding groove, leaves us caught in psychological limbo.

This ominous, experimental track immediately signals Bowie and Iggy's shift away from The Stooges' anarchic sound towards a brooding, dispassionate style. Bowie later repurposed it as 'Red Money' on *Lodger* (1979), and revived Iggy's version during his 2003 *Reality Tour*, further securing its place in the art rock canon.

'Nightclubbing' (Pop, Bowie)

Enter this nocturnal zombie dance 'like the nuclear bomb'. While working on the final track for *The Idiot*, Iggy and Bowie, both in a playful mood and donning fright masks, stumbled upon a preset on a Roland drum machine. Iggy insisted on keeping it, a rare moment where he steered Bowie's choices. Bowie protested, Iggy recalled in a 2019 SiriusXM interview: 'David said, 'I can't put out something with *that* as a drum track', and I said, 'No, but I can!'' What began as a placeholder became the track's backbone, setting its automated mood for a repetitive two-chord progression over glacial synths. Bowie's sparse piano evokes a Weimar-era cabaret-meets-noir vibe, with a bluesy bar-room swing that drips with ironic decadence. The sloppy guitar functions more as ambient noise than melodic centrepiece, while a deep bass anchors the track with a droning pulse, adding to its sinister undercurrent. Iggy's deadpan tone underscores the song's irony. 'Oh isn't it wild?' mocks the hedonism of nightlife, presenting it as both alluring and empty. 'We walk like a ghost' adds an eerie touch, portraying the cruisers as drugged, detached and dehumanised. There's humour in his laconic manner, turning the nightclub scene into a parody of itself. The Bowie-Pop duo embraced its simplicity and etched a sonic snapshot of their after-hours drift.

Decades later, 'Nightclubbing' experienced a resurgence through its inclusion in the 1996 film *Trainspotting*. By then, it had already been covered by Grace Jones and The Human League, while Trent Reznor famously sampled its drum pattern for Nine Inch Nails' 1994 hit 'Closer'. That same beat also pops up in Oasis' 'Force Of Nature', illustrating the track's enduring influence across genres and generations.

'Funtime' (Pop, Bowie)

First titled 'Fun Fun Fun', 'Funtime' was Iggy's sly response to The Sex Pistols' take on The Stooges' 'No Fun'. It also echoes Sly & The Family Stone's 'Fun', and most clearly channels Neu!'s 'Lila Engel'. Stripped of its warped, industrial sway, it might channel the blueprint of a Stooges stomper, reimagined through Bowie and Iggy's experimental spirit. The song opens with a giggle or sob, quickly giving way to the abrupt 'Fun! Baby, baby, we like your lips'. Bowie provides synthesisers, piano and guitar, adding a touch of Keith Richards' 'Satisfaction' riff, and anchors the party call: 'All aboard for funtime!' He also told Iggy to sing the song 'like Mae West, like a bitch who wants to make money', as quoted in Pegg's *The Complete David Bowie*. With that cue, Iggy delivers the lines with deadpan flair. He shifts between singular and plural perspectives, hinting at the pair's hedonistic escapades during Bowie's tour: 'Last night I was down in the lab/Talkin' to Dracula and his crew'. Iggy projects his signature mix of irony, levity and clinical restraint, charging the piece with both exhilaration and unease.

The track cycles through a four-bar chorus and verse, ruptured in the bridge by a guitar striking a wrong note before quickly resolving, where Iggy utters 'We're having fun'. Harmonised drums pound a suffocating beat, punctuated by treated cymbal strikes, as quavering guitar overdubs, piano and bass thrum together to form a dense soundscape. As it hurtles towards its frenzied finale, Iggy grows increasingly monotonous, like a wind-up corpse clinging to the illusion of fun. His final screams teeter between unbridled excitement and total collapse, heightening the song's demented energy.

Multiple artists have covered 'Funtime', including Boy George, Peter Murphy, R.E.M., The Cars and Blondie, who named their 2002 tour *Camp Funtime* in its honour.

'Baby' (Pop, Bowie)

The most forgettable track on an album full of experimental highs. It has the essentials: layered synths, distorted bass and off-kilter guitars, yet it lacks the alienating pull and intensity that define the album's highlights. In the original press release, Iggy reflected on the spontaneous nature of the sessions:

> When we went into the studio, we didn't have any finished tracks at all. We just strolled in with a lot of themes and feelings we liked. David would work on the music at one time, and I would drift in and out and listen to it. Then, I would come in on my own and put on the vocals. Then, he would hear what I had done, and, of course, that would change the nature of the music. So, the tracks grew from that kind of back and forth.

Recorded early in the sessions, 'Baby' feels more like a testing ground for their collaboration. Bowie's atmospheric touch is present, but it feels tentative rather than transformative. Iggy's Morrison-esque delivery leans into indifference, mirroring the track itself: repetitive, monotonous and missing the sharp wit or insight he otherwise brings. It's just a weary Iggy, seasoned by disillusionment, cautioning his baby that the world deals in slim odds on 'the street of chance' – echoing a phrase from Burroughs' *The Soft Machine*. As a love song, it sways, at least as much as Iggy's jaded, cynical style allows. The track drifts along without much development, never quite finding its footing.

'China Girl' (Bowie, Pop)
One night at Château d'Hérouville, Iggy and Bowie, a few drinks in, stumbled into a room with a toy piano and a child's drum kit. They laid down a groove dubbed 'Borderline', which became a haunting standout, reworked by Bowie into a global hit in 1983. Both versions are meticulously crafted and packed with hooks, but Iggy's original is grittier and tenser.

A killer bassline anchors the foreboding atmosphere, while guitars shift between delicate plucks, galloping rhythms and moody swells. The drums attack with fury, and Bowie's East Asian-tinged toy piano hammers in and out, like an auxiliary gear in a finely crafted engine. At the end, he also punctuates the track with saxophone blasts before Palmer's spiralling guitar line locks into a final, gripping motif. Every element fuels the track's ominous, propulsive power. It's a Bowie trademark: starting with restraint and building to a storm of anguish, here propelled by Iggy's impassioned delivery. His ambiguous lyrics, partly inspired by his brief liaison with Nguyen, seethe with strain. Exploring obsession, power and control, the tension peaks with:

> My little China girl
> You shouldn't mess with me
> I'll ruin everything you are

These words blend tenderness and threat, while Iggy's voice channels their volatile dynamic.

At the time, the Chinese government had begun opening shops in Western capitals to sell robes and Little Red Books, a symbolic soft-power move that struck Iggy as part of a coming cultural shift. 'The line, 'I'll give you television' was about that,' he told *The Times* in 2023.

Then there's the infamous 'Visions of swastikas in my head'. Jarring and provocative, the line stirs anguish and a fractured post-war psyche. It may also nod to the swastika's sacred Hindu origins – echoed in the mention of 'a sacred cow' – and to how the West defiled this Eastern symbol: a grim mirror of how Iggy foresees himself corrupting his China Girl. Above all, it's a tortured monologue, laced with menace and the lingering shadow of destructive ideologies. Whether grappling with internal conflict or reflecting on Western imperialism's subversive influence, the line shifts the song from a brooding love ballad into something far more sinister.

We could go even darker. Neither Bowie nor Iggy ever adhered to Nazi ideology, but both engaged at times with fascist imagery and provocation, inviting chilling readings of the song. Iggy's associative writing, combined with their historically laden interests and surroundings, opens the door to unsettling interpretations. Could the lines 'It's in the white of my eyes' and 'I'll give you eyes of blue' evoke Mengele's grotesque ophthalmic experiments at Auschwitz? Even his vainglorious ambition finds a twisted echo in 'I'll give you a man who wants to rule the world'. Paired with the swastikas and 'plans for everyone', these disturbing undercurrents deepen the song's already complex layers – intended or not. (Notably, Iggy sings 'men who want to rule the world' on the record, but 'a man' in most live versions, while Bowie does the same in his rendition.)

Revealing yet another connotation this song plays on, Nile Rodgers, producer of Bowie's version, suggested in *Le Freak* that it references speedballing: heroin was nicknamed 'China White' and cocaine 'Girl' at the time. He described it as 'a junkie's ode if ever there was one'. This casts a drug-fuelled twist on 'I'm a wreck without my little China girl', not to mention:

And when I get excited
My little China girl says
'Oh Jimmy, just you shut your mouth'
She says, 'sh-sh-shhh'

The track unfolds further, but there's more to explore. Conclusively, 'China Girl' is like a broken-down car: each part may seem ragged, rattling or barely holding on, yet together, they roar with mesmeric force. A dark, cinematic epic: profound, catchy, intimate and unflinchingly brilliant.

'Dum Dum Boys' (Bowie, Pop)

Side two opens with Iggy in a street-corner exchange with himself, slack-jawed hoodlums trading news over finger snaps:

'What happened to Zeke?'
'He's dead on Jones, man.'

'How about Dave?'
'O.D.'d on alcohol.'
'Oh, what's Rock doing?'
'Oh, he's living with his mother.'
'What about James?'
'He's gone straight.'

This roll call isn't just a status update; it is a eulogy for The Stooges' disintegration. Zeke Zettner, a former roadie turned short-term bassist, died of a heroin overdose in 1973. Original bassist Dave Alexander succumbed to pneumonia in 1975 after alcohol-induced pancreatitis. Drummer Scott 'Rock Action' Asheton ended up back in Ann Arbor, while guitarist 'Straight James' Williamson managed to clean up. Their former frontman opens the song acknowledging the void left by the band's collapse: 'Well, things have been tough/Without the Dum Dum Boys/I can't seem to speak the language'. Cut off from his outsider tribe and their instinctive, uncompromising chemistry, he feels disconnected, adrift in a world that never understood them. He recalls the boys breaking down, and the criticism: 'People said we were negative/They said we would take but we would never give', another line lifted almost verbatim from 'Beyond The Law', on *Kill City*. A dubious charge, given the unfiltered ferocity they poured into every performance. As Iggy's delivery intensifies, 'Hey, where are you now when I need your noise?' is wrenched from deep inside, the stretched-out 'neeeed' turning it into one of the album's most thrilling vocal moments. With the Dum Dum Boys gone, he faces the walls closing in. The noise was more than loud rock 'n' roll: it was identity, grounding, purpose. A lifeline ready to snap. 'Da, da, da, da, da/Dum dum day' is a sonic echo of their shared past, hummed through the graveyard of their history.

The heaving riff that defines the song was originally laid down by Bowie. As Iggy recalled in 1997, as quoted in Pegg's *The Complete David Bowie*:

> I only had a few notes on the piano and couldn't quite finish the tune. Bowie said: 'Don't you think we could make a song with that? Why don't you tell the story of The Stooges?' He gave me the concept of the song and he also gave me the title. Then, he added that guitar arpeggio that metal groups love today.

Listening back to his tentative playing, Bowie wasn't satisfied and called up Palmer, Ray Davies' nephew, to overdub the riff with added licks and hammer-ons. As a result, its unvarnished rock feel is drenched in distorted guitars, fittingly for a track about The Stooges. The bass lolls beneath them, sliding down in three-note patterns with occasional flurries, mostly leaving space at the end of measures for the drums' rumbling transition fills. Beyond the title – originally 'Dum Dum Days', a nod to dumdum bullets, designed to expand on impact – Bowie adds guitar, synth textures, treated electric piano and his distinctive backing vocals, soaring over 'Dum dum day'. 'There was a power to the music he was willing to provide for me', Iggy reflected in *Mojo* in 2012. 'It was perfect, and I loved it.'

'Tiny Girls' (Bowie, Pop)

The melancholy of a French chanson and the decadent haze of a Berlin nightclub, with vocals by an American proto-punk and saxophone from a British eclecticist, draped in a 1950s doo-wop sway. This border-blurring song drifts in like the first light of dawn after a night gone wrong, lingering in Bowie's husky sax solo. Slipped between the album's two longest tracks, this understated gem is often overlooked, perhaps because it does not share the sonic experimentation that defines much of the record. It's a fine example of how the Bowie-Pop collaboration produced songs neither could have written alone. Iggy had never attempted anything like this lilting ballad, while Bowie would hardly have penned such blunt lyrics about 'tiny' girls.

Iggy's opening lines reflect the album's catatonia: 'Well the day begins, you don't want to live/'Cause you can't believe in the one you're with'. His voice, though, sounds clearer than elsewhere; the undead crooner seems slightly more alive as he fixes his gaze on callow girls, a theme that is only just getting started. The 'tiny girls' appear as archetypes: symbols of purity, free from hidden motives, with no tricks and no past. But it's an illusion he clings to, only to meet the same hollow disappointment. The final, sneering 'Ah what did you think?' is pure self-reproach, exasperation at his own gullibility. Yet he knows he'll try again. The saxophone cries to the end, echoing Iggy's disillusionment, though perhaps it weeps for the pitiful man himself.

'Mass Production' (Bowie, Pop)

The final track to be completed makes a strong case as one of the most unnerving album closers in rock history. Its industrial repetition and disconnection didn't just foreshadow the future; it helped to shape it, becoming a blueprint for post-punk and industrial music in the decades to come.

Frustrated in his search for the right sound, Bowie seized on a tape loop of industrial noise from Thibault. In *Muziq* in 2020, Thibault recalled Bowie was 'like a child transfixed by a train set', watching the tape spool and listening to its drone. Spliced into sections, it became the song's ominous backdrop. Its oppressive atmosphere mirrors Iggy's lyrics, partly inspired by a third-grade field trip to Ford's River Rouge plant in Dearborn, Michigan: 'It was the sound it made. That had a big effect on me', he told *GQ* in 2011. 'These giant metallic castles, these castles of hell.' Iggy described to Bowie the decaying beauty of American steelbones culture: towering smokestacks, rusting factories, entire cities once built on production, now crumbling into industrial relics. In a 2016 interview with *The New York Times*, Iggy recalled how Bowie had shaped the album's lyrical direction: 'He subsumed my personality, lyrically, on that first album,' adding, 'It was like having Professor Higgins say: 'Young man, please, you are from the Detroit area. I think you should write a song about mass production."

The result is no heroic vision of blue-collar diligence. It is a manic-depressive soundscape shaped by monolithic forces that pulse like ravenous gods demanding sacrifice. Iggy delivers a grim portrait of human connection distorted by cold machinery, echoing the brutal dehumanisation of *Metropolis*. He starts in a drained monotone, then shifts into the voice of a torch singer on the brink, as if the words rise from a post-coital void:

Before you go
Do me a favour
Give me a number
Of a girl almost like you
With legs almost like you
I'm buried deep in mass production
You're not nothing new

The lines land with a dull thud. Everything is interchangeable; lust collapses into hollow ritual, stripped of meaning by endless sameness. Death seems the only escape, but even that autonomy is denied. Iggy's identity fractures under the weight, splintering like a fabricated part. Then, with a casual masterstroke, he snaps back to the surface: 'Oh by the way/I'm going for cigarettes'. The mundane remark slices through the haze with a shrug of resignation: back to the cogwheel. The girl about to leave is just another product in the assembly line of intimacy, while he, too, has been reduced to an ambiguous copy: 'And I'm almost like him'.

The manufactured nightmare drags itself forward through a synth-doubled guitar riff, locked in a cycle that refuses to evolve. Occasional shifts, marked by an opening chord change and brief guitar arpeggios, feel like fleeting glimpses of daylight before the nihilistic pull grinds everything back into itself. Bowie's freakfest of warped synths grates through like a malfunctioning engine. Their off-kilter screeches fray the edges, escalating the tension, turning routine into a parody of progress. As the song winds down, it collapses into the same lifeless gloom where it began. Foghorns wail like factory ghosts, blasting from spewing smokestack spires on the outskirts of town.

Lust For Life (1977)

Personnel:
Iggy Pop: vocals
David Bowie: keyboards, piano, organ, backing vocals
Carlos Alomar: guitar
Ricky Gardiner: guitar
Tony Sales: bass, backing vocals
Hunt Sales: drums, backing vocals
Recorded at Hansa Studios, Berlin, between May and June 1977
Producers: David Bowie, Iggy Pop, Colin Thurston
Release date: September 1977
Label: RCA
Chart places: US: 120, UK: 28
Running time: 41:53

In early 1977, the former UFA studios in Berlin, once the nerve centre of Goebbels' propaganda empire, sat largely abandoned: cavernous and crumbling, with peeling walls and rusting cabinets still stuffed with Nazi paperwork. A grim proving ground for Iggy's first real test as a solo act, rehearsing for *The Idiot Tour.*

He and Bowie had assembled a tight, no-frills band: Scottish guitarist Ricky Gardiner, fresh from *Low*, and a powerful rhythm section of Tony and Hunt Sales, sons of Soupy Sales, one of Iggy's childhood comedy heroes. Their father's rule of keeping fan letters under 25 words was a lesson in brevity that stuck with Iggy and often found its way into his songwriting. The Sales brothers had played on two tracks from *Kill City* before reuniting with Iggy here. In the late 1980s, they would join Tin Machine with the most unexpected member of Iggy's new lineup: Bowie himself. He would be the biggest name on stage but planned to stay in the background, keeping the focus on Iggy and limiting himself to keys. It was a deliberate gesture of support: the tour they were about to go on wasn't just about the music, but about giving Iggy the momentum to expand his reach.

After 29 shows across Europe and North America in March and April, the band returned to Berlin, fired up to make another Iggy Pop album just as the first was hitting record stores. Following the success of *The Idiot*, RCA had handed Iggy an advance for the follow-up. He put his share into fixing up his newly rented apartment: a cramped fourth-floor flat at the back of Bowie's building. For 170 DM a month, he got three tiny rooms linked by a narrow hallway: a kitchen, a bedroom and a space that barely passed for a living room. Cold water, a coal stove and a kitchen floor buried under decades of linoleum. And there, in that Spartan hideout, running on beer, hash, wine and wurst, he sketched out ideas for *Lust For Life*.

With some new songs already road-tested, Iggy was ready to bottle that energy with his well-oiled band. The impact of *The Idiot* and the tour had brought him more fame and money than he had ever seen with The Stooges. But in interviews, Bowie's name started overshadowing his own. Their next collaboration had to be on his terms: the music had to be harder, trashier, faster. Determined to outrun Bowie's notorious recording speed and controlling vision, Iggy immersed himself in every detail, taking the tapes back to his apartment and working at a feverish pace, charged with intent – and whatever fuelled his intensity.

Sessions moved fast in June at Hansa Studio by the Wall. The album was cut and finished in two weeks with the touring band plus guitarist Alomar, whom Bowie had brought in as musical director. Iggy had prepared only fragments of lyrics and essentially improvised at the microphone, with most vocals captured in a single take. Bowie himself had scaled back his role from *The Idiot*, sticking to keyboards, as he had on stage. Yet, besides co-producing, he remained the main composer, writing or co-writing seven of the nine songs and adding his unmistakable backing vocals. The black-and-white cover photo was once again shot by Kent. Taken in Iggy's dressing room during the UK tour, it captures him buzzing with energy, a stark contrast to *The Idiot*'s hollow-eyed degenerate. Here, Iggy is sharp, grinning, exuding life. It mirrors *Lust For Life*'s brighter tone, though you have to wonder who feels more unnerving in the dark: the 'idiot' or this hypercharged self-help messiah.

Only six months after *The Idiot*, its successor was released on 9 September 1977. But it took a major hit almost immediately: RCA's biggest act, Elvis Presley, had died three weeks earlier, and the label was now fully focused on reissuing his catalogue. Although RCA had pressed decent quantities of Iggy's album, once the first pressings sold out, stores were soon empty as pressing plants worked overtime in the wake of Elvis' death. Despite little promotion and limited availability, *Lust For Life* reached number 120 on *Billboard* and peaked at number 28 in the UK, where it remained Iggy's highest-charting release until 2016's *Post Pop Depression*. Though some critics overlooked it, those who did respond were largely positive. *Rolling Stone* judged that 'purely on its own terms, *Lust For Life* is a successful album', while *The Village Voice* called it more consistent than Iggy's work with the Stooges. *Sounds* praised the band's performance and Iggy's 'jagged but powerful' vocals, and *NME* ranked it the eighth best album of the year.

The Idiot is still too often dismissed as a Bowie album with Iggy as a guest. This is understandable given Bowie's dominant role, but an oversimplification: that record wouldn't have been the same without Iggy's musical ideas, his lyrical bite and his freewheeling spirit. With *Lust For Life*, the balance shifted, yet neither album would have taken form as it did without Bowie and Iggy's competitive mutual influence. The two records belong together like night and day: opposites in tone, yet inseparable, best heard as a pair to fully grasp the high-voltage creativity that shaped them. Recorded in Hansa's technologically advanced lower Studio 3, its 'Berlin sound' is massive. Most monstrous of all: the title track's hammering drumbeat, set up in the main room and captured with an array of microphones for maximum impact. Iggy's voice, run through a guitar amplifier, carries a ragged edge with a gritty bite, while the songs themselves spew timeless, exuberant, infectious rock 'n' roll. *Lust For Life* gained lasting recognition in later years: ranked 21st in *Sounds'* 1986 list of the 100 Greatest Albums of All Time, and 44th in *Mojo*'s 1995 equivalent. In 2004, *Pitchfork* placed it 64th among the best albums of the 1970s, and in 2013, *NME* included it in their 500 Greatest Albums of All Time.

By the summer of 1977, with two strong records to his name, a successful tour behind him and a heroin habit under control, Iggy seemed to be in a solid place. If a relapse loomed, Bowie, his assistant and Esther kept constant watch, like trusted sentries. At the time, he had high hopes for his new release, but soon found himself stalled by RCA's half-hearted promotion and botched restock. It fizzled out fast. Having tasted success, he suddenly decided the album wasn't up to scratch – at least, according to himself. After more than a year of near-constant collaboration, the partnership with Bowie had loosened for now. Iggy was growing weary of seeing his success credited to Bowie, while Bowie had moved on, gearing up for his *"Heroes"* promo run, with a world tour six months down the line. Meanwhile, Iggy – now with real money in his pocket for the first time – was burning through it just as fast, pouring it into booze and cocaine. Less than a week after the album's release, he was already back on the road to support it. The tension between him and RCA led to an easy way out: the label handed him at least $75,000 to wrap up his contract with a live album. Like giving a pyromaniac a match.

'Lust For Life' (Bowie, Pop)

This is the monster. The spine of the myth. In a recording career spanning more than half a century, this is *the* quintessential Iggy Pop song. Decades from now, it will still be the one playing when his name comes up.

It was born in Bowie's Schöneberg apartment, as the Bowie-Pop duo waited for their weekly dose of *Starsky & Hutch*. Bowie picked up his son's ukulele and began strumming along to the Armed Forces Network's interval signal. That peculiar Morse code riff became the song's backbone. With Bowie's quick suggestion to name it 'Lust For Life', the blueprint was set.

Drummer Hunt Sales lays down a groove that fuses the swagger of *George Of The Jungle,* the rhythm of Motown staples 'You Can't Hurry Love' and 'I'm Ready For Love', and a flicker of The Doors' 'Touch Me'. It's a Teutonic, militaristic onslaught that doesn't just grab you but clobbers you with unstoppable force. Tony Sales' rumbling bassline locks in, shadowing the beat with a push-and-pull energy. Alomar and Gardiner's layered guitars provide rollicking riffs and subtle interplay, while Bowie's R&B-inflected piano injects staccato shots of adrenaline. The result is invigorating and relentless, its celebratory vitality ironically contrasting with the song's self-destructive themes. When Iggy finally enters, he bursts onto the track brimming with attitude, casting himself as Johnny Yen, immersed in a world of excess:

Here comes Johnny Yen again
With the liquor and drugs
And the flesh machine
He's gonna do another striptease

Many of Iggy's lyrics were improvised on the spot, blending personal turmoil with absurdities like 'hypnotizing chickens' and 'flesh machine', drawn from Burroughs' *The Ticket That Exploded*. Johnny Yen, too, is lifted from Burroughs' twisted world, an ambisexual hustler who embodies untamed hedonism. The admission 'Of course I've had it in the ear before' is both surreal and ambiguous, nodding to a scene where Yen is tortured with a scalpel. 'That's a common expression in the Midwest', Iggy told *Rolling Stone* in 2011. 'To give it to him right in the ear means to fuck somebody over.' The defiant 'I'm worth a million in prizes' boldly affirms Johnny's worth, despite – or because of – his torment and self-abuse. There's dry irony in the fact that his anarchic, exuberant lust for life is funded by a government loan. Yet, beneath the bravado, Johnny Yen, battered by rock 'n' roll, longs for escape. 'I'm through with sleeping on the sidewalk' and 'No more beatin' my brains' lay bare his yearning to break free from the endless cycle of self-destruction. With its ferocious drive, absurd imagery and visceral punch, 'Lust For Life' remains an immortal anthem: bloodied, brilliant and forever Iggy's signature song.

The song's title originated with Irving Stone's 1934 novel about Vincent van Gogh, later adapted into a Vincente Minnelli film, linking the song to another poor bastard who's had it in the ear. Its inclusion in the iconic opening of *Trainspotting* has frequently been praised by critics as one of the most striking uses of music in film, and *Rolling Stone* ranks it among their 500 Greatest Songs of All Time. Over the years, the distinctive drumbeat has been borrowed, adapted and reimagined by countless bands. The influence of 'Lust For Life' stretches far beyond music, appearing in films, TV series, video games and advertisements, with numerous cover versions solidifying its legacy. Not bad for a track about liquor, drugs, flesh machines and stripteases. And chickens.

'Sixteen' (Pop)

The album's only track solely credited to Iggy offers an undressed glimpse into his songwriting. Hunt Sales spoke on Produce Like A Pro in 2022 about the album sessions: 'That record came together really fast. I worked my ass off, we're talking ten hours a day or more. Everything was written on the spot. Iggy had a couple of ideas, and he'd go, 'Yeah, that chord!" That relentless pace bled straight into the music. Built on a loose B minor progression with grimy guitars and a stripped-down arrangement, 'Sixteen' is simple yet strikingly effective. Hunt slams a cowbell into the mix, anchoring the groove and amplifying the track's ragged texture, while slashed riffs add sharp stings. Iggy's anguished vocals are funnelled through a guitar amplifier outside the control room, adding another layer of distortion. The lyrics tread unsettling territory, centring on a 16-year-old girl in a 'funky bar', reflecting a recurring and controversial theme in Iggy's work. 'And they don't need me' and 'Everywhere I go, I'm lonely' reflect the song's rough-hewn mix of longing and isolation, while the fixation on her 'leather boots' exposes the misfit's predatory yearning. At least 'Now baby I know/That's not normal' acknowledges a shred of self-awareness amid the obsession.

'Some Weird Sin' (Bowie, Pop)
A carryover from *The Idiot Tour*, this muddled rogue shifts quickly into high gear, radiating lean, propulsive energy cloaked in a ramshackle glam rock guise. After a surprisingly cheery guitar line, the sombre shadow of Johnny Yen emerges, embodying rejection and alienation: 'I never got my license to live/They won't give it up' – an echo of Iggy's tangle with the *Ausländerbehörde* while trying to secure a West Berlin residence permit. Where the title track revels in chaos and hedonism, debauchery here becomes a coping mechanism, 'just to relax with', against the crushing monotony of 'things getting too straight'. Teetering on society's margins, 'With my head on the ledge/That's what you get out on the edge', he feels both shut out of conventional life and repelled by it. This tension, a desire to belong clashing with disdain for conformity, drives him to indulge in 'Some dumb weird sin/ For a while anyway'. As Sales pummels the cymbals in the outro, the track becomes both a cry for escape and a lament for its cost.

'The Passenger' (Gardiner, Pop)
Over one of the era's most recognisable guitar riffs and a mesmeric pulse, Iggy takes us on a nocturnal journey through the city's underbelly. A snare reinforced with tambourine accents, crashing cymbals and low-slung bass lock into a driving, bare-bones cadence, fuelling Gardiner's taut, lilting guitar riff. The looping, clipped progression churns like endless train tracks, hypnotic and unyielding, propelling the song's unstoppable momentum. When Iggy first heard it, he caught the riff on his mono cassette recorder and scrawled down lyrics on the spot, drawing from Antonioni's 1975 film, S-Bahn rides with Esther and shotgun trips in Bowie's car – unlicensed as he was. He also found inspiration in Jim Morrison's *The Lords And The New Creatures*, which reads:

> Modern life is a journey by car. The Passengers change terribly in their reeking seats, or roam from car to car, subject to unceasing transformation. Inevitable progress is made toward the beginning (there is no difference in terminals), as we slice through cities, whose ripped backsides present a moving picture of windows, signs, streets, buildings.

The recording came together swiftly: Gardiner's reggae-tinged part on his '68 Strat, along with bass and drums, was cut live, with Iggy's vocal, the backing harmonies and Alomar's Alembic overdubs added soon after. With no middle eight and a single progression throughout, the song risks feeling overlong, but Iggy's escalating delivery drives it towards a fervent climax, as the communal 'lalala' choruses evoke a feeling that's both euphoric and indifferent. Trapped 'under glass', Iggy gazes out with a mix of alienation and wonder, where bright stars and 'the winding ocean drive' feel distant yet strangely intimate. 'Over the city's ripped backsides', the world unfolds as a jagged spectacle. He's drawing beauty from decay, claiming the theatre of life as his own: 'So, let's take a ride and see what's mine!' His shift in perspective – from 'I' to 'we' to 'he' – is an intriguing touch. The 'we' hints at another passenger, perhaps Esther, Bowie, or Jim Osterberg, hitching a ride with Iggy Pop. The lens then pulls back to 'he', as if Iggy steps outside himself, blurring the line between observer and participant.

Never an A-side single until 1998, this standout became one of Iggy's defining songs and a live staple. On Stoogesforum in 2010, Gardiner described it as 'the junction of classical harmonic structure with 20th-century urban imagery', adding that it 'forms a bridge between Europe and America.' Covered by artists from Michael Hutchence and Alison Mosshart to the unlikely David Hasselhoff, it has appeared in a wide range of films, games and advertisements, including a haunting 2024 version featuring Siouxsie Sioux arranged with strings. 'The Passenger' captures the universal pull of movement, alienation and ethereal thrill. Mean and magnificent, it leaves Iggy prowling the neon-lit Straßen of 1977 Berlin, lost in motion, untethered in time.

'Tonight' (Bowie, Pop)

Road-tested during *The Idiot Tour*, this haunting junkie lament plays like a funeral dirge for a love claimed by heroin. The desperate sung-spoken intro, laid over Bowie and the Sales brothers' wailing choir, sets a tragic scene:

I saw my baby
She was turning blue
I knew that soon, her
Young life was through
So I got down on my knees
Down by her bed
And these are the words
To her I said

Then, the song kicks in with Iggy's simple, moving line comforting his dying lover: 'Everything will be alright tonight'. The words, though, echo as much for himself, with the next fix already in mind. The promise to 'love her 'til the end' becomes bitterly ironic, as her death turns 'tonight' into both a vow and a farewell, transforming the track into an unexpected break-up song. The music, with its sweeping cinematic quality and subtly uplifting tone, contrasts with the surrounding gloom. Funky guitar licks and hovering synths lend the song an ethereal feel as Iggy's resigned baritone blends with Bowie's harmonies. In the chorus, the vocal line gracefully descends, making it *Lust For Life*'s most compelling melody, with a line that subtly echoes a phrase from Burroughs' *Naked Lunch*. Bowie's 1984 remake, featuring Tina Turner, reimagines this elegy as reggae-flavoured light fare, stripping away the original's opening and emotional depth. Devastating yet beautiful, Iggy's version remains peerless.

After Bowie's death in 2016, Iggy told *The New York Times*: 'The friendship was basically that this guy salvaged me from certain professional and maybe personal annihilation – simple as that.' That same year, at the Tibet House Benefit, he paid tribute to his fallen friend with a performance of 'Tonight'. He described it as 'a wonderful, elegant song with a deceptively simple lyric.'

'Success' (Bowie, Gardiner, Pop)

Instead of promoting obvious hits like 'Lust For Life' or 'The Passenger', RCA chose to push the album's quirkiest track. Unsurprisingly, it never charted. Closing side one, the song is a goofy, hand-clapping anthem, with Iggy and the band belting out lines like 'I'm gonna do the twist/I'm gonna hop like a frog'. Not exactly hit material. It's an offbeat invocation of success, slipping into a playful bit of autobiography with 'Here comes my Chinese rug'. Iggy wasn't just name-dropping; he actually invested some of *The Idiot*'s album and tour earnings in Chinese rugs, reasoning they would hold their value. That gamble paid off quicker than expected, a year later, when he found himself strapped for cash just before his move to Arista and the release of *New Values* in 1979. 'I hocked my Chinese rugs to stay alive when I lived like a pauper in Berlin', he told WHFS in 1980.

Originally written by Bowie, the track started with a different vision, but Iggy rejected Bowie's initial arrangement and melody. He stripped it down: fewer chords, no verses, just looping refrains and two punchy guitar solos. Again, many of his lyrics were improvised, and the Sales brothers delivered their backing vocals in one spontaneous take, hilariously echoing Iggy's off-the-cuff lines. Looking back, 'Success' still hits as a big, irreverent slab of rock 'n' roll, stomping and strutting in absurdity. But there's an edge of irony, considering the commercially rocky years Iggy was about to face.

'Turn Blue' (Bowie, Peace, Pop, Lacey)

An example of live vamps that defy studio capture, this nearly seven-minute soul confessional, reimagined as an unhinged junkie's cabaret spectacle, stands as the album's longest and most divisive track. A revived relic from Iggy and Bowie's abortive 1975 LA sessions, written at the peak of Iggy's heroin addiction. The track trudges through a stop-start structure, with arpeggiated guitar, synths and organ swells rolling out a carpet for Iggy to sprawl on. His loose, meandering delivery veers between despair and absurdity ('Jesus? This is Iggy'), while the repetition of 'stepping on our hearts' deepens the song's anguish. Oppression and helplessness seep through, whether from society, personal demons or drug-induced paranoia. Among the utterances, including his repeated cries for mamma, the lines 'What color will the lights be?/Will they turn blue on me?' and 'I didn't mean to, but I did it/I shot myself up' are laced with the spectre of an overdose. Wrestling with guilt, self-destruction and fetishisation, ambiguous lyrics like 'How come the blacks copy you so good?/They get off on you so sexually' sit uneasily in the mix. At 4:34, the track shifts into double time, building to a crescendo that feels more exhausting than cathartic. Though Iggy sought more control on this album, the song's slow-building intensity drags, never quite landing as either brooding rock or soul ballad. Played live during *The Idiot Tour*, its theatrical passion could be gripping, but here it stumbles with fragmented indulgence. And then there's the feral screech Iggy rips out, not once but twice – the kind of yowl that makes you check if your own cat's still breathing.

'Neighborhood Threat' (Bowie, Gardiner, Pop)
This garage-rocker is a welcome jolt after the weariness of the two preceding tracks, ripping like a rambling bar band spilling venom in an overcrowded Kreuzberg beer hall. The lyrics sketch a raw portrait of exclusion, centring on a figure pushed to society's margins. The neighbourhood doesn't just look down on him – it looks *past* him. He's ignored, scrutinised and judged: 'Did you see his crazy eyes?' The song exposes privilege's arrogance: 'You're so surprised he doesn't run to catch your ash/Everybody always wants to kiss your trash'. But as the outcast realises 'there's nothing to get', scorn gives way to fear: 'Will you still place your bet against the neighborhood threat?' Is he truly powerless, or is he a ticking time bomb? Its dirty, snarling guitars, overdriven vocal, spectral backing and dark piano chords create a vigorous ride, while rumbling low toms lend an ominous edge. Still, the mix feels muddy and chaotic, crying out for tighter compression and more balanced stereo panning. There is a sharper, more focused song buried here, something Bowie must have sensed, given his later cover on *Tonight*. A shame he could not quite carve it out either.

'Fall In Love With Me' (Pop, Bowie, Sales, Sales)
The album-closing extended jam finds the band swapping roles in a freewheeling, improvised session. Gardiner moved to drums, Hunt traded his kit for bass, his brother picked up guitar and Alomar handled lead. Bowie added his signature descending organ lines, while Iggy did what he does best: riffing on the mic. The result is a smoky, evocative sketch of longing and

fleeting connection against the backdrop of Berlin nightlife. Mentions of 'white wine', 'a table made of wood' and 'this old saloon' pull us into its palpable, cinematic setting. They form a triadic evocation, where recurring sensory elements not only strengthen the imagery but make it feel inevitable. 'I do think it's about us', Esther told *Humo* in 2016. 'There are references to little things I had bought: boots and a plastic raincoat.'

Riding on a stomping four-to-the-floor groove, choppy guitars, bounding organ and Iggy's clipped vocal delivery, the track exudes a playful, rambling charm. Iggy's lyrics are sparse yet vivid, evoking a wistful yearning: 'And when you're tumbling down/You just look better'. As a closer, 'Fall In Love With Me' mirrors the spontaneity of the Berlin era, its off-the-cuff charm tying the album together. If 'Sister Midnight' opened this chapter with haunting intrigue, the finale bids it farewell with a buoyant, bittersweet plea.

TV Eye 1977 Live (1978)

Personnel:
Iggy Pop: vocals
David Bowie: piano and synthesisers on 'TV Eye', 'Funtime', 'Dirt', 'I Wanna Be Your Dog'
Ricky Gardiner: guitar on 'TV Eye', 'Funtime', 'Dirt', 'I Wanna Be Your Dog'
Stacy Heydon: guitar on 'Sixteen', 'I Got A Right', 'Lust For Life', 'Nightclubbing'
Scott Thurston: guitar, piano, harmonica, synthesiser on 'Sixteen', 'I Got A Right', 'Lust For Life', 'Nightclubbing'
Tony Sales: bass
Hunt Sales: drums
Recorded at The Agora, Cleveland, Ohio, on 21 and 22 March 1977; The Aragon, Chicago, Illinois, on 28 March 1977 (according to album credits); The Uptown Theater, Kansas City, Missouri, on 26 October 1977
Producers: Iggy Pop, David Bowie
Release date: May 1978
Label: RCA
Chart places: US: did not chart, UK: did not chart, Aus: 89
Running time: 36:01

The Idiot Tour took Iggy, Bowie, Gardiner and the Sales brothers to six UK dates, three in Canada and 20 across the US, in a run stretching from early March to mid-April 1977. Bowie's presence remained a rumour until the night before the tour opened. From then on, the audience would surge to the right side of the stage, where he would take his place behind his keyboards, smoking Gitanes. At his request, he stayed in the shadows. This was Iggy's show. Now with black hair, a stark contrast to the blonde crop from *The Idiot* sessions, he emerged bare-chested, twisting his body like a jungle cat: fluid, tense, unpredictable. Not as manic as in his Stooges days, but still a live wire. The set leaned heavily on Stooges material, with Gardiner tasked with summoning the band's fury from his guitar. The UK dates were well received, reinforcing Iggy's reputation as a dangerous, exhilarating performer. This was no comeback; it was a rearmament.

After he arrived in Canada, Iggy sat down for an interview on CBC's *90 Minutes Live*. When host Peter Gzowski asked about the rise of punk rock, Iggy didn't hold back. 'Well, I'll tell you about punk rock', he said coolly. 'Punk rock is a word used by dilettantes and heartless manipulators.' He had no problem with the bands themselves, but the term, he argued, was rooted in 'contempt', 'elitism' and 'satanism'. He made it clear he wasn't interested in being boxed in. His performance in Toronto carried that same defiant spirit. *The Globe And Mail* described it as 'relatively bloodless', observing that 'Iggy shouted, growled, screamed and threw his body at solid objects within staggering distance.'

Next came the US leg of the tour, where he performed solo in his hometown of Detroit for the first time. During this stretch, he reconnected with his son and arranged for his enrolment in a private boarding school. With two gigs left, Iggy and Bowie landed in an unlikely setting: *The Dinah! Show*, a haven of daytime TV wholesomeness. Dinah, elegant and Southern, looked baffled by Iggy's reputation. The man who once turned stages into bloody battlefields had somehow ended up on her couch. With motherly concern, she asked about his history of self-harm. He answered with disarming honesty: 'I've had treatment for that sort of thing.'

Following the release of *Lust For Life*, Iggy hit the road again in September. The 40-date tour kicked off in Germany and ended in the US before the year was out. Early on, his now legendary *TopPop* appearance on Dutch TV ended in chaos: wrecking the set, trashing a studio plant and racking up 2,000 guilders in damages. According to *Oor* magazine, after the shoot, he walked up to the floor manager and said politely, 'Thank you very much, sir.' Fans who had seen him controlled and focused on *The Idiot Tour* six months earlier now witnessed a different Iggy: wilder, more unhinged, thrashing through every night. For this new run of shows, Bowie and Gardiner had stepped aside, making way for Scott Thurston on keys, guitar and harmonica. A member of the final Stooges lineup, Thurston had also contributed to *Kill City* in 1975. On guitar, he was joined by Stacy Heydon, who had played with Bowie on the *Station To Station Tour,* where he and Iggy first met. In a 2017 article on The Fat Angel Sings, Heydon was quoted on the *Lust For Life Tour*:

> Jimmy was and is quite the entertainer. On countless occasions, he would be sharing his extensive knowledge on things like French Impressionists, psychology, various political systems, specific museum pieces and the like. Two steps later, as soon as we'd taken the stage, all bets were off. Being on tour with Mr Osterberg was not for the faint of heart, but it did open my eyes to the immense wit and chameleon-like qualities that he could extract from his psyche at will, and was the very fabric of his being.

Though Iggy's first two solo albums had received positive reviews, their sales fell short of RCA's expectations. The label saw a live album as the fastest route to get his contract done. With a budget for the project, Iggy compiled soundboard tapes from three 1977 concert dates, spent $5,000 tweaking them in Berlin and pocketed the rest. In 1980, he told WHFS: 'I did *TV Eye* just to rip off as much money as I could from the record company before I left. So I made a lot, actually, I lived like a king, baby!'

For all its force, *TV Eye* is remembered less for its performances than for its harsh, lopsided mix. The sound is thin and hollow, with Iggy's vocals often floating above the band, as if singing along to a cheap TDK cassette recording. What should have been a blistering live document, building on the momentum of his two solo records, instead feels like an afterthought, weakening rather than solidifying his resurgence. Reviews were largely negative, with critics bemoaning its poor sound and how it failed to capture

Iggy's legendary stage presence. Yet, despite its flaws, *TV Eye* has a strange kind of merit. It embodies Iggy's total disregard for industry expectations: grating, reckless and defiantly unpolished. Its cheap, no-frills cover, assembled by Iggy and Esther, mirrors the botched mix: indifferent and thrown together, daring you to take it or leave it. More than a live album, it plays like an act of sabotage, a sneer at commercial gloss. And in that, there's something almost admirable. It may not stand as a worthy successor to his two studio albums, but its abrasive, scathing edge earns it at least one listen – just to catch a legend in motion, even if the tape recorder was barely keeping up.

To promote the album and keep the relentless stage beast fed, Iggy assembled another formidable lineup. Thurston returned on keys, joined by three members of Sonic's Rendezvous Band: MC5 guitarist Fred 'Sonic' Smith, who would marry Patti Smith in 1980, Gary Rasmussen, formerly of The Up, and Scott Asheton, the stalwart Stooges drummer. The *TV Eye Tour* began on 3 May 1978, a six-week run through ten European countries. Just before kick-off, Iggy once again performed on *TopPop*. There were no more flower pots on the stage.

'TV Eye' (Alexander, R. Asheton, S. Asheton, Pop)
The album kicks off hard with Iggy's wild 'Looord! You gotta stomp on it, bitch!', launching the first official live release of this Stooges powerhouse. Bowie's wailing synth sweeps give the track a rousing new dimension, but when the lines shadow Iggy's vocal, it throws in a flourish that doesn't quite fit the bill. Fortunately, a riff this tough wouldn't flinch if a cement truck ran it over. At 2:17, Gardiner slams the accelerator, propelled by Sales' exhilarating drums, followed by Iggy shrugging off TV with a sneer. Partly playing on the CBS eye logo, 'TV Eye' was never about the medium, though; it was about sexual desire and being watched. Ron Asheton's sister Kathy once coined the phrase, short for 'twat vibe'.

In 1998, the track was covered for the glam rock film *Velvet Goldmine*, with Ewan McGregor on vocals as Curt Wild, a character heavily based on Iggy. The song's impact spread further: Rage Against The Machine's 'Sleep Now In The Fire' echoes its relentless riff, and it later featured in *Grand Theft Auto IV*, where Iggy himself hosts the fictional Liberty Rock Radio 97.8. After a long absence from his live sets since 2004, Iggy brought the track back in 2017, making it the show opener on his 2025 tour.

'Funtime' (Pop, Bowie)
Performed alongside 'Sister Midnight' on *The Dinah! Show*, this is one of only two tracks from *The Idiot* on what Iggy called a 'nasty little rock 'n' roll album' in a 1996 interview on STV. For all its immediacy, this rattling live blast feels superfluous next to the studio take. Iggy's undercooled, mechanical tone in the original is what lends the 'we' in 'we like your lips' and 'we like

your pants' its creepy undercurrent. His nonchalant delivery of 'I just do what I want to do' rings as a narcissistic declaration of freedom as well as an offhand justification for pursuing his unhinged impulses. That matter-of-factness deepens the song's lurking menace and emotional numbness. Here, that tension dissipates, leaving only speed without shadow.

'Sixteen' (Pop)
Sure, this recording is from a different date, but who introduces the third song on a live album with the MC declaring, 'Ladies and gentlemen: Iggy Pop!'? Less funny, but just as subversive, is the sound quality, which takes a dumpster nosedive here. In return, this version fights harder and leaves more wreckage in its wake than the original. It barrels forward like a beast prowling for prey. The tempo lags slightly behind the studio take, but Iggy sounds possessed and the band advance with grim determination. 'Sixteen' went on to become one of Iggy's most-played live songs.

'I Got A Right' (Pop, Williamson)
MainMan's Tony Defries, The Stooges' manager at the time, had written off this ripcharger in 1972 as too violent and unrelenting. As a result, it remained unreleased until 1977, when it finally surfaced and was later recognised as a proto-punk classic. Fuelled by Iggy's resolve after Elektra dropped the band following *Fun House*, it was a full-throttle statement that The Stooges weren't done yet. On the song's inspiration, Iggy explained in *Interview* magazine in 1990:

> Freedom was very, very important to me when I was young. When I did 'I Got A Right', I had come to the conclusion that the freedoms that we were taught about in civics class didn't actually exist, and so I was going to have to declare my own. That song was my little declaration of independence.

Jumping on the single's release, Iggy wasted no time adding it to the setlist. The tempo is slightly slower than the single, but the band deliver a killer take. Iggy spits and snarls with a feral urgency that bypasses thought, electrifies the nerves and makes every word sound like a birthright. It perfectly distils why he hits so hard: untamed individuality and a voltage that sears.

'Lust For Life' (Bowie, Pop)
Even at the time, Iggy felt that both 'Lust For Life' and 'The Passenger' had been recorded just a touch too slow, and from the very first live shows, he pushed the tempos up. While that cranked the heat on stage, it never made them any better, as this trainwreck of a version shows. The sound is dreadful, Thurston's harmonica is grating and out of place, and the band stumble through the performance. The first ten seconds of the original alone make

this butchery even harder to excuse. In a 1995 *ABC Australia* feature, former Doors manager Danny Sugerman recalled that Iggy, who had briefly been considered as a possible frontman for The Doors after Morrison's death, had shared a heroin dealer with the band, 'Gypsy Johnny', who was nicknamed 'Yen', a name Iggy later reused in 'Lust For Life'. Sugerman's anecdote only underscores the song's darker themes, which makes it all the more baffling that 'Lust For Life' later ended up in a Royal Caribbean Cruise Lines TV ad, voted by *Slate* listeners and readers in 2005 as the most incongruous advertising soundtrack ever. Iggy found no issue with the commercial. In 2007, he told *Rolling Stone*: 'I was thrilled. And the song sounds great in there.' A shame this version missed the boat.

'Dirt' (Alexander, R. Asheton, S. Asheton, Pop)
The album's high point is the psychedelic slow burn of *Fun House*, musically primarily a composition by bassist Dave Alexander, wrapped in a nocturnal, lurching version that could have fitted right onto *The Idiot*. A possessed, trance-like confession of self-destruction and desire, where pain, lust and indifference fuse into an unquenchable fire. Iggy's vocals are at their peak, and when he improvises with 'The sky is blackout and it's raining, and I'm trying/Yes, I'm crying', it is almost spellbinding.

'Nightclubbing' (Pop, Bowie)
After months of cruising through divided Berlin with Bowie, drinking KöPi at Joe's Bierhaus, drifting through the cabaret drag bar The Lützower Lampe and descending late into Schöneberg's nightclub haze, starting this song in wonky German feels like a fitting touch. Too bad this version drags into plodding, overlong sludge. It lacks the smoky cabaret feel, the prowling nocturnal groove and the distorted disco pulse of the drum machine. The terrible sound of this live album is one thing, but the fact that its already questionable audio quality fluctuates between tracks makes for an even rougher listen.

'I Wanna Be Your Dog' (Alexander, R. Asheton, S. Asheton, Pop)
The most played song of Iggy's career, this take on The Stooges' three-chord beast was recorded at Mantra Studios in Chicago for a radio broadcast, taped without an audience, which likely explains the abrupt fade-out. The album credits this version to the live show at the Aragon Ballroom, but if Iggy doesn't care, why should we?

During the North American leg of *The Idiot Tour*, Blondie had handled the opening slot, and Iggy would go on to forge a friendship and collaborate with several of its members. A week after the tour wrapped, Debbie Harry was still deep in Iggy mode. At the Whisky a Go Go, she invited Joan Jett on stage for an encore of 'I Wanna Be Your Dog'. Harry sank to all fours, tongue out, panting like a stray in heat. 'Debbie was an American ponytail girl as seen through the lens of Roger Vadim, Barbarella on speed, or something like that',

Iggy recalled in the 2006 documentary *Blondie: One Way Or Another*. 'Bowie and I both tried to hit on her backstage. We couldn't get anywhere, but she was always very smooth about that.' Harry summed it up in *The Independent* in 2006: 'The whole thing was mind-blowing, to be on tour with them in the first place. And to have flirtations with guys like that was just the icing on the cake.'

New Values (1979)

Personnel:
Iggy Pop: vocals
Scott Thurston: guitars, harp, keyboards, synthesiser, vocals, horn arrangement
Klaus Krüger: drums
Jackie Clark: bass
John Harden: horns
David Brock: strings, string arrangement
Earl Shackelford: backing vocals
The Alfono Sisters (Anna and Mary): backing vocals on 'Don't Look Down', 'Angel'
James Williamson: guitar, horn and string arrangement
Recorded at Paramount, Hollywood, California, in January 1979
Producer: James Williamson
Release date: UK: April 1979; US: October 1979
Label: Arista
Chart places: US: 180, UK: 60, Aus: 36
Running time: 39:26

First Patti Smith, then Lou Reed, now Iggy Pop. When Arista signed Iggy in 1978, it felt like a natural extension of the label's downtown rock 'n' roll credibility. But Iggy came with baggage. Arista president Clive Davis had already tangled with Iggy's chaos when he bankrolled *Raw Power*, an expensive disaster in his final year at Columbia. So when UK A&R man Ben Edmonds signed Iggy without Davis' prior approval, he was resistant. Rather than blocking it altogether, he stalled the US release of *New Values*, waiting to see how it would perform. It peaked at number 60 in the UK, with 'I'm Bored' making it onto *The Old Grey Whistle Test*. American fans started importing the album, and stations like WBCN in Boston picked it up. When import sales proved there was demand, Davis relented. Six months after its UK debut, *New Values* finally saw a domestic release, landing at number 180 on *Billboard*. Hardly a blockbuster, since the novelty had worn off after half a year. Yet it was enough to confirm that Iggy was still a going concern.

Before the RCA deal, back in late 1977, CBS had rereleased *Raw Power* in the UK, riding the wave of punk's explosion and capitalising on its newfound influence. That year, James Williamson, needing money, saw an opportunity in Iggy's rising profile following his two albums with Bowie. He dusted off *Kill City*, recorded in 1975 but never properly released, and put it out through Bomp! Records, credited to 'Iggy Pop and James Williamson'. He later recalled to *Clash* magazine in 2010:

> When I released it, Iggy had a fit because he and Bowie were making so-called professional albums at that point. That was his first take. And then what started happening was that kids started buying it, and all of a sudden,

> it became an underground thing, and Iggy started thinking, 'Shit, well, this is kinda cool.' He and Bowie used it to get another record deal for him. So now he kinda liked it, and he thought, 'Well, you know what? I'll try calling up my old buddy James and see if he'll produce the record for me.'

Williamson took the job. With Sonic's Rendezvous Band unwilling to record an album, he and Iggy had to assemble a new lineup. Thurston stayed on board as a versatile musician and songwriter, taking on guitar and keyboards. The rhythm section featured bassist Jackie Clark, formerly with Ike & Tina Turner, and drummer Klaus Krüger, a Berlin associate who had played with Tangerine Dream and was known for blending percussion with electronics. To broaden the vocal palette, Williamson brought in three backing singers. Earl Shackleford, a music industry veteran, had cut the garage single 'Pretty Little Thing' with The Deepest Blue in 1966, before The Stooges even existed. Williamson had caught his band, The Strutters, at a club gig and invited him to contribute vocals. The group's other singers, Anna and Mary Alfono, added their voices to two tracks, softly offsetting Iggy's baritone. John Harden, already heard on *Kill City*, returned on horns, while David Brock handled strings.

Recording in the US was the most practical option, and in January 1979, Paramount Studios in Hollywood became their base of operations. Cocaine flowed freely. The group were repeatedly kicked out of hotels for attracting too many groupies and making too much noise, like Iggy, sprawled out naked at 3 am, hacking away at his guitar. Still, the sessions stayed focused, and the band shaped Iggy's tunes into a fierce, wry and oddly touching collection. On tour, Fred Smith had encouraged Iggy to pick up a guitar. Eager to rely less on others for his songs, he spent months honing his skills in his Hinterhof apartment, where Esther had moved in. With his Fender Telecaster, he practised for up to nine hours a day, drawing on Keith Richards' riffs as he worked on new material. Thurston had flown over to collaborate, with three of his contributions making the album, while two *Kill City* leftovers – 'Curiosity' and 'Angel' – were revived.

Often labelled Iggy's new wave album for its jagged grooves, it also channels his feral punk pulse, laced with Dionysian Everyman observations. Still, too untamed for pure new wave, too controlled for straight punk, *New Values* ultimately stakes out its own territory. 'There were no tricks on it', Iggy told *Mean* magazine in 2001. 'It's a very particular sound on that record.' It ranks among his best albums, if one can look past its disappointingly flat mix. Professionally balanced but sonically uninvolving, it offers angular, percussive and tight guitars, yet their lack of sustain and heft leaves them sounding somewhat thin. The bass lacks depth, and the drums sound papery and underpowered. By contrast, Iggy's voice is pushed forward in the mix, at times dulling the impact of the instrumentation. The result is a stripped-down, controlled and subdued sound, almost tame at times, that doesn't always do the songs justice. But great songs they are.

While it wasn't the US breakthrough Arista had hoped for, the album did moderately well in Australia and New Zealand, leading to Iggy's first visit there to promote it. In Melbourne, he made a bouncy appearance on ABC's *Countdown*, greeting the host with, 'Hiya, dogface!' During his lip-synced performance of 'I'm Bored', he shoved the microphone down his pants and reached out to the bewildered teenage girls in the audience. Iggy's appearance left a mark on Australian punk fans, and he has made the country a regular stop ever since.

The cover, plucked from a Trevor Rogers photoshoot, captures him in a compelling contradiction: bare-chested yet poised, wild yet elegant, stretched in ballet tights like a feral danseur. Although *The New York Times* considered *New Values* 'bland' compared to the Bowie-produced albums, the overall critical reception was positive. It was praised for its sharp, heartfelt and humorous blend of raw energy and nuanced ballads. *NME* hailed the album for affirming the balance between Osterberg the thinker and Iggy the performer. The *LA Times* described it as a key part of Iggy's re-emergence, while *Rolling Stone* listed it among the best albums of 1979. Since then, it has remained highly regarded by critics and fans alike. Rather than fully embracing his newfound Godfather of Punk status, Iggy took a bold step, shifting his sound yet again. More importantly, *New Values* shattered any lingering doubts that he could only function under Bowie's wing. He had proven he could write, focus and deliver without his mentor's assistance. And despite Davis' initial reluctance, Arista now had reason to believe that with the right push, Iggy could evolve into something more marketable: a sharper, more mature version of himself, still wild but no longer a walking disaster.

'Tell Me A Story' (Pop)

Iggy's new chapter opens with a clean sound after the garage grit of *Lust For Life*. In no-frills production, the song crackles with brattiness and sly humour: 'What must I do to take a holiday?/Show me a bill that they can make me pay, ha!' Its ironic, performative tone draws us into Iggy's world, where he hunts for stories – true or not – to distract him, amuse him, or simply give him something to believe in. Framing himself as 'too dumb to cry', he leans into the bravado of being young, free and invincible. Onstage, he winks at The Stones' 'It's Only Rock 'N Roll' with 'I like, I like it', quickly tempered by 'What did they do to chill the joy away/What did they do to say you had to pay', exposing the tension between his love for the spotlight and the burdens of his persona. Playful and cheeky, the song carries a subtle touch of yearning that adds an extra layer to the mix. 'He has a very strong imagination and the ability to paint a picture with words', Williamson noted to Songfacts in 2018. The first of six Iggy-penned tracks, it's a jangly, Stones-esque number with playful piano, synthesiser touches and a blend of live and electronic drums. Shackleford's soaring backing vocals punctuate Iggy's delivery of 'too hard' and 'too tough', a savvy touch in Williamson's production. Concise, witty and buzzing with the renewed energy of Iggy's post-Bowie reinvention, it's a strong opener.

'New Values' (Pop, Thurston)
Next up is the title track, which thrives on tension. Built on Thurston's circular bass-doubled riff, a stinging guitar solo, buzzing synths and canned handclaps, this punk-new wave blend delivers a sinewy sound and incisive lyrics. The opening 'I'm healthy as a horse, but everything is spinnin'' meets the deadpan punch of 'If I use a gun, I'm sure to go to prison', hinting at Nietzsche's analysis of passive nihilism: the impulse to act, even destructively, to escape stagnation, paired with the awareness that this offers no real solution. The recurring line 'I'm lookin' for one new value/But nothing comes my way' underscores both stagnation and yearning for renewal. According to Nietzsche's philosophy, old values must collapse to make room for new ones. In *The Will To Power*, he writes: 'The new values must first be created – this task awaits the philosophers of the future.' Recorded in 1979, the line 'We were young in the 20th century' conveys a sense of history yet to come in an era still unfolding. Delivered in a robotic, megaphone-like tone, it evokes the voice of such a philosopher from the future. This detachment sharpens the tension between meaning-seeking and the inertia of the present. The riff's anxious repetition intensifies this conflict, leaving Iggy trapped in a loop that embodies both progress and paralysis.

'Girls' (Pop)
Iggy had been constantly listening to The Stones' *Some Girls* at the time of writing songs for the sessions. While 'New Values' features a riff reminiscent of 'Shattered', this song channels The Stones through Richards-style licks and playful lyrics hinting at their title track. As *New Values* points towards growth, Iggy's usual celebration of sexual lust, or the paradox of corrupting and preserving purity, takes on a lighter tone. 'Girls' revels in female beauty with pure, unfiltered delight. 'I love girls/They're all over this world' is wide-eyed and eager, driven by amazement and admiration rather than conquest. 'You're somebody to talk to' shifts it from simple infatuation, suggesting genuine appreciation alongside the thrill of attraction. There's an ease to Iggy's conversational delivery and spontaneous energy, while the interpolation of Gershwin's 'Summertime' gives this freewheeling track an unexpected wink. The song doesn't take itself too seriously, but its infectious vibe keeps it from falling flat, coloured by exquisite rhymes like: 'Some have beautiful shapes/I wanna live to be 98'.

'I'm Bored' (Pop)
A snotty anthem for the disaffected, Iggy unleashes a near three-minute war cry against enthusiasm itself. With a sneer you can hear, he transforms boredom into identity, art and maybe even a weapon. The killer line 'I'm the

chairman of the bored' turns simple disinterest into absurdist poetry, a sarcastic badge of honour in a world of try-hards. Iggy's deadpan verses and hilarious exclamation of 'I'm BORED!' teeter between self-parody and disdain, lampooning both boredom and the bland world around him. Crisp guitar riffs and a propulsive rhythm inject playful energy, paradoxically making this ode to apathy irresistibly punchy. Hovering between punk and new wave, it's sharp, mock-heroic and cheeky: a masterclass in ironic apathy.

'Don't Look Down' (Pop, Williamson)

It opens with a nod to the previous song: 'So why be bored?/Who scared you and why stay there?/It's no piece of cake'. The recurring 'don't look down' serves as both warning and advice, urging defiance of the ambiguous 'crazy sound', a force that could represent societal pressure, personal demons or life's turbulence. 'From Central Park to shanty town' suggests this cryptic presence transcends social and geographical boundaries. Iggy's visit to the cemetery 'to see old Rudy Valentino buried' takes some creative licence, as Valentino is interred in a crypt. The reference winks at Valentino's 1926 defence of his masculinity after critics accused him of feminising American men. Challenging a writer to a boxing match (and winning against a stand-in), Valentino became a symbol of standing firm against ridicule, a legacy Iggy mirrors with flair.

The laid-back arrangement, featuring sax and organ, frames Iggy's confident delivery. The Alfono sisters' harmonies add just the right sweetening, while Shackleford belts out another striking sweep. With music written by Williamson years prior to the sessions, it's the only track on the album to showcase his guitar playing, apart from a few additional rhythm parts. Bowie's stripped-down reggae cover on *Tonight* left Williamson unimpressed: 'I always thought it was kind of lame,' he told Songfacts in 2018, 'but I loved the royalties.'

'The Endless Sea' (Pop)

The late 1970s marked a shift in popular music, as punk gave way to the layered sounds of post-punk and new wave. In the midst of this transition, an exploratory Iggy took a more refined approach on 'The Endless Sea', a move reflected in the album's title. This tightly focused production holds back sax and violin as extra colour, opening with Krüger's 1-2-3-4-5 rhythm: a quintuple time signature. This uncommon metre creates immediate tension, pulling us into the unsettling mood of the cosmic synths, accented by the sound of waves. The track stands as a key moment on *New Values*, resonating with the existential concerns of contemporaries like Joy Division and early Talking Heads. Like them, Iggy grapples with alienation and societal constraints, pushing back with a fierce insistence on freedom and refusal to conform. Following a verse weighed down by frustration and fakery, the song's emotional core peaks in its fervent climax: 'You better go home, buddy', a line that breaks through the surrounding pressure with stark finality. Though 'The Endless Sea' lacks the playful irony of other tracks on *New Values*, its slow-burning intensity signals a turning point in Iggy's output. Some may see this earnest tone as a departure from his usual irreverence, but for others, the contrast between rebellion and introspection makes it the album's high point.

Covered by The Church and Cat Power, the song also appeared in the 1986 film *Dogs In Space*. Though not performed since 1983, Iggy revived it to great effect in 2019, turning it into a staple of his 2022 and 2023 tours.

'Five Foot One' (Pop)

The band are razor-sharp throughout *New Values*, but never tighter than on this five-minute burst of short-guy complex, punctuated by Iggy's animalistic grunts, gulps and yelps. With jerky guitars, brassy interjections and a jittery pace, the track mirrors the uneasy defiance of a scrappy rebel navigating a towering, mechanised world:

> I'm only five foot one
> I got a pain in my neck
> I'm looking up in the city
> What the hell, what the heck?
> I stare at the concrete
> The girders rise high
> The steel's above me
> There's love in my eyes

With sardonic precision, Iggy blends humour and frustration to sketch the small man's life: late nights working at an amusement park, armed with 'a bottle of aspirin/A sack full of jokes' and yearning for connection 'with all the big folks'. This desire surges into the brilliant refrain: 'I wish life could be/ Swedish magazines'. It conjures a fantasy world of unattainable beauty, glossy perfection, idyllic forests and perhaps a dash of late-1970s erotica. The bittersweet cry 'I wish life could be/Anything!' sharpens the longing to transcend one's shortcomings, tempered by the sobering self-awareness of 'I won't grow anymore'. This is a wry ode to the underdog: defiant in its embrace of smallness, unflinching in its portrayal of life and aching in its dreams for more. It's a standout moment and one of Iggy's finest.

'How Do Ya Fix A Broken Part' (Pop, Thurston)

Where The Bee Gees' 'How Can You Mend A Broken Heart' is steeped in sincerity, Iggy takes a satirical detour. 'How can you stop the sun from shining?' they ask wistfully; Iggy retorts, 'How come the sun's too bright to bear?', twisting their lament into something harsher. 'Broken, it's broken, what good is it broken?' drains heartbreak of grandeur, turning it into a mundane inconvenience, worlds apart from the sentimentality of The Bee Gees' 'How can a loser ever win?' Iggy's 'Get out your toolbox boys, I know you can fix things' reframes heartbreak as a mechanical task, mocking the idea of a noble struggle with pain. It's a fun, simply structured track built on a four-note piano motif, closing with a coda that flirts with jazz-fusion. Ultimately, it's undemanding and fairly forgettable, hinting that the album's stellar streak softens from this point onward.

'Angel' (Pop, Thurston)

Iggy's closest foray into torch song territory, this slow-burner evokes Alice Cooper's 'You And Me' while channelling, yet again, the essence of a Stones ballad, with piano and twangy guitar licks woven into swelling strings. His tender crooning sounds almost uncharacteristic as he laments, 'When I was crying, you were on my side', his sweetness later matched by silky backing vocals. Iggy exposes a rarely seen openness: 'I never thought I'd be free and clear/Except for you, I doubt I'd be here'. While the angel could be Esther, a muse, or even a metaphorical saviour, it clearly represents the elusive source of salvation Iggy believes he needs. Even as he elevates it to a celestial guardian, 'Still I'm needing somebody else/Again' exposes a longing this figure can't satisfy. While the song threatens to drown in schmaltz, not one for the syrup-intolerant, Iggy's vulnerable delivery keeps it afloat. For all its devotion, it still leaves the sense that Iggy's redemption is just out of reach.

'Curiosity' (Pop, Thurston)

This short, energetic rocker, driven by his lively Jerry Lee Lewis-style rollicking piano, had been shelved in Thurston's head since 1974. It opens with a tongue-in-cheek glance at the Vandals' sack of Rome, reframing history as a parable of destructive curiosity. From this lofty reference, Iggy pivots to the personal, diving headfirst into his own obsessive tendencies. 'I'm just riddled with anxiety/I'm the lowest level' and 'When I see your smiling face, I'm so disgraced' expose the emotional toll of his uncontrollable curiosity. But who cares? 'I'll meet you at the old mouse hole' is a delightfully cartoonish, cryptic image, evoking a secret rendezvous and a chance to start over. The witty nod to the adage 'Curiosity killed the cat, but satisfaction brought it back' captures the ambivalence of, well, curiosity: dangerous yet irresistible. Like the song, it's a playful nudge to embrace curiosity, even just for lightweight fun.

'African Man' (Pop, Thurston)

Afrobeat grooves, funk basslines and instinctual vocals merge in this track, notorious for its racially charged and offensive imagery. The words and delivery are so outrageously ridiculous and theatrical that it is clear they were never meant to be taken seriously. And yet, the lyrics degrade African people and culture, reducing them to a primitive, savage caricature and reinforcing colonial absurdities. This grotesque portrayal echoes a long history of blatant misrepresentation in Western culture. In *The New York Times Magazine* in 2023, Iggy recalled seeing an African artist perform in a tiny Berlin club and admitted he had nicked a lyric for his own track. 'I couldn't think up anything else to go with that music … and I thought, Boy, that's fun, and why can't I sing that too?' He called it the weakest song on *New Values* and said he had no objection to its removal, framing it as an ill-conceived experiment born of impulse rather than an attempt to provoke or perpetuate racism.

While punk has often confronted race and politics, 'African Man' backfires. Instead of challenging norms, it entrenches racist tropes, lacking the self-awareness or intent to critique them. But rather than erase it, we might keep it in circulation to confront what it exposes: the persistence of racist archetypes and the ethical responsibilities of artists, whether dismantling or reinforcing them. Acknowledging its toxic content could offer insight into how racial representation in art has evolved, and why it continues to matter. Open dialogue and thoughtful critique remain essential for reckoning and renewal.

'Billy Is A Runaway' (Pop, Thurston)

Closing out, we're urged on by sampled handclaps and angular riffs, while Clark's loose, slap-style bass adds a funky edge. When Clark switched to guitar for the *New Values Tour*, ex-Sex Pistol Glen Matlock was brought in to handle bass duties. Unfamiliar with the style, he struggled in rehearsals, hammering away at the part during a lunch break until he finally locked it in, just as Iggy returned with an unexpected Bowie in tow. Startled, Matlock wavered for a second before snapping back into Clark's infectious groove.

The track itself unfolds in brief, cinematic scenes, introducing Billy as he pulls up in a flashy Bonneville, exuding freedom and bravado:

Billy pulled his wallet
Full of hundred dollar bills
Took me for a joyride
Talkin' 'bout the stereo
Drivin' in the left lane
I'm thinkin' 'bout my burial

With Iggy's sly slant rhyme of 'stereo' and 'burial', the ride ends at a liquor store, where Billy's confidence masks his underage status. A glimpse into his toxic family reveals the roots of his turmoil: threats to 'skin him alive', and a drug-dealing sister pressuring him to join her schemes. Dubiously, Iggy the narrator invites him for a drink, where trembling hands expose the scared, damaged kid beneath. Billy's fleeting, restless nature as a 'bird dog' is underscored by a recurring chirp effect – a subtle wink in the arrangement.

After an electrifying 25-minute opening and a more uneven remainder, Iggy's third strong solo album draws to a close. 'I had a lot of fun writing it. It got a tiny bit overprofessionalised for my taste. But all in all, it came out pretty well', Iggy remarked in *Rip It Up* in 1979. Balancing newfound reflective maturity with the volatile energy of his past, it proves his new direction had legs. Nothing seemed to stand in the way of a breakthrough to wider success. Or did it?

Bonus Tracks

'Chains' (Pop, Williamson, Thurston)

A pleasant enough soulful, rocking ode to self-reflection, built around the contrast between freedom and the comfort of confinement. Iggy questions love's binding forces, while the refrains evoke transformation and emotional weight. Catchy enough, but the lyrics feel cursory and uninspired. Written by three ex-Stooges, it sounds more interesting on paper than in practice. Its omission from the album was the right call.

'Pretty Flamingo' (Pop)

The piano-led, humdrum B-side to 'Five Foot One' is the second bonus track on the 2000 Buddha reissue. Framed as a sultry, voyeuristic ode to obsession ('You locked the door on me so I crawled in your window'), Iggy turns the titular bird, presumably Esther, into a symbol of fragile beauty, restraint and desire, though without much conviction. He even serves up one of his feeblest lines with 'I, I will protect you/As you, you are so worth protecting': a discount-store take on Bowie's '"Heroes"'.

Soldier (1980)

Personnel:
Iggy Pop: vocals
Glen Matlock: bass, backing vocals
Ivan Kral: guitar, keyboards
Klaus Krüger: drums
Steve New: guitar
Barry Andrews: keyboards
Jim Kerr, Derek Forbes, David Bowie, Patti Palladin, Glen Matlock, Steve New, Ivan Kral, James Williamson: backing vocals on 'Play It Safe'
Henry McGroggan: chorus on 'Loco Mosquito'
Recorded at Rockfield Studios, Wales, in August 1979
Producer: Pat Moran
Release date: February 1980
Label: Arista
Chart places: US: 125, UK: 62, Aus: 78
Running time: 37:00

Before *New Values* had seen its US release, Iggy promoted it on the road across the UK and Europe from late April to early July 1979. The band were reinforced by Matlock on bass, shifting Clark to guitar. During the UK leg, certain hotels refused to host them, not because of Iggy Pop but simply because an ex-Sex Pistol was in the lineup. Even Iggy couldn't compete with that backstory. Under pressure from Arista, Iggy was rushed back into the studio right after the tour. Recording took place in August at Rockfield, a residential studio in a former farm in the Welsh countryside. Thurston and Clark had left, with Thurston fed up with Iggy's decisions and unwilling to record in Wales. To fill the gap, Matlock brought in former Rich Kids guitarist Steve New. The new roster was further expanded with XTC's Barry Andrews on keys, while guitarist Ivan Kral from The Patti Smith Group arrived later in the sessions. Also on the studio grounds were Simple Minds, who were recording their sophomore album. 'It was unimaginable to us that Iggy Pop would be in the Welsh countryside, where there's nothing going on except sheep and hills', Jim Kerr recalled to *Billboard* in 2018. 'Every night he would come and take all our goodies and all our women and head into the night.'

From the start, tensions were brewing. Producer Williamson had no real interest in the project, had taken the job for the money, was still frustrated by Thurston's departure and hit the vodka harder as the sessions dragged on, waving around a pellet gun. Iggy had yet to write most of the songs and was, as he told *Mean* magazine in 2001, 'unsound at the time.' The band were struggling to find their footing and lacked a clear musical leader. Isolated in the middle of nowhere, the studio drove everyone to the brink, fuelling arguments and pushing them towards substances to keep the madness at bay. Under pressure from Arista to deliver a radio-friendly album, Williamson became fixated on new recording techniques, causing delays that frustrated Iggy and the band. The budget spiralled out of control, with Clive Davis monitoring the situation closely and tightening the pressure from afar.

When Bowie unexpectedly dropped by and began interfering with the sessions, Williamson had had enough and walked out. Convinced Bowie was after his girlfriend, New jumped on him, sending both men tumbling down the stairs. Iggy, far from amused by the outburst, grew increasingly resentful when, at the last minute, New informed him he wouldn't be joining the already planned US leg of the *New Values Tour*. With no producer, Rockfield engineer Pat Moran stepped in to help Iggy finish the album. After the US gigs, with Brian James from The Damned replacing New, Iggy and Thom Panunzio mixed the album in New York. Iggy, still annoyed by New's departure, retaliated by all but erasing his guitar parts from the final mix. Given the tensions and disarray that plagued the project, it's a wonder the album was ever completed, yet it surfaced in February 1980. That same month, Iggy packed for another punishing tour, with an altered lineup and a gruelling schedule across the UK, Europe and North America. The slumped album cover photo was taken by Brian Griffin in London's Notting Hill Gate, with the sleeve designed by Alex McDowell. Iggy asked them to create three improvised promo videos for £3000, a request that would set McDowell on the path to becoming one of Hollywood's most acclaimed production designers. Their paths would cross again in 1995 when he worked on *The Crow: City Of Angels*, in which Iggy co-starred.

In the UK, critics and polls saw Iggy's new record as a solid effort, with *Record Mirror* praising his humour and individuality, and *NME* placing it at number 28 in its Albums of the Year. Reception in the US was less favourable. Although *Rolling Stone* gave it a positive review, the album failed to make major year-end polls or critics' lists. It was absent from *The Village Voice*'s 1980 Pazz & Jop Critics Poll, where *London Calling* and *Remain In Light* dominated, leaving *Soldier* without enough support to rank.

More than 45 years after its release, *Soldier* still sparks wildly different opinions. It is one of the few Iggy albums people either hail as a flawed gem or write off entirely, with little middle ground. This book makes the case for the former: born out of chaos it may be, but it is a dynamic, ragged and eccentric record that only sinks in deeper with every listen. It has a murky, battered weight that reflects the damp, corroded atmosphere of the early 1980s. The lyrics are unpredictable, shifting between offbeat satire, splintered visions and Iggy's penchant for inserting words no other rock record would consider. His voice sounds weathered and dark, carrying the rasp of a washed-up AWOL ghoul trooper as he survives on a nocturnal diet of drugs and booze, hiding out in the Welsh countryside, waiting for nightfall before crawling back to life.

'Loco Mosquito' (Pop)

My momma told me
If I was goody
That she would buy me
A rubber dolly

There's an opening line! Absurd and ironic, these words mock childhood ideals and the simplistic rewards of conformity. This is quintessential Iggy Pop: using nonsensical imagery to comment on societal conformity. A sharp way to set the tone for the chaos and estrangement that runs through this song. The snappy title captures Iggy's erratic, restless energy, buzzing with aimless drive and cyclical frustration. It mirrors his own persona, defined by rebellion and volatility. Iggy vacillates between feeling out of place, being too old for the military, unease around 'old transvestites' and the absurdity of repeating empty patterns: 'Here I go, in love again'. Romantic and sexual encounters, far from fulfilling, only deepen the tension and dissatisfaction.

Punk's vigour fuses with flashes of new wave, driven by a bouncy rhythm, jagged strumming and carnival ride-like keyboard swirls. More polished than Iggy's work with The Stooges or even Bowie, the song retains its visceral edge, despite the absence of electric lead guitar. His vocal delivery shifts between snarling aggression and sardonic playfulness, matching the frenetic 'mosquito' vibe. Though overshadowed by Iggy's iconic hits, 'Loco Mosquito' is a zany triumph. Its off-beat lyrics, quirky humour ('Hirohito!') and dynamic pulse illustrate Iggy's mix of defiance and innovation in the 1970s, pointing to the artistic path he would explore in the decade to come, with mixed results.

'Ambition' (Matlock)
With most of New's guitar parts removed and only some replaced by Kral's, *Soldier* stands out for its focus on bass, drums and keys: rare for an Iggy record. Matlock considered New's contributions among the best of the sessions, calling Iggy's decision both childish and self-defeating. 'That annoyed me because it spoiled my songs, as far as I was concerned', Matlock told fan site God Save The Sex Pistols in 2000, admitting it was one reason he chose not to work with Iggy again.

Nowhere is the absence of a fuller guitar line felt more acutely than here. Instead, strummed acoustic guitars follow a tango-like 4/4 pulse, while ominous organ underscores Iggy's delivery of Matlock's anti-establishment lyrics. Singing from a girl's perspective, Iggy stakes her claim on 'that whole wide world', rejecting mediocrity with a smirk and a bite. Fierce and cunning, she channels betrayal into fuel, proving that ambition never plays fair, but she plays to win. A rare case where Iggy didn't write the lyrics, but he liked them and they fit him well, even if the song itself isn't particularly memorable. Reflecting later, Matlock said: 'I realised after we did it with Iggy that it should have been in 6/8, a waltz-time kind of thing', though he remained fond of the song and has performed it live ever since. Iggy, however, did not.

'Knocking 'Em Down (In The City)' (Pop)
The album catches fire here with Iggy in familiar skin, unleashing his soaring Stooges voice over a chugging punk-infused rocker. With its defiant, anthemic backing vocals, catchy chorus and gutter guitar solo, this might just be the song that gave birth to Jane's Addiction. Although unlikely to bother a Stooges fan out of bed, it's a solid, spiky call to arms. The track thrives on urban hustle, favouring forward motion over finesse and grime over precision. 'You can change situations/Go ahead and knock 'em down' is a rallying cry, aimed at nothing in particular yet everything at once, both internal and external. With 'I don't care what your name is', obstacles are stripped of individuality, reduced to mere targets. The focus is clear: stop hesitating and take control. In its promotion, Iggy re-staked his claim for the title of cheapest music video ever. Ironically, in a song urging action, he spends most of it in bed.

'Play It Safe' (Bowie, Pop)
One of the album's stronger tracks took shape after an unexpected spark from Bowie. Dropping by during the album's chaotic sessions, he lifted Iggy's spirits with a night of wild stories from London's underworld: tales of the Krays, John Bindon and even whispers of royal scandal. Fired up, Iggy crafted an ironic 'Americanised' ode to the allure of crime, improvising lyrics spun from Bowie's vivid monologue. With Bowie himself playing on the recording, the track rides on his descending chord progression, anchored by a four-on-the-snare beat layered over a brooding synth drone. Iggy delivers his lines with dry, sardonic wit: 'I want to be a criminal/Play it safe'. He turns rebellion on its head, suggesting that breaking the rules might just be the safest bet. Two members of Simple Minds, recording next door, joined the fun with cheeky faux-Cockney backing vocals, dialling up the song's playful absurdity. Though Bowie reportedly had some of the sharper edges smoothed out by cutting references to Princess Margaret, the track kept its bite. Iggy's wild, name-dropping finale, shouting out Al Capone, Joe Gallo, Son of Sam and Jim Jones, ensures it ends gloriously off the rails.

Bowie's long drive to see his friend was greatly appreciated by Iggy, but Williamson saw his visit as nothing more than interference. For him, it was simply the last straw in an already frustrating ordeal. He hadn't wanted to record in that studio, felt the material was half-baked and had little respect for the musicians involved. Frustrated, he walked away from the project, dismissing it as a mistake altogether. Iggy wasn't particularly fazed at the time: 'He got carried away, wanted to make it 48-track, bring in an orchestra', he recalled on Nardwuar's radio show in 1996. 'Seemed a bit much for a song like 'Dog Food' or 'I Snub You'.'

'Get Up And Get Out' (Pop)
A bit rich coming from Iggy, whose own past with groupies does not reflect well on him. Yet in this over-caffeinated pep talk, he warns of the fallout from misogyny and abuse, declaring that women will 'be leaving this town, if you don't treat 'em right'. His voice snarls and growls, teetering between motivation and menace, as if he's shaking you by the shoulders. It's not pretty, but it's undeniably Iggy: part unhinged preacher, part overzealous fitness coach. Pure bedlam wrapped in a brassy riff with a dash of avant-funk, it's as messy as it is infectious. The production struggles to contain the song's chaotic spirit, as if trying to trap wildfire in a dumpster.

'Mr. Dynamite' (Matlock, Pop)
Despite sharing a nickname with one of his main influences, James Brown, Iggy's 'Mr. Dynamite' charts its own dangerous territory, sketching a character who wreaks havoc only to be discarded once the initial shock fades. Iggy channelling his own worst prophecy here? He unleashes his self-destructive tendencies through an unpredictable mix of punk, rock and jazz. A nervous, menacing bass underpins the track, constantly reprimanded by militaristic snare shots. Crabby guitar and fluttering trumpet weave a jagged, discordant texture, while eerie piano and vibraslap add to the creeping unease. Together, they feel like a powder keg ready to blow. The tension never fully resolves, leaving a lingering sense of unrealised potential. And yet, the line 'Yesterday he changed/Today he is betrayed' captures the arc of a figure of fire and fallout in a single sharp line.

'Dog Food' (Pop)
Iggy Pop at his most feral, a snarling, unhinged hammering punk stomp, thrashing like a wild animal locked in a cage. The opening growl is less an intro and more a warning, setting the stage for a song that feels like it has been dragged through a pile of scrap metal. The guitars buzz like a faulty electric fence, and the rhythm section thud with a ramshackle urgency that threatens to fall apart at any moment, yet somehow it holds. Iggy's voice, part beast, part madman, barks and snarls:

> I'm hanging around, that same old scene
> My girlfriend Betsy, she's just fourteen
> There's nothing better for me to do
> I'm living on dog food (so what?)
> Dog food is so good for you
> It makes you strong, and clever too
> Dog food is a current craze
> Eat some every day

An autobiographical song, according to Iggy, reflecting the dark days when he drifted through LA. It was prompted by the housing projects he encountered there, where people weren't allowed to keep pets but bought more pet food than anywhere else. For Arista, this revised leftover from The Stooges' days must have hit like a brick through a boardroom window. After *New Values* teased a move towards accessibility, *Soldier* demolished that notion with this 1:47 blast of unfiltered, rabid chaos. Still, it was backed by a video, equally bizarre, featuring nothing but Iggy, a toy dog and a refrigerator.

'I Need More' (Matlock, Pop)
Over a strutting bass and relentless beat, Iggy lays it bare: he's not just hungry for more, he's starving for it. The song stomps forward with urgency, as if he's pacing a dingy room, hunting the next thrill or escape. 'I walk around, I flop around, I need something that will be found', he sneers, daring the world to meet his demands. His voice teeters between a growl and a command, making it clear he's not here for subtlety or compromise. The lyrics begin as an anarchist's wishlist, 'More venom, more dynamite, more disaster', then spiral into the cluttered visions of a junk-drawer prophet: 'More floors, more doors/More mustard, pickle, and relish'. It's Maslow's hierarchy of needs rewritten by a punk-rock madman, and it's thrilling. Spiky guitars pierce through the verses while the rhythm section pound like a clenched fist on a bar table. There's no build, no release, just forward momentum: demanding attention and leaving no room for reflection. An in-your-face reminder that sometimes wanting everything is more punk than pretending to want nothing at all. In hindsight, Iggy prophesies the decade to come: a Reagan-era binge of greed, gloss and gimme-more materialism disguised as the American Dream.

'Take Care Of Me' (Matlock, Pop)
This riff-driven rocker at a runner's pace began life under the working title 'Forget Me Not', a song brought in by Matlock, who nudged Iggy to write new lyrics. Hesitant at first, Iggy delivered words much to Matlock's approval: 'The lyrics to that are great. He was still living in Germany and starting to get a bit fed up with it', he noted on God Save The Sex Pistols. Iggy pours his frustration into these bitterly funny lines:

International garbage man
I've decided that's what I am
I need somebody to pull me out
I'm sinking like crazy in my sauerkraut

Beneath the humour lies a jagged autobiographical confession: Iggy, worn down by excess, calls for salvation while owning his duplicity. He confronts the 'heavy price' of his choices and the cracks in his intimacy. These surface in the middle eight, where he likens himself to a 'little boy', admitting that fleeting sexual thrills mean little: 'Benwa balls and bugs that crawl/I can't enjoy them without love'. The overdubbed lines might even hint at echoes of his lover's thoughts. The song's duality emerges as a plea for help, contrasting with a warning of unreliability: 'Sometimes I'm a snake/Just after the take'. This tension is deepened in the refrain, 'Take care of me', shifting between vulnerability and demand, exposing the contradictions of someone craving stability yet undermining it: 'I've done my best/Now you do the rest'. By the early 1980s, Iggy had left Berlin and was spending time in the UK with no fixed address, accompanied by Esther, before the two eventually settled in New York. Looking back on his final period in Berlin, Iggy told *Zeitmagazin* in 2016:

> I only let myself go toward the end of my time there. The city was changing, and the people, too. From one day to the next, Berlin was flooded with drugs, and I did not always make the best decisions. To cut it short: I came to Berlin totally fit and left it as a wreck.

The song's closing line, 'I'll never forget', lingers in ambiguity, suggesting gratitude, regret or an inevitable farewell, likely all at once. This unresolved tension mirrors the fractured persona at the song's core.

'I'm A Conservative' (Pop)
Iggy opens quietly, contemplating that he has had enough of his wild ways. Suddenly, the guitars kick in, and he smirks: 'Hello, my friends, is everybody happy?' What follows is a cheeky jab at political and social conformity, complete with chirping backing vocals singing 'lalala' like gleeful schoolgirls. When Iggy declares, 'I'm in the clear/'Cause I'm a conservative', it drips with irony, especially from a punk icon who built a career railing against authority. Over a straightforward beat and bare-bones guitar, the piano hammers away, a sly callback to 'Raw Power'. Its tone and attitude recall Patti Smith's controversial 'Rock N Roll N*****', released a year prior to the *Soldier* sessions, but while she hailed rebellious outsiders, Iggy plays the part of the traditionalist. His delivery treads sincerity and satire, making it clear he's not just mocking the system but grinning as he toys with it.

'I Snub You' (Andrews, Pop)
Soldier wraps up with a sneering kiss-off delivered with all the subtlety of a middle finger in your face. It's Iggy at his bratty best, strutting through a punk-fuelled assault and lashing out:

> You most deplorable glaring example
> Of a degenerate narcotic influence
> My seething hate is driving me nuts
> What can I do to obliterate you
> I snub you

His voice is pure attitude, half-spat, half-snarled, dripping with mockery and venom. He doesn't just sing the words; he weaponises them. With flashes of absurdism and theatrical flair, the track fires intense disdain at a bullying 'beast' and 'pig', though the subject remains ambiguous. Whoever it is, the target is doomed to 'look like watercress' after being snubbed by Iggy. A tighter low-end and punchier drums might have made it truly lethal, driving the mayhem to full potential.

Bonus Tracks

'Low Life' (Pop, Kral)

A digitally remastered edition of *Soldier* was released by Buddha Records in 2000, including two bonus outtakes. Little is known about these tracks, with even Matlock unable to recall their creation. 'I have cassettes of some great unreleased stuff we wrote in my apartment between 1979 and 1981', Kral recalled to Dangerous Minds in 2015. 'He has a sweet side and it shines through all that blood, guts and cocaine.' Much of it remains unreleased, though tracks like 'Puppet World' occasionally surfaced in live performances. 'Low Life', however, made it to the studio, with production credited to Thom Panunzio, which likely places it in the *Party* era. It's an acoustic, country-tinged campfire strum where Iggy balances isolation and ambition. Wandering Times Square 'wearing no underwear' and stalling in bed, he sketches a fragmented identity, caught between invisibility and vague dreams of 'planning great things'. Somehow, the dreams stayed on.

'Drop A Hook' (Unknown)

This inessential, driving instrumental new wave piece in E minor remains even more enigmatic. A looser demo circulates online, suggesting it preceded the fuller band version included here, featuring Kral on guitar, possibly with New before his parts were wiped or reduced in post-production. It might even be Rob Duprey, who joined immediately after the *Soldier* sessions to prepare for the tour. With no lyrics or vocals ever added, the working title remains a trace of a song that never quite showed up.

Party (1981)

Personnel:
Iggy Pop: vocals
Ivan Kral: guitar, keyboards
Rob Duprey: guitar
Michael Page: bass
Douglas Bowne: drums
Jimmy Whizner: arrangements on 'Sea Of Love', 'Bang Bang', 'Time Won't Let Me'
The Uptown Horns: brass on 'Pleasure', 'Sincerity', 'Houston Is Hot Tonight', 'Happy Man'
Recorded at Record Plant, New York City, in August 1980
Producers: Thom Panunzio and Tommy Boyce
Release date: UK: June 1981; US: September 1981
Label: Arista
Chart places: US: 166, UK: did not chart, Aus: 93
Running time: 35:23

Having left Berlin in a state of transience, Iggy spent the first half of 1980 relentlessly touring *Soldier*. Struggling to cut back on hard drugs, he battled insomnia, fuelling himself with heavy drinking and a revolving cast of groupies. His band featured the ambitious Kral on guitar and keyboards, alongside ex-Mumps guitarist Rob Duprey. Matlock left soon after, replaced briefly by Billy Rath, whose heroin habit was barely manageable. Both he and Krüger, who had never felt at home in rock 'n' roll excess, were soon dismissed. Their replacements, Michael Page and Douglas Bowne, rounded out the lineup. With *Soldier* barely promoted and the tours running on fumes without label support, finances were tight. Arista's managing director and Clive Davis wanted an album with stronger commercial potential. In August 1980, under mounting pressure, Iggy took his touring band into the Record Plant studio in New York. The result is often seen as the nadir of his studio output. As the slicker, pop-leaning side of new wave gained ground in the early 1980s, Iggy found himself caught in the crossfire. Part wildman, part eager experimenter, and now given a final shot at hitmaker status, he lived up to none of it.

Hungry for a banger, Arista had put up the money. Preparations were hopeful: the band were far more tight-knit than the thrown-together lineup on *Soldier*, and Iggy and Kral had come up with a promising batch of songs. But it didn't take long for Kral to realise that Iggy had no real desire to be in the studio. Once he tore down walls with reckless abandon, now he was a hired decorator, repainting them in radio-friendly pastels. Iggy's mental state was unsteady, and he struggled to balance his earlier edgy, instinctive lyrics with a more accessible approach that would fit into relatively upbeat songs. Panunzio, who had mixed *Soldier*, returned as producer, but Duprey later called it a poor fit on The C86 Show in 2020: 'He didn't really have the force, personality or vision for what to do with the record, and the people at Arista weren't happy.' Hoping to steer the sessions towards the elusive crossover hit, the label wanted a more proven name. Iggy brought in The Monkees hitmaker Tommy Boyce, chosen for his 1960s sentiment, after reaching out by letter. But as the recordings progressed, it became clear to everyone involved: this record wasn't going to be good. Looking back, Kral told Dangerous Minds in 2015:

> Who else can say they wrote Iggy's worst album? It became his joke album. I didn't know he had a personal vendetta against the record company and intended to record a lousy album. I wasted all that time trying to write great songs, but he wanted the opposite. However, 'Pumpin' For Jill' and 'Bang Bang' get licensed often, so it can't be too bad.

Iggy ultimately sabotaged his own shot at success. Struggling with poor sales, executive meddling and an expiring contract, he grew spiteful and apathetic towards finishing the album, with a pharmacological blur only intensifying his mindset. When it came out in summer 1981, Kral, disillusioned by the record and fed up with the backstage tour dynamics, left soon after. The *Party* cover portrait of Iggy was shot by Masayoshi Sukita during the same session that produced Bowie's *"Heroes"* cover, taken while the two were in Japan promoting *The Idiot* in 1977. Iggy's face is trapped in a preschooler's planetarium poster, staring into the future, wondering what the hell he ended up releasing in 1981.

'Iggy is driving himself harder than ever in search of thrills', said the *NME*, and Robert Christgau of *The Village Voice* sneered that 'it took him longer to get The Uptown Horns on the telephone than to write these lyrics.' Though Lester Bangs placed *Party* at number ten on his year-end list in *The Village Voice*, the record was otherwise mostly panned and a commercial failure. The album advance had already been burned on recording expenses and Iggy's anything-but-frugal lifestyle. To keep the cash flowing, a *Party* tour followed immediately. Former Blondie bassist Gary Valentine took over guitar from Kral, and Richard Sohl of The Patti Smith Group briefly joined on keyboards. After a two-month break in September and October, it resumed as the *Follow The Sun Tour*, with Carlos Alomar joining alongside Blondie drummer Clem Burke. Speaking with *Classic Rock* in 2024, Burke recalled: 'Iggy was basically out of his mind. There was no food allowed backstage, only drugs and booze. It was 'no blow, no show', and his only mandate was: 'Play as loud and as fast as possible." The Old Waldorf performance of 25 November 1981 was released on VHS as *Iggy Pop – Live!!!* in 1991. It captures Iggy in suspenders, fishnet stockings and a leather cap, visibly gaunt, his voice ragged and worn: a glimpse into the toll years of touring, drugs and alcohol had taken. Yet the gig – later issued as *Live In San Fran 1981* – features far stronger versions than the album's. *Party* is a surreal oddity: so sanitised and anti-Iggy that its stronger songs never stood a chance, drowned in forced cheerfulness. Time to drag them back up.

'Pleasure' (Pop, Kral)
Arista bet big on *Party*, hoping for a polished, mainstream Iggy Pop, but 'Pleasure' smirks at the idea. The album opener twists lust into absurdity, with Iggy promising to 'squeeze you just like a tomato' and 'peel you like some old potato'. What begins as playful innuendo spirals into a manic plea: 'Just give me some pleasure, it's my life'. The childlike yearning perhaps masks a flicker of truth, a flash of loneliness, as he blurts out: 'I got no wife'. Chugging guitars and brash horn blasts match the lyrics' primal simplicity. The song channels Iggy's unruly core: hungry, giddy and slightly unhinged. It's both hilarious and uncomfortable, clear proof that even when aiming for pop, Iggy couldn't resist, or help, making it weird.

'Rock And Roll Party' (Pop, Kral)
Half-celebrating, half-mocking the rock 'n' roll lifestyle, this underrated cut is essentially the album's title track. It rides on a scruffy riff and a rhythm that thuds like a party lurching towards dawn. Iggy's straightforward lyrics graze the hollowness beneath the revelry: 'Where is the wine?' and 'Where we gonna go tonight?' echo the restless pursuit of indulgence, always just out of reach. Asked about the stylistic shift of *Party*, Iggy told *FFanzeen* in 1988: 'It was supposed to be a commercial album. I did my best to give the record content; every track is about somewhere in America', adding, 'My definition of a rock 'n' roll party is not all fun and games.' Despite clear attempts to shape it for radio play, the song didn't deliver the commercial impact Arista had hoped for. Like the rest of *Party*, it was either too offbeat or simply not hooky enough for mainstream tastes. Meanwhile, many Iggy Pop fans found it too slick, too radio-friendly. Sometimes, you just can't win.

'Eggs On Plate' (Pop, Kral)
Originally a simple riff without a melody by Kral, written with either Mick Ronson or Patti Smith in mind, Iggy quickly turned it into a jittery new wave romp through fame, identity and absurdity. This off-kilter track starts with mundane imagery – eggs, four walls – before spiralling into cryptic references like jewel thief Murph the Surf and cult musician Nash the Slash, who would open for Iggy on his 1982 tour. A clear sneer at Clive Davis, a Colonel Parker-type promises Iggy a spot on the 'hit parade' and all the fame that comes with it. His sceptical reply cuts to the heart of it: 'So who does my name belong to then?' Equal parts autobiography and satire, he embraces his four walls, though with doubt, while skewering the hollow promises of success. Though the thin mix dulls the punk edge, the track rushes through Iggy's one-of-a-kind perspective, but is ultimately forgettable.

'Sincerity' (Pop, Kral)
Kral added a distinct touch to *Party* by bringing in his pals, The Uptown Horns, then just starting out as sidemen. But here, their brass doesn't just land; it crashes through the track like an uninvited guest knocking over the furniture. This limp jam stumbles under its own banality, dragged down by sluggish rhythms and a meandering structure. More filler than anything on an already polarising album, 'Sincerity' is a throwaway, with Iggy reduced to a goofy caricature. Lyrically, it's nothing but a drunken voicemail.

'Houston Is Hot Tonight' (Pop, Kral)
Side one wraps up with a Stonesy riff cruising over a smooth groove that oozes a steamy, nocturnal vibe. Backed by a coiling bass line, this slinky track glows like neon-lit asphalt on a late-night drive. A 1960s soul feel seeps through, courtesy of its horn bursts and handclaps. Tired of Chicago winters, Iggy weaves through images of Houston's oil empire and space programme, his doubled vocals laced with a hint of cynicism, all while simmering in a core theme of heat: intensity, ambition and a dash of danger.

'Pumpin' For Jill' (Pop, Kral)
This hypnotic side two opener is pleasantly quirky, with sparse lyrics laced with innuendo, hinting at affection and frustration. It wastes no time in getting strange, opening with:

> When I'm asleep, you touch my feet
> You let me know that I am no creep

The bottom-rung romantic here is an unappreciated gas station worker, pledging his devotion to a certain Jill, recalling their fleeting Mardi Gras kiss and wondering if she'll ever hear his song. The ambiguity of her existence adds to the overall surreal, dreamlike mood. It's a steady mid-tempo drift, with a thudding bass and a welcome guitar break slicing through the haze. A modal guitar line, faintly echoing Robert Fripp on '"Heroes"', floats in sustained waves. Iggy's subdued delivery fits the song's cool, minimalist charm, leading to a 'lalala' coda that keeps the groove 'pumping' to the very last beat.

'Happy Man' (Pop, Kral)
As the 2 Tone movement rose in the UK in 1979, this track was about as 'on trend' as Iggy gets. With chipper rhythms, peppy guitar strums and horns blaring like a parade, the song seems eager to be fun. And then there's Iggy. With 'I'm a happy man, don't it look that way?', he botches the very notion of happiness, tossing out nonsense so absurd it begs to be quoted:

> I can make her scream
> 'Cause she's my only machine

I'm her confidant
And she's my only cream

If this is the sound of domestic bliss, it should come with an escape plan. With another brass arrangement by The Uptown Horns, it's a peculiar mix of big band swing and Iggy's spectacularly hollow delivery, like a ska band forcing a twitchy frontman through a polka. Whether intentional or not, 'Happy Man' finds Iggy at his most bizarre: a sappy, upbeat misfire that refuses to take itself seriously, or so one hopes.

'Bang Bang' (Pop, Kral)
Unhappy with the initial results of the *Party* sessions, a frustrated Arista sought a high-profile producer to salvage the project. Although Iggy pitched Phil Spector and Mike Chapman, the job ultimately went to Tommy Boyce. Boyce zeroed in on 'Bang Bang', dressing it up with strings, tambourine and handclaps, polishing it into a pop single. The original lyrics, written by Kral and centred on the emancipation of women, were slightly twisted, Iggy-style: 'It's about the appetites of young women', he mused on MTV in 1981. Inspired in part by his reading of *The Right Stuff* by Tom Wolfe in a bookstore, Iggy's version reflects the cold, clinical mindset of a character on a (rather phallic) mission, whether launching rockets, driving fast cars or pursuing groupies. Whatever the intent, the arrangement, with its spidery sound effects, heavy reverb and funereal organ, shapes an eerie, detached atmosphere, which works in its favour. The anthemic 'bang bang' refrain lifts it further with a hook that lingers.

Released in the spring of 1981, the single was accompanied by a bizarre performance on Germany's *Bananas* TV show. A toothless Iggy bounces through a bleak set under the unsettling gazes of Vivian Girls, as if plucked from a Henry Darger fever dream. At the climax, ping-pong balls inexplicably rain down. The result is both whimsical and captivating. Although it reached number 35 on the *Billboard* Club Play Singles Chart, 'Bang Bang' failed to make a commercial impact, leaving Boyce flabbergasted: 'I'm surprised – shocked – that English radio wouldn't play something so commercial', he told *NME* not long after the single had already faded. 'Not because it's something I've worked on but because it's just better than what I'm hearing.' Bowie's 1987 album version on *Never Let Me Down* didn't fare much better. Still, it stands as one of the stronger tracks on *Party*, offering a glimpse of hope that not all was lost.

'Sea Of Love' (Khoury, Phillips)
Pushed by Arista and chosen by Boyce, Iggy's cover of Phil Phillips' 1959 hit is like a leather-clad punk trying to woo you with plastic flowers: equally curious and baffling. The production is slick and sterile, morphing Iggy into a guest crooner on the soundtrack to David Lynch's prom-night slow dance. At

2:05, the solo kicks in, and schmaltz officially eats itself. In the end, it's a curio in his discography. Worth a listen, if only to wonder: did Iggy serenade us, or was he trolling us all along?

'Time Won't Let Me' (King/Kelly)
Another cover, another attempt at accessibility. Here's the musical equivalent of a friend crashing a wedding, stealing the mic and belting out a garage-rock tune with almost enough reckless charm to make you forgive the intrusion. This time, Boyce picked The Outsiders' 1966 hit, a 'commercial' choice that isn't exactly a reinvention but is undeniably Iggy-ised: scrappy, swaggering and a little rough around the edges. Love it or leave it, it's another reminder that when Iggy shows up, he's always going to make it his own, even if just barely.

And with that, the Arista trilogy was over. His contract was terminated and Iggy was once again adrift, with no commercial footing. Asked in 2001 by *Q* magazine to name his worst album, he laughed and said: 'Probably as a whole album, it would be *Party*. The title was a poor choice of word to apply to my output.' If nothing else, the next one had a title that fit. *Zombie Birdhouse* was about to see the light.

Bonus Tracks
'Speak To Me' (Pop, Kral)
In the same vein as 'Low Life', this track leans on a mostly acoustic strum, with clunky, fleeting synths dropping in to add a touch of charm. With lyrics by Iggy and music by Kral, it was inspired by Iggy's intent, before the *Party* sessions, to take bohemian folk music and twist it. The song reflects a quiet longing for connection and a hope for a spark amidst an awkward, slow-moving 'party' (funnily enough), brushing once again against Iggy's fixation on a teenage girl. Kral appreciated the folky songs, believing they could broaden Iggy's left-field audience, but Iggy ultimately rejected them. Kral later re-recorded 'Speak To Me' for his 1995 album *Nostalgia*, while his versions of four other *Party* tracks appeared on his 1999 album *Dancing Barefoot*.

'One For My Baby' (Arlen, Mercer)
The second bonus track on the 2000 Buddha reissue is a studio take of this jazz standard, sometimes listed as 'Set 'Em Up Joe' on bootlegs and semi-officials, after its most quoted line. Iggy had been performing it live since the 1978 *TV Eye Tour*, sometimes to hostile reactions. Originally written for the 1943 film musical *The Sky's The Limit* and first performed by Fred Astaire, the song was later popularised by one of Iggy's earliest influences: Frank Sinatra. In a 2022 interview on Vinyl Writers, he recalled:

> I remember how my father always sang along to 'Young At Heart' in the car; he loved that song. When I was five or six, my parents asked me what I

wanted to be in life. And I just said: 'I wanna be a singer!' That was Frank's fault. He belongs everywhere and nowhere; he is not really a blues singer, not really a crooner. A wanderer between the worlds. The personification of American culture at its peak.

With a soft brushed drumbeat and smoky sax lines, Iggy might seem an unlikely interpreter of the song, yet he fares better with this cover than either of the two misguided oddballs that somehow made it onto the album.

Zombie Birdhouse (1982)

Personnel:
Iggy Pop: vocals
Rob Duprey: guitar, keyboards, background vocals
Chris Stein: bass on 'The Ballad Of Cookie McBride', 'Ordinary Bummer', 'Bulldozer', 'Platonic', 'Street Crazies'
Clem Burke: drums, percussion
Recorded at Blank Tape, New York City, in June 1982
Producer: Chris Stein
Release date: September 1982
Label: Animal Records
Chart places: did not chart
Running time: 42:08

After the *Follow The Sun Tour* wrapped in December 1981, Iggy was nearly broke, without a label and deep into drugs. Record sales were poor, and following his fallout with Arista, his last three albums would soon disappear from stores. Unable to afford the pricey Manhattan hotels where he and Esther had stayed between tours, they moved to a small apartment in Bensonhurst, Brooklyn, which reminded him of Berlin. There, he reconnected with his 12-year-old son and began working with Anne Wehrer on his biography, offering some financial prospects. He drifted: unmoored and aimless. Esther put him on a budget of 20 dollars a day, a familiar constraint from his Berlin years. Looking back in *The Ticket* in 2008, Iggy said:

> I was sleeping on the floor in Bensonhurst, which was like a Mafia neighbourhood in Brooklyn. Basically, I was living hand to mouth, my health was going and I realised I couldn't take on the world anymore. I was going to lose.

Although his recent tour had included a few nights opening for The Rolling Stones in front of 70,000 people, where his miniskirt had provoked a dismissive reception, Iggy felt stuck and dissatisfied with his career. Blondie founder Chris Stein, who had just launched Animal Records, approached him about making an album. Stein laid out the structure of his small operation, and while Iggy knew the budget would be tight, he jumped at the opportunity. Stein knew him, was a fan and would give him the freedom to make a record that stayed truer to his instincts and heart than anything Arista had overseen. With Kral out of the picture, Duprey became Iggy's new songwriting partner, co-writing much of *Zombie Birdhouse:* a strange and compelling descent into his fractured, fevered mind. The small crew was rounded out by Stein on bass and Burke on drums. At Blank Tape Studios in New York, they recorded obscure, Afrobeat-infused new wave songs on 16-track tape, defined by a sharp electronic edge, layered lyrics and an idiosyncratic spirit.

Shortly after finishing the album, Iggy and Esther left for Haiti, where they planned to shoot the cover and recuperate, with Wehrer initially joining them to continue work on *I Need More*. In 1982, Haiti was under the rule of President Jean-Claude 'Baby Doc' Duvalier, a brutal regime marked by economic decay and social unrest. The country was also reeling from the AIDS epidemic, fuelling stigma and crippling tourism, while drug use remained rampant. It was in this environment that Iggy spiralled, unravelling into mania and reckless abandon. Esther described it in a 2013 interview with *Die Zeit*:

> On our first night there, we went to a voodoo ceremony. Jim immediately stripped and started dancing. The voodoo priest didn't think it was very funny. He put a curse on us. I don't believe in things like that, but still, the following weeks were unbelievable. Jim was always getting lost. He spent all our money on drinks, and eventually we found him on one of the streets.

One night, as they were dining with a group, a boat docked on the beach. Suddenly, the conversation stopped as an imposing entourage entered the restaurant. At the centre of the group was Duvalier himself. Fearing for their lives, Esther begged Iggy to stay in line: 'Luckily, Jim listened to me this time. But Haiti was a nightmare.' Short on money, as Iggy had either given theirs away to locals or spent it on booze, Esther took a job as a dentist's assistant in a dingy clinic, pulling teeth to scrape together their return fare. With a borrowed credit card, Esther managed to get them to New York, then put Iggy on a flight to LA, where he was admitted to Northridge Hospital. As he later told *The Ticket*:

> I decided to try to go straight; it was a good decision, although it took three or four years of adjustment and probably led to a fairly long period of mediocrity in my music. But it also led to my survival as a person.

The disorienting trip to Haiti, the mental collapse that followed and Esther's striking photo series remain a vivid reflection of *Zombie Birdhouse*. Few records fuse imagery, title, lyrics and music so seamlessly, forming a delirious *gesamtkunstwerk* on the brink of madness. Critics couldn't quite agree: *Rolling Stone* praised it as 'a brainy, well-plotted collection', while *Sounds* found it less challenging than his earlier records. *The New York Times* called Iggy 'one of rock music's more forceful misanthropes' and *The Village Voice* labelled it his most experimental work to date, adding pointedly, 'which sucks.' Too much and too weird for the general record-buying public, it failed to chart and disappeared when Animal Records folded. For years, it remained lost, overlooked and unappreciated before finding recognition in the next century. It had always been ahead of its time.

'Run Like A Villain' (Pop, Duprey)
Zombie Birdhouse hits hard right out the gate with a sharp post-punk edge, leaving *Party* in the rearview mirror. It's a strong yet relatively conventional track considering what follows. Its oddball energy echoes Devo's 'Whip It', while the sharp bass channels Gang Of Four's 'Damaged Goods'. The track's sound and chaotic undertones also recall Pere Ubu's 'Non-Alignment Pact', blending influences into a taut, kinetic whole. Duprey's edgy guitar injects bite, as a Suicide-like drumbeat pushes with urgency. With a wink (or was it?) to Dick Tracy, the song introduces two characters, sparsely drawn but effective:

Big Dick is a thumbs-up guy
He shot a missile in the sky
It functioned just as advertised
Until the fire made him cry

A product of Cold War bravado, he embodies toxic masculinity with destructive results, while Tracy is the face of consumer culture:

Tracy got an Afghan, pedigreed
Prescription shades and designer jeans
A Sony Walkman on her head
All she wants is to be fed

The lyrics lampoon shallow lifestyles with wry humour and outright aversion: 'Run like a villain 'cause you can't adjust/To a saccharine suburb in the mush'. The song, like the entire album, brims with disorienting yet playfully cryptic language, sometimes pieced together on the spot. Iggy swiped 'Buried in a melting coffin' from a *New York Post* headline on the morning of the recording, about the HMS Sheffield and its doomed crew in the Falkland conflict. And with a brief hesitation after 'zombie', he spontaneously threw in 'birdhouse', inadvertently giving the album its name. 'Darker than the tombs of Egypt' may, in turn, have been sparked by Stein, who once aspired to be an Egyptologist.

A 2019 reissue of the album featured a striking animated video for the song by Polish visual artist Marta Kacprzak, the creative force behind Motion Picture Stories.

'The Villagers' (Pop, Duprey)
Like much of the album, this track pulls us into a stifling, disquieting space. Driven by an Afrobeat groove, a trotting bassline and Burke's uncompromising drumming, it generates a hypnotic, looping current. Iggy's voice toys with pitch, weaving through layered guitar textures and employing rubato phrasing that unsettles the groove, creating an eccentric edge.

Above: *The Idiot Tour*, with Bowie on keys and Gardiner on guitar in his trademark dungarees. Seneca College Field House, Toronto, March 1977. (*Bob Gruen*)

Below: The Ramones opened, Iggy took over. Lust For Life Tour, Aragon Ballroom, Chicago, October 1977. (*Paul Natkin*)

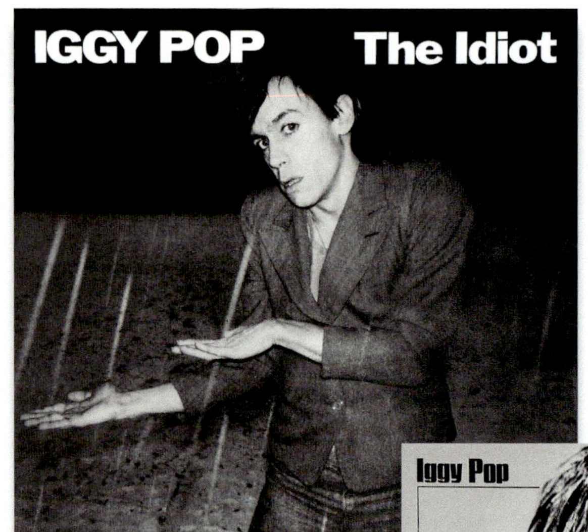

Left: Alien, angular, alive. *The Idiot*, 1977. (*RCA, Sony Music*)

Right: This time, Iggy's driving. *Lust For Life*, 1977. (*RCA, Sony Music*)

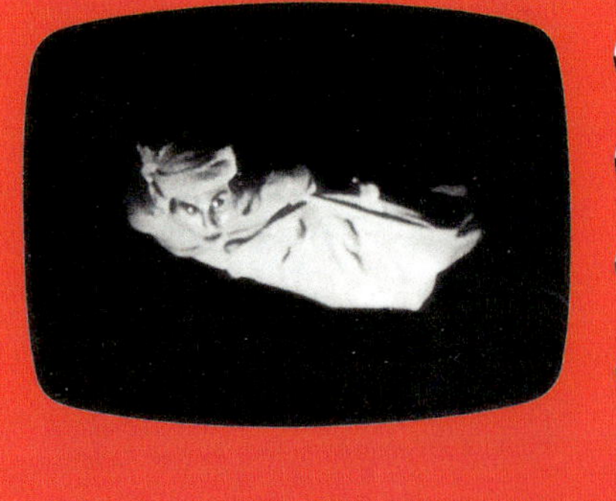

Left: Live, loud and barely held together. *TV Eye Live*, 1978. (*RCA, Sony Music*)

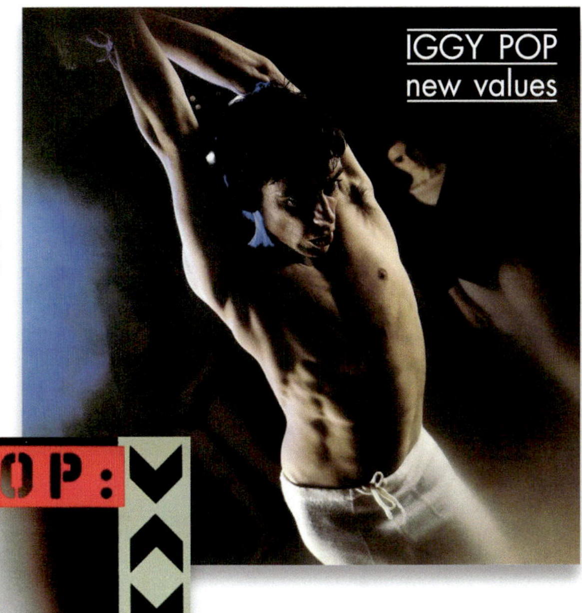

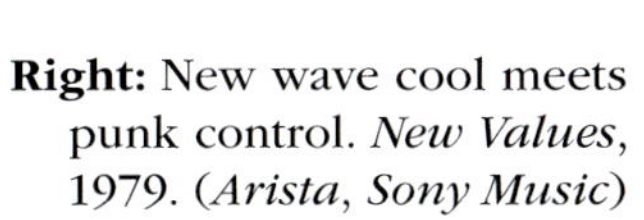

Right: New wave cool meets punk control. *New Values*, 1979. (*Arista, Sony Music*)

Left: Disorderly conduct in uniform. *Soldier*, 1980. (*Arista, Sony Music*)

Right: Dancing on the edge of disinterest. *Party*, 1981. (*Arista, Sony Music*)

Above: Wearing his German helmet, gleaming with sweat. Live in Chicago, 1977. (*Paul Natkin*)

Below: Raw power meets red spandex. The TV Eye *Tour*, Edenbaan, Amsterdam, May 1978. (*Photos by Jilles van Houten*)

A well-shod Iggy promotes *New Values* in New Zealand. White Heron Hotel, Auckland, July 1979. (*Bruce Jarvis*)

Left: Glen Matlock in the background on bass, New Values Tour, Park West, Chicago, November 1979. (*Paul Natkin*)

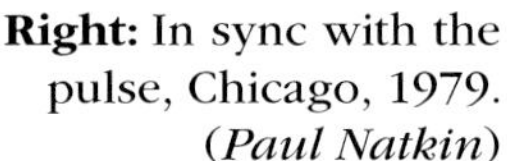

Right: In sync with the pulse, Chicago, 1979. (*Paul Natkin*)

Above: Caught between tension and poise on the Soldier Tour, Riviera Theatre, Chicago, March 1980. (*Paul Natkin*)

Right: Berlin snapshot: Bowie, Iggy and Ivan Kral, 1980. (*CC: Ivan Kral Archive*)

Left: The toll of the years, written across his face. *The Breaking Point Tour*, Commodore Ballroom, Vancouver, February 1983. (*Rob Gander*)

Below: Beer can inbound. Iggy doesn't flinch. (*Rob Gander*)

Right: A fever dream in lo-fi incantations. *Zombie Birdhouse*, 1982. (*Animal Records, Chrysalis Records*)

Left: Cleaned up and radio-ready. *Blah-Blah-Blah*, 1986. (*A&M, Universal Music*)

Right: Heavy sound, light footprint. *Instinct*, 1988. (*A&M, Universal Music*)

Left: A body rebuilt, a voice reborn. *Blah-Blah-Blah Tour,* Vredenburg, Utrecht, November 1986. (*Frans Schellekens*)

Right: The cartoonish metal look in full effect. Instinct Tour, Aragon Ballroom, Chicago, September 1988. (*Paul Natkin*)

Right: Crossing paths again, two icons of different stripes: with Joey Ramone, Chicago, September 1988. (*Paul Natkin*)

Below: Dedicating 'High On You' to his fans, with Andy McCoy. Instinct Tour, Paradiso, Amsterdam, November 1988. (*Frans Schellekens*)

Above: Dressed for duty. Farm Aid, Hoosier Dome, Indianapolis, April 1990. (*Paul Natkin*)

Below: 'He's gonna do another striptease'. As promised. *Brick By Brick* tour, Ahoy, Rotterdam, January 1991. (*Photos by Rob Verhorst*)

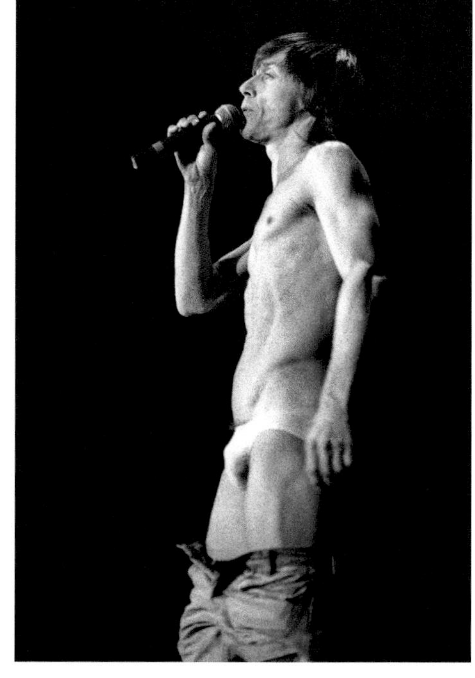

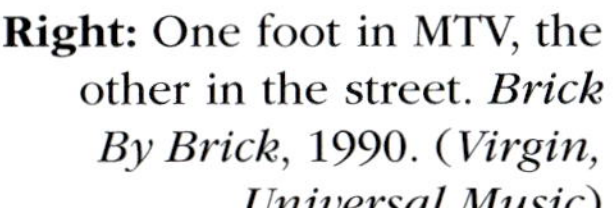

Right: One foot in MTV, the other in the street. *Brick By Brick*, 1990. (*Virgin, Universal Music*)

Left: The US, reimagined as grunge theatre. *American Caesar*, 1993. (*Virgin, Universal Music*)

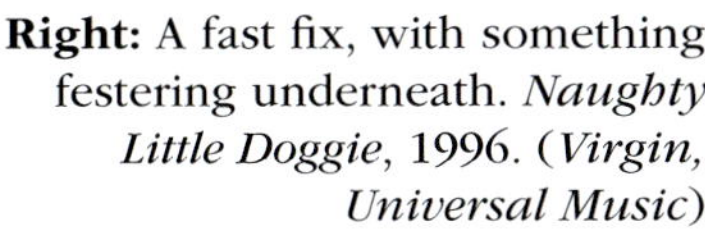

Right: A fast fix, with something festering underneath. *Naughty Little Doggie*, 1996. (*Virgin, Universal Music*)

Left: With Eric Schermerhorn on the American Caesar *Tour* front line, 1994. (*Eric Schermerhorn Archive*)

Right: Hail Caesar! Field Commander Iggy at Lowlands Festival, Biddinghuizen, August 1993. (*Frans Schellekens*)

Right: A low-lit journal from the Lower East Side. *Avenue B*, 1999. (*Virgin, Universal Music*)

Left: Leaning into the next century. Avenue B Tour, Paradiso, Amsterdam, December 1999. (*Frans Schellekens*)

Thirty years to the month after completing *The Idiot*, still going strong. Lowlands, Biddinghuizen, August 2006. (*Rob Verhorst*)

The lyrics dissect a hostile village mentality, where 'sneaking peeping toms' are 'united by the glue of our loathsome qualities' and trapped in cycles of distrust. As the 'village idiot' transforms into a figurehead of media culture in the 'space age', the song veers into dystopia. This absurdity recalls the warnings of Orwell's *1984* and Huxley's *Brave New World*, where oppressive systems thrive on conformity and superficiality. Iggy's wild howl of 'the viiiillagers' evokes a rogue town crier, rousing the village from 'sleepy malice' with drunken fervour. The closing lines, 'You can't get lost/In the village of space', deepen the claustrophobia of a society trapped in uniformity. Drawing on the sociologist Émile Durkheim's idea of a repressive collective consciousness, the song reflects how social cohesion often silences individuality: 'They live to die anonymous/And muted to villagers'. A wry reflection on humanity's lack of progress, even in a so-called enlightened age, this piece showcases the album's bold artistic steps. It illustrates Iggy's creative freedom at this point, his risk-taking and his impulse to venture into new sonic and conceptual terrain.

'Angry Hills' (Pop, Duprey)

Over yet another motorik drumbeat, Iggy sets the scene: dawnlight shines over a distant 'movement in the brush', followed by 'Watering graves of the people who read in the book of forbidden content'. This wonderfully ambiguous line suggests transience, censorship and the silencing of defiance. Under the watchful gaze of the angry hills ('In a gentle way hear them laughing'), Iggy slurs and slides through the album's loveliest melody, framed by chiming guitars. The second verse deepens the theme of repression with 'Imagination under attack/For the pictures I can't even think/I don't even know them', touching on a stifling of free thought and access to suppressed knowledge. By the end, Iggy joins the laughter of the hills. Was it his anger and laughter all along? Is he laughing in relief or sarcasm? In a 1982 interview with *The New York Times*, Iggy fittingly described *Zombie Birdhouse* as 'a kind of audio movie.' Anyone hoping for linear storytelling will be disappointed, but the first three tracks already deliver a feast of free-flowing lyrics and hallucinatory imagery.

'Life Of Work' (Pop, Duprey)

'There are no synthesisers on this record', the sleeve notes insist. Who are we to argue? Yet, with so many treated, looped and distorted sounds, they might as well have smuggled one in. Reflecting on the origins of the album, Duprey recalled in a 2020 interview on The C86 Show:

> After *Party*, I lived on oatmeal in my little rent-controlled apartment in New York, where I started making these goofy recordings with pro Walkmans. I kept bouncing them until the sound was totally transformed into something else. Iggy got interested in these homemade electronic sound processes I made and said, 'Gee, I like to do this on my next record.'

Iggy took the tapes home, focusing purely on lyrics and melody with just a typewriter and a guitar. Feeling like his last two albums hadn't fully captured what he wanted to say, he was determined to reclaim his voice. For six weeks, he commuted from Brooklyn to Manhattan, spending hours each day in Duprey's cramped spare bedroom, sifting through ideas, scrapping what didn't work and shaping what did. Perhaps 'Life Of Work' was born from a late-night drinking session, since its vocal melody borrows heavily from the sea shanty 'What Shall We Do With A Drunken Sailor?'.

Over a persistent drone, a stair-step piano, a metronomic beat and an array of clinical tones, this track firmly belongs in early 1980s industrial electronics. Iggy presents work as a battlefield where routine swallows struggle and people fade into anonymity. He opens with the quasi-heroic 'Riding in the saddle, henchmen at your side', casting the worker as a gunslinger, only to undercut the image with the outlandish 'Holy macaroni, hose you on your back'. Stripped of dignity, he's sanitised like livestock or a machine, while bystanders just stand there 'like oysters on a shelf'. Its cartoon absurdity heightens the monotony and ruthlessness of labour. The repeated 'What do you do with a life of work?' only deepens the sense of endless drudgery. If only machines could do your work for you. Like, maybe some sort of synth?

'The Ballad Of Cookie McBride' (Pop, Duprey)
This conventional, accessible composition is completely upended by Iggy's hillbilly gnawing delivery. It's as if Blondie's 'Heart Of Glass' got mangled at a backwoods hoedown. Over a fairly unassuming backdrop of drums, bass and twangy guitar, woven with Duprey's high-pitched backing vocals, Iggy yodels the tale of Cookie McBride: a 'hermit of Burial Ridge' who abandoned society for life in the wilderness. Bears, wolves and brutal conditions paint a picture of danger and isolation. Aware that he's heading for an 'unmarked', 'unhappy' and ultimately 'rain-filled' grave, he still chooses freedom. Near the song's end, he makes it clear what following his path will cost: we, too, will end up 'high, wet and hanging like Cookie McBride'. A wry parting shot in the face of death wraps up the yarn: 'Who will remember the money you saved?' An uncompromising, goofy and unexpected allegory of Mr Pop himself? Five songs in, it's clear: all bets are off.

'Ordinary Bummer' (Pop)
Stein reflected on Iggy's vocal performance in *NME* in 1982:

> I think Ig really got pushed into this American mainstream rock 'n' roll thing the last couple of albums. I just wanted to see him be really free to go crazy. When we did his vocal sessions, he really was just totally crazy.

Yet here, wrapped in a loose, melancholic atmosphere, Iggy carries a wistful tone, musing on the ebb and flow of joy with understated resignation. The spidery guitar adds texture rather than melody, weaving like a ghost in the machine. The laid-back drums steer the slower tempo, while subtle piano lines drift in and out, deepening the languid feel. It's not a banger, but it lingers, brooding and subdued.

In 1997, before their official reformation, Blondie (under the pseudonym Adolph's Dog) covered the song for the Iggy Pop tribute album *We Will Fall*. Years earlier, Debbie Harry also performed 'Cookie McBride' live as a solo artist, with Stein on guitar, showing that his love for the album remained strong despite its poor reception at the time.

'Eat Or Be Eaten' (Pop, Duprey)

Side two opens with this dog-eat-dog track that showcases both the primal force and contradictions of the album. Cryptic and predatory, the lyrics paint a world ruled by instinct. The opening lines set a scene of hunger and desperation, bringing the animalistic drive for survival into focus: 'I got nothing to eat in this old house/I gotta go out and catch a mouse'. What follows continues in the same vein, offering a quirky nihilism rather than, say, a profound philosophical exploration. To get the gist:

Strike or be stricken
Eat or be eaten
Yum yum yum yum
Eat or be eaten

There's a ritualistic streak here: 'just the night for a conquering tribe' blurs sex and violence, stylised like pulp fiction and curling through the city haze. The nervy music centres on a punk-funk groove, built on two simple chords and a sense of unease. It's a humorously compelling, skeletal piece for fans of Iggy's more avant-garde work and those keen to hear him scat. While it establishes a hypnotic vibe, it ultimately lacks memorability, feeling too sparse and repetitive to rise above its minimalism. This fleeting impact extends across the whole album, meaning 'Eat Or Be Eaten' fits within the experimental context of *Zombie Birdhouse*, but fails to stand out as one of Iggy's more enduring works. However, notable live performances include a show at The Ritz in New York in December 1982, where Iggy's untamed fury elevated the song's urgency immensely. Another great rendition was on the British TV show *The Tube* in December 1983, where he blasted it alongside savage, face-melting versions of 'Run Like A Villain' and 'Sixteen'. Photographer Virginia Turbett, present that day, recalled for this book: 'During the shoot, the producer said: 'The second he goes for his trousers, cameras off him!'.'

'Bulldozer' (Pop, Duprey)

A punk riff so forgettable, it's hard to tell whether it's an unfinished leftover or a deliberate base for what's about to unfold. Either way, what follows defies all expectations. Channelling Zappa's 'The Central Scrutinizer', Iggy descends into a spoken-word jazz piece with a full-blown Bogart-Bacall syndrome, starring a bulldozer urged to 'Run that girl over'. His delivery is so unhinged, you'd swear the alleged Haitian voodoo curse that would soon haunt him had already taken hold. Halfway through, Iggy chuckles, then folds it into the character's voice. Is he leaving it in to show he's in on the absurdity of the track? Maybe. But then, it happens again at the end! Has he lured us into some avant-garde experiment on chaos theory, where order emerges from disorder? Compelling and bat-crazy, this track was recorded, released and even performed live. Audacity, stupidity, genius? This is Iggy, man. For Ripley's enthusiasts: the six-CD box set *Where The Faces Shine – Volume 2* includes a live version of the track, recorded during the 1982 *Zombie Birdhouse Tour*, with heavier drums and guitars, plus that cryptic laugh.

'Platonic' (Pop, Duprey)
With its sleek, refined sound, 'Platonic' exudes late-Roxy Music sophistication. Shimmering guitars, textural keyboard sounds and a tight rhythm section create a dreamy, meditative atmosphere that feels effortless yet elegant. This dreaminess carries into the lyrics, introducing a philosophical layer rooted in Plato's concept of the 'Platonic ideal': perfect, unchanging forms beyond the physical world. The lyrics describe a figure embodying this ideal beauty: 'Oh, the coronation when she walks by/Even if it's private miss you and your mind'. Iggy's awe frames her as a muse or near-divine figure, both untouchable and deeply inspiring. She transcends imperfection and time, as 'time has no pull on her soul'. A reference to geometry ('angles indirectly revealed') echoes Plato's belief in geometric order as a path to understanding perfection. Meanwhile, the tension between timelessness and immediacy ('buy in a hurry') reflects the human urge to grasp something as abstract and unchanging as an ideal. The song cleverly plays with the double meaning of 'Platonic', contrasting abstract perfection with lived admiration. In this peculiar track, where Iggy sounds so awestruck that he barely lands in key, it adds a philosophical shade that enriches its surface-level allure. The result is both fascinating and just disorienting enough to keep you guessing.

'The Horse Song' (Pop, Duprey)
One of the few tracks where you can actually tell the drums are played by a real human, confirming Clem Burke is, in fact, not a machine. It struts along with a hard-strummed acoustic, a warped electric riff and punchy chords popping in and out unexpectedly. Iggy delivers one of the album's most disarming moments. It's not about heroin, as that would feel almost pedestrian in this hall of warped visions. Instead, it's about Iggy framing *himself* as a horse, curious and sensing spring for the first time. He stands at a door, caught between two worlds: 'And when you nicely ask me in/I'm staring at your shoes'. Part stallion, part pet, he wonders which life calls to

him more: the open range or the soft brush of a loving gaze. The song drifts between tenderness and absurdity, comfort and unease. There is a striking honesty in Iggy's outcry: 'I think you've noticed/That I don't wanna be a bad guy anymore!' A moment of self-awareness that foreshadows his check-in at Northridge for rehab later that year. The results were short-lived, but lasting salvation lay just around the corner. For now, a fleeting moment of relative clarity before the chaos closes in once more.

'Watching The News' (Pop, Duprey)

The mechanical rhythm and authority of typewritten text naturally lend a sense of intention, making even mundane words seem more profound. Hammered out on his second-hand Smith Corona, it may have looked like a poetic masterpiece to Iggy, but for mere mortals, there's little to cling to.

Over Duprey's patchwork of pulses and frequencies, he drags us into a feverish media storm, spiralling through a manic transmission where war, politics, capitalism and anxiety blur into one. 'His most pretentious record', Duprey is quoted as saying in Trynka's *Open Up And Bleed*. That may be, but it's of no concern if it treats us to a delightfully deranged gem like 'My daughter's not some damn hamburger chainsaw' in a track that casually lifts from 'O Come, All Ye Faithful'. Iggy's disjointed phrases mirror the media's distortion of reality, locking us into a cycle of consumption and desensitisation. Fuelled by Cold War tensions, he echoes the album's opener: 'The president today announced that he's pushing all the buttons, in a giggling fit'. The absurdity hits harder as nuclear paranoia and the news cycle collide. 'Links, rechts, links, rechts!' yanks us into military drill mode, a cold, mechanical order imposed on a society marching to a rhythm not of its own making. Iggy doesn't just critique media saturation, he embodies it: lost in mantras and monologues, spitting out fragments of a world that no longer makes sense. After four minutes of this broadcast, you agree.

'Street Crazies' (Pop)

During the early 1980s, homelessness across the United States became increasingly visible, driven by economic policies, a decline in affordable housing and inadequate governmental responses. In New York City, numerous individuals slept on streets and church steps, a sight that didn't escape Iggy. Looking back in 1995, he said in *Plazm* magazine:

> I'm not sure, but 'Street Crazies' may have been one of the first songs anyone ever wrote about homeless people. They weren't really capital H, known as homeless then. But I saw these people around and thought, 'these are the most important people in America', so I just wanted to sing about them. The way it went with the music, it just felt a little Indian, like being in Calcutta besieged by people with outstretched hands, only you didn't have to go to Calcutta anymore.

The music is heavily influenced by Afrobeat, recalling Talking Heads/Byrne/Eno experiments from the same era and the unified primitive/futuristic vision of Jon Hassell's *Fourth World* music. Both the instrumentation and Iggy's vocals surge and recede like a hallucinatory incantation. He chants, growls, ululates, moans, shouts and shrieks, shifting between shaman, mystic and absolute nutcase. Then, mid-flow, he snaps the spell with a street preacher aside:

> Yes, they're cropping up now with alarming frequency
> These little group eyes, wasted people standing around
> Those who've been kicked ass backwards hard out of our society
> As we try for the better, for the higher in man
> They may as well be apes, you know
> Trying to comprehend a way of death...

He rambles on for a moment but fades out, making way for the returning chant, a piercing yelp and screeching guitars and keyboards, like fingernails on a blackboard. At 3:08, the ritual frenzy nearly grinds to a halt. Iggy hacks, then picks up the thread again. The album's feverish clash of jungle delirium, voodoo trances and mechanised dystopian surrealism culminates in Iggy's cracked, despairing cry: 'Is this vision I've seen really here?'

Bonus Track

'Pain & Suffering' (Pop, Kral)

The origins of this track are muddled. Some *Zombie Birdhouse* CD releases credit Kral as co-writer, while others list Duprey. Some feature Iggy's solo version, while others include an alternate take with Debbie Harry's backing vocals. To complicate matters further, some releases cite the *Birdhouse* musicians, while others reference *Party*'s lineup. Originally featured in *Rock & Rule*, a now cult-status 1983 Canadian animated film, the version with Harry's vocals first appeared on a promotional cassette, as the official soundtrack was never released. In 2019, it was issued on 7" vinyl as the B-side to 'The Villagers', coinciding with Iggy's birthday and Record Store Day. It served as a teaser for the forthcoming album reissue, where it is credited to Kral and the *Party* musicians, likely the most accurate attribution.

Ultimately, the music is what matters, and this intriguing anomaly, particularly the version with Harry, remains essential. In the 1983 documentary *The Making Of Rock & Rule*, Iggy explained that he was trying to draw on nature in his lyrics, because it was something anybody could relate to: 'Just of how bad nature could go. How sick could I feel?' With its steady rock backdrop, bizarre animal sounds and Iggy's Beefheart-esque delivery, the track perfectly aligns with the film's dystopian essence and stands as a fitting postscript to *Birdhouse*. Grotesque imagery and apocalyptic themes collide: 'Red wine turns to blood' twists sacred symbolism, while a cow floating in mud and a goat's skull 'making love' heighten the song's macabre absurdity. The violent threat to 'rip you limb from limb/and tear you up', and the claim 'I am black Armageddon', drive a manic, visceral narrative of collapse, topped off with a dessert of shouted German, leaving a ghostly stamp of unease.

Blah-Blah-Blah (1986)

Personnel:
Iggy Pop: vocals
Kevin Armstrong: guitar, backing vocals
Erdal Kizilcay: synthesiser, bass, drums, string arrangements, backing vocals
Steve Jones: guitar solo on 'Cry For Love'
David Bowie: backing vocals
Recorded at Mountain Studios, Montreux, Switzerland, in May 1986
Producers: David Bowie and David Richards
Release date: September 1986
Label: A&M
Chart places: US: 75, UK: 43, Aus: 34, Can: 61
Running time: 46:12

Barely recovered from his breakdown in Haiti, Iggy spent the better part of late 1982 through mid-1983 on the road, playing sweaty, shambolic shows to keep the money coming in. He kept pushing the edge, wrecking himself in every sense. As the *Zombie Birdhouse Tour* wore on, it morphed into the aptly named *The Breaking Point Tour*, taking Iggy from the US to Hawaii, Japan and Australia. In Tokyo, his eyes fell on a girl in the audience: Suchi Asano, who followed him to LA after the tour ended abruptly when Iggy cancelled the final show. The exhaustion of touring, the shadow of darker days and the pull of a new relationship ended his time with Esther. She went on to run galleries in Heidelberg and Frankfurt, where she became an independent art consultant. After cleaning up in LA and getting physically back on track, Iggy and Suchi moved to a tidy high-rise apartment in Greenwich Village, Manhattan. After years of nomadic living, drugs, groupies, label clashes and self-destruction, he didn't set foot on stage for the next three years. He got a new manager, joined SAG, took acting classes, auditioned for films and landed small parts in *Sid And Nancy* and *The Color Of Money*. For the first time in his life, he handled his own finances, signed a lease, did his own grocery shopping and vacuumed the apartment, a domestic rhythm he found oddly satisfying. His relationship with Suchi, unfamiliar with the US and still struggling with the language, gave him someone to take care of instead of the other way around. Not being able to talk about sobriety or career frustrations with her proved unexpectedly liberating. To keep her in the country, they decided to get married.

With his new manager in place, royalty payments began flowing more smoothly, and his earlier albums and covers by Grace Jones and The Sex Pistols were finally bringing in some money. But once again, it was Bowie who did the most to help. His global success with their co-written 'China Girl' meant Iggy no longer had to tour just to survive. For the first time in years, he could actually settle down. That winter, he and Suchi joined Bowie on a vacation to Bali and Java. The trip inspired 'Tumble And Twirl', which Bowie recorded for *Tonight*, along with two more of their songs: 'Tonight' and 'Neighborhood Threat', as well as Iggy's 'Don't Look Down'. During Bowie's recording of *Tonight* in the spring of 1984, Iggy joined him in Canada for a week. They wrote and recorded 'Dancing With The Big Boys', both contributing vocals. Although *Tonight* is widely seen as one of Bowie's weakest albums, it sold well in the wake of *Let's Dance* and hit number one in the UK, bringing Iggy yet another wave of royalties.

He used the windfall to record demos with Steve Jones in LA. A rock artist approaching 40, with two flopped albums and a drug-ridden past, was hardly what labels were looking for. Many would have called it quits. Iggy was ready to fight his way back up. When Bowie heard the new songs, he was impressed by their melodies and charged lyrics and offered to produce Iggy's next album, saying he could shape the material into commercially viable songs and proposing to co-write new ones. The two friends retreated to Bowie's holiday home in Mustique, where they started recording rough ideas and took the work with them on a skiing trip to Gstaad. In the spring of 1986, they began recording at Queen's Mountain Studios in Montreux, near Bowie's home. Bowie assembled a skeleton crew: guitarist Kevin Armstrong, who had played with him at Live Aid, and multi-instrumentalist Erdal Kizilcay, already familiar from earlier Montreux sessions. A borrowed Linn drum machine from Roger Taylor stood in as the drummer. Programming and technical production were handled by David Richards, Mountain's in-house engineer, while Bowie oversaw the album's creative direction.

Without a label advance, Bowie personally covered a significant share of the costs. In the studio, he was focused and fast, chain-smoking, drinking coffee and scribbling notes, determined to help Iggy make a hit. His investment paid off when A&M took the bait. Drawn by the album's sleek, accessible production and boosted by Bowie's name, they offered Iggy the best contract of his career. The cover, a Michael Halsband photograph, showed Iggy in hardware-store gear: stripped of drugs, dressed for errands, yet far from defanged. It became a solid success, going gold in Canada and performing well in both the UK and the US. Reviews were largely positive, with occasional reservations. While *Rolling Stone* predicted Stooges fans might see it as a major sellout, *Sounds* countered with: 'Iggy Pop is back with a slam.' The *LA Times* praised its emotional undercurrents, while *Creem* leaned positive, too, calling it 'an Iggy-flavoured Bowie album', a sentiment echoed by critics and fans alike, both as praise and critique. Looking back in 1990, Iggy told the *Chicago Tribune*:

> Bowie set up a good framework for me to tell my story in a way that people could hear. It got on the radio. At times, we got a little too meticulous in the studio. But 'Shades', 'Winners & Losers', 'Cry For Love' and 'Wild Child' sum up my story at the time.

Blah-Blah-Blah has faced increasingly critical reactions in the years since, including from Iggy himself later in his career. Too poppy, too slick, the least Iggy-like album he ever made (*Party*, anyone?). But after years of personal and professional struggle, he needed a record that would put him back on the map and keep him from fading into the long, unceremonious list of rock stars whose careers sputtered out, left to peddle covers or trade on nostalgia. With Bowie's guidance, a focused Iggy and a strong batch of songs, the album's contemporary, glossy packaging did exactly what it was supposed to do. It gave Iggy fresh wind in his sails. And beneath the sheen, he delivered emotionally direct lyrics and some of his strongest vocals in years. He sounds sharp, expressive and fully committed, without being intoxicated. Now that the sounds of the 1980s have resurfaced in a new generation of artists, from mainstream pop to synth-influenced indie, its once-dated corniness has taken on a different charm.

'Real Wild Child (Wild One)' (O'Keefe, Greenan, Owens)
The opener plunges us into a reverb-soaked, slicked-up Iggy Pop, wrapped in the lacquered laminate of commercial rock on this lively cover of Johnny O'Keefe's 'The Wild One', a 1958 staple often dubbed the birth of Aussie rock 'n' roll. Retitled 'Real Wild Child', Iggy's version drips with mid-1980s flash: drum machine, electronic bass and clean-lined synth chords over serrated guitar riffs. The irony, of course, is that it sounds anything but wild. Which may be why it became Iggy's biggest hit, cracking the UK top ten and edging into US rotation. Its lyrics and dancefloor pulse channel the juvenile instinct, but Iggy valued it for another reason. He noted how the words referenced 'the world gone crazy and everything hazy' even before 'Purple Haze' had emerged. Its afterlife in pop culture was sealed: the song featured in films like *Problem Child*, *Clueless* and *Five Nights At Freddy's*, and served as Australia's *Rage* theme for over 20 years. Future collaborators Jet marked its 50th anniversary with Iggy in 2008, and Kesha adopted it as her walk-on music. In 1987, it powered Iggy's notorious appearance on the UK kids' show *Number 73*, where he stomped, strangled and dry-humped a giant teddy bear: a moment of live TV chaos proving you can lacquer Iggy, but thankfully, you'll never sand him down.

'Baby, It Can't Fall' (Pop, Bowie)
An oddly sleek pop-rock track built on a chugging rhythm that bounces forward with a catchy groove: think dated synths with a pinch of punk. Its clean production affirms the opener as a clear shift in Iggy's sound, blending polished, commercial stylings with his signature edge. The cheerful organ riff, uncannily reminiscent of Huey Lewis And The News' 'Heart And Soul', does it no favours, and neither do the canned horn blasts. The mix feels unresolved, its sound effects bordering on grating. Armstrong's guitar, becoming more prominent at 3:02, sparks a flicker of tension towards the end. A welcome ascending break at 3:28 launches Kizilcay's Hammond with a burst of energy, but it's all too little, too late.

The rather uplifting lyrics reflect love's enduring strength amid life's uncertainties. Given Iggy's often turbulent personal life, there's a layer of vulnerability in his delivery, though it's masked with cool detachment. The result is an intriguing contrast: a track that's both slick and muscled, like Iggy in a designer suit doing things his way. It offers an infectious snapshot of his unpredictable journey through the decade, but not much else.

'Shades' (Pop, Bowie)
Once a street-walking cheetah with a heart full of napalm, Iggy Pop now delights in the simple gift of sunglasses. The premise might seem absurd, yet his delivery radiates sincerity, and he sells it with conviction. The production feels fuller and more balanced than the previous track, allowing this love song's structure and melody to shine. The key line 'I like these shades' rises from a reflective build-up, with octave-high echoes of 'pain' and 'mirror', delivering a straightforward but resonant payoff.

Inspired by a moment of affection between Iggy and Suchi, and the riff for 'Cry For Love', Bowie composed much of the music and penned the first verse. The lyrics reflect his view of Iggy's rehabilitation over three years, portraying him as a bruised but ordinary Joe, savouring life's small moments with humility. Iggy liked the idea of a 'reformed guy' song but pared down Bowie's ornate lines, scrapping references to Saint Francis and Baudelaire for simpler, heartfelt expressions:

These shades say something
I'll bet they cost a lot
I hope I don't break 'em
I hope we don't break up

As throughout the album, most of the instrumentation is handled by wizard-of-all-trades Kizilcay, who contributes keyboards, synthesisers, percussion, bass and subtle touches like the recurring bending two-note bass motif. A 'French horn' countermelody in the chorus plays off Iggy's vocal rise and fall, adding elegance. The machine-driven beat provides a steady undercurrent, giving Armstrong's mildly dissonant riff room to cut through. Though it received some airplay as a single in 1987 (edited to protect us from the soul-crushing obscenity 'it makes me come in the night'), the excellent 'Shades' failed to leave a mark. Its low-budget video, featuring Iggy behind a chain-link fence, happens to predict the fleeting nature of his cleaned-up, everyday-man persona. It presents a confined reflection of Iggy, one destined to break free. And soon enough, it would.

'Fire Girl' (Pop, Jones)
A recurring theme on *Blah-Blah-Blah* is Iggy's conflicted relationship with television, a symbol of both seduction and rot. From 'bad TV that insults me

freely' ('Cry For Love') to 'raw greed and king TV' ('Hideaway') and the rant on TV in the title track, the album frequently critiques the medium's trivial grip. In 'Fire Girl', however, Iggy sets the screen aside, declaring: 'I have no time to watch TV'. It's a tender moment, as his focus shifts entirely to his love interest, portrayed as a force of nature. With the direct opener 'I loved you when it was alright/I'll love you when it all goes wrong', Iggy pledges devotion through all circumstances. His desire is absolute, yet a quiet loneliness seeps through, culminating in the plaintive 'I'm so lonely'. The track is a light, melodic could-have-been-but-wasn't single, tinged with vulnerability. Its insistent, trebly synth pulses and lifeless drumbeat, embalmed even by drum machine standards, undercut its potential, while the production drains the song of its natural flow. Written with Jones during the pre-album sessions, it remains an unassuming but heartfelt moment, though the thin mix and abrupt fade-out leave it trailing off rather than landing.

'Isolation' (Pop, Bowie)
A stunning melody, anchored by a beat that's as firm as it is measured, blending emotional vulnerability with structural strength. Its reflective tone and steady build evoke echoes of pop melancholy, with a touch of grandeur. Iggy, reflecting on past work, admitted he had neglected melody but made it a focus during this period (perhaps taking cues from The Alan Parsons Project's 'Don't Answer Me'?). While Iggy claimed the melody as his own, Bowie's imprint is unmistakable. With him in the backing vocals, as integral as the lush synths, the song surges towards its explosive chorus, nodding to the sax arrangement of 'Absolute Beginners' released two months prior. Bowie's vocal interplay with Iggy, breaking the title into rhythmic fragments and tossing it back and forth, creates a dynamic exchange, giving Iggy room to pour his isolation into long, aching notes. It's a masterful construction, with Bowie's push for sustained notes and extended phrases helping to craft what may be Iggy's most compelling vocal performance. In the verses, Iggy assumes the role of a wanderer seeking love, navigating a loop from heartbreak to freedom to renewed longing, only to return to solitude. The choruses lay bare the paradox of craving intimacy while knowing its futility. Yet amidst the sorrow, there's humour: 'I need some lovin'/Like a fastball needs control' surely provoked laughter in the studio. In 1988, Iggy told *FFanzeen*:

> I sincerely believe the lyrics on the album to be the best since my work on *Raw Power*. I worked very hard to make my point clear on each lyric. I'm interested in dealing with one-on-one situations that I was too frightened to deal with before.

Bowie's affection for 'Isolation' remained undiminished. While curating the 2002 Meltdown Festival, he tried to recruit Iggy, unsuccessfully due to touring commitments. Bowie told him he'd hoped to hear what he fondly called 'a damn good song', as Iggy later recalled to *The Word* in 2009.

'Cry For Love' (Pop, Jones)

'I beg your pardon!?' Iggy laughed during a 1986 Radio Luxembourg interview when the host asked him about his 'second Sex Pistol'. Following Matlock's work on *Soldier*, Steve Jones was indeed the second ex-Pistol to collaborate with Iggy. Three of the songs they had crafted together in LA in 1985 made it onto the album. When Bowie based the sessions in Montreux, visa issues and scheduling conflicts prevented Jones from recording. His blistering guitar solo on 'Cry For Love', along with Iggy's vocal, was flown in from their demo.

The album's lead single, peaking at number 34 on *Billboard*'s Album Rock Tracks chart, stands out as one of the album's heavier cuts. A hybrid of Billy Idol swagger and The Cars' refined drive, it's a powerful track built around a surging guitar riff, a string arrangement and a kinetic backbeat. It captures an aching urgency, while Iggy's composed baritone channels a yearning for connection in a cold, hollow world. The chorus lingers through repetition of the title, ultimately offering reassurance to fellow cravers. Beneath the surface, the lyrics balance defiance and confession. 'Every stinking bum should wear a crown' rejects societal hierarchies, while 'Been searching for a meaningful embrace/Sometimes my self-respect took second place' exposes both longing and compromise. Although stripped of its atmospheric strings, the Iggy-Jones demo drives the song in a darker direction. Its aggressive power chords and fiercer drums make it the stronger version, with its sturm und drang hinting at Iggy's next chapter: a no-frills, chest-thumping heavy-rock sound.

'Blah-Blah-Blah' (Pop, Bowie)

Imagine a 1986 arcade machine in meltdown, spewing synth-driven, dance-rock chaos over a steroid-fuelled 'Footloose' beat. That's the title track: frenetic, prophetic and experimental. A sonic hurricane of Linn drums, bouncy organ, disruptive guitar, conjoined textures and fragmented lyrics, it shreds through the information clutter of its time. Iggy's snarling vocals, colliding with sped-up and delayed echoes, latch onto consumerism, media overload and the absurdity of modern spectacle. He likely employed the cut-up writing technique Bowie adopted from Burroughs here, resulting in a deliberately scattered effect. References to Shimon Peres and 'Senator Rambo' conflate geopolitical power with violent posturing, while 'Johnny's' illiteracy, consumer goods and spectacular violence dissolve into the same trivialisation:

Johnny can't read
Blah blah blah
I can't see

Blah blah blah
Tuna on white
Guns all night
Blah blah blah

The recurring 'blah blah blah' isn't just grating; it's the point. It mocks the numbing churn of empty slogans and hollow rhetoric ('We are the world/We are so huge'), reinforcing the diatribe's critique of cultural noise, strikingly prescient in a pre-internet world. It all builds to Iggy's cutting verdict: 'The most spoiled brats on God's green earth', before he circles back to his opening line. What makes the track stand out is its audacious production, shaped by Bowie's creative touch as he twisted the controls of a modulation pedal that captured fragments of Iggy's voice and spat them back at unpredictable speeds and pitches.

Though dated now, the track captures a moment of candid studio experimentation. Layered keyboards, distorted voices, bark samples and clattering effects forge a dense, collaged soundscape. A daring time capsule of sound and satire, it finds Iggy skewering societal superficiality with wit, disarray and a knowing smirk.

As for 'Johnny': the name may nod to Johnny Yen, or to Don Henley's 1982 single 'Johnny Can't Read', which had already cast it as shorthand for American cultural decline. The phrase itself dates back to Rudolf Flesch's 1955 bestseller *Why Johnny Can't Read*, a scathing critique of the education system that turned 'Johnny' into a byword for national failure. Iggy, for his part, turns it into a symbol of the culturally stunted everyman: overfed, undereducated and gun-happy. Notably, a decade later, Bowie's paranoid sketch of US culture, 'I'm Afraid Of Americans', would revolve around an emblematic character with the very same name.

'Hideaway' (Pop, Bowie)

This simple, diatonic structure grooves with a smooth bassline, pierced by a sharp five-note guitar figure, creating a pulse like a heartbeat beneath a silk shirt. Iggy's controlled vocals wind through the verses, crooning about the damage wrought by 'big industry', 'king TV' and the greed-fuelled sprawl of 'concrete strips'. Disillusioned by apathy ('They say 'so what' I say 'so this''), he yearns for a retreat, clinging to what little purity and grace remain in a world that has lost its way. There's a winking self-awareness beneath it all, as if Iggy's too cool to care, but just enough to sing about it. The real treat lies in the song's elements. The rhythm section drives forward with tight control; the backing chorus is irresistibly catchy; the bridge at 2:41 screams Bowie; and Iggy's slightly ragged vocals and Armstrong's guitar outro add just a bit of bite, all wrapped in a glossy 1980s package. It's another glimpse of Iggy trying on new clothes without shedding his true identity, a man trapped in his own reinvention.

'Winners & Losers' (Pop, Jones)
For newcomers to Iggy Pop in 1986, this album might have raised an eyebrow: how had this 39-year-old crooner once stood at punk rock's blood-soaked edge? Its longest and fiercest track offered a rare flash of Iggy's untamed past. A solo wink to The Stooges' 'Scene Of The Crime', it delivers a jagged reflection on life's divide between success and failure. It opens with the reflective line 'Winners and losers, which one am I?/Is it the same under the sky?' before spiralling into sharp critiques, dark humour and vivid imagery:

In this glass and wire world
Surely leeches gain the right
To send their message screaming
One that has no meaning
To people who feel
Questions and questions
Plain as your nose
But who would believe a little rose?
Winners and losers in love with themselves
No Santa Claus, no happy elves

An arresting tableau of a world filled with hollow noise, where exploiters thrive, genuine beauty is dismissed and self-absorbed vanity takes centre stage. Later in the song comes a moment of cold-eyed nihilism, echoing the emotional dead ends of his past – like his relationship with underaged lover Betsy:

She gave me money
She gave me head
She gave me everything
And then she went dead

The final verse suggests that, despite the senselessness of it all, life rolls on as people cope with their lot, caught in the endless cycle of winners and losers. For the song's construction, Iggy drew inspiration from an unlikely source: Bo Diddley's call-and-response format, which he had used to great effect in the original Stooges shows. Lyrically and stylistically intertwined, 'Scene Of The Crime' and 'Winners & Losers' occasionally found themselves side by side in Iggy's late-1980s live sets. It is undeniably the darkest track on the album, and one of its finest.

'Little Miss Emperor' (Pop, Bowie)
This B-side to 'Real Wild Child' was tacked onto CD and cassette versions of *Blah-Blah-Blah*, upsetting the sequencing by bumping 'Winners & Losers'

from its rightful closing slot. Often dismissed as filler, it still has its moments, especially in Iggy's vocal delivery and lyrical scope. 'I think he's getting better and better as a songwriter, substantially as a lyricist', Bowie told *Music & Sound Output* in 1987. 'There's a fabulous maturity around what he's doing. He's my favourite contemporary songwriter.'

A staccato bass rumbles and pushes against the rigid beat, while sharply voiced piano, synth washes and string flourishes weave through the dense mix. Iggy riffs on Ginsberg's *Howl*, channelling its critique of conformity and societal decay. 'I saw the best minds of my generation/Learn how to crawl across our nation' nods to *Howl*'s iconic opening, while 'But babies mostly drown/It's a company town' and 'Conformity falls like one wet blanket' reflect Ginsberg's despair over a corporate world. The title figure blends ambition with self-delusion and control. Her struggle reflects both societal pressure and personal rebellion while still remaining the object of Iggy's desire. Despite its ambition, the track stumbles: the chorus stagnates, and the overstuffed mix buries its impact under too many competing elements. Still, as a B-side, it intrigues. Six months later, Bowie lifted a line from its chorus melody for ''87 And Cry', a song more justifiably forgotten.

Instinct (1988)

Personnel:
Iggy Pop: vocals
Steve Jones: guitar
Seamus Beaghen: keyboards
Leigh Foxx: bass
Paul Garisto: drums
Recorded at Sorcerer Sound and BC Studio, New York City, in April 1988
Producer: Bill Laswell
Release date: June 1988
Label: A&M
Chart places: US: 110, UK: 61, Aus: 82, Can: 34
Running time: 43:38

In 1986, Iggy hit the stage sober for the first time. 'He was fit, newly married, doing ballet stretches and exercises, eating right, no funny stuff', Kevin Armstrong recalled on The Hustle podcast in 2018. Credited as bandleader on the *Blah-Blah-Blah Tour*, he led a lineup featuring Phil Butcher on bass, Gavin Harrison on drums and Seamus Beaghen, who had played with Madness, on keyboards and guitar. They played over a hundred shows between October 1986 and November 1987, across the US, Canada, the UK, Europe and Japan.

The tour was matched by a long string of press interviews, TV appearances and photo ops, all handled with unflagging patience and charm by a trim and alert Iggy. The US leg included a three-month stint supporting The Pretenders. Each night, Chrissie Hynde kissed the stage Iggy had just left. The gruelling schedule soon took its toll, and before long, Harrison and Butcher were replaced. Andy Anderson, formerly of The Cure, took over on drums while Barry Adamson, recently out of The Bad Seeds, stepped in on bass. The set centred on a mix of Stooges rippers and tracks from the three Bowie-Pop albums. While the band sounded most at home on the latter, their tight performances earned praise worldwide. Iggy was less volatile, more in control, which left disaster-lovers disappointed, but he remained convincing and energetic, delivering a solid dose of rock 'n' roll that brought his music to a new generation. Iggy told *The Gavin Report* in 1988:

> I was playing almost all new stuff at first, a lot of the technically oriented material off *Blah-Blah-Blah*. But I noticed the audience were responding more strongly to the simpler, more basic songs. So as the tour went on, I thought: 'Let's try 'I Wanna Be Your Dog'.' I hadn't played that in years. But I did it, and I liked it a lot. Then we tried 'No Fun'. After steering in that direction, I saw people accepting it. A lot more than when I first brought those songs on stage. They're real simple. Just a couple of chords.

Knowing Iggy wanted a similar back-to-basics, guitar-driven sound for his next record, Bowie suggested Bill Laswell, whose production on PiL's *Album* they both admired. Laswell had once played bass in R&B and funk bands around Detroit and Ann Arbor, where he had seen The Stooges and MC5. His influences ranged from Coltrane and Ayler to Miles Davis, and he had recently worked with Motörhead. It all struck a chord with Iggy, who now had a real sense of choice: a hit to his name, some financial breathing room and growing recognition from younger bands citing him as an influence.

With that security came new surroundings. He and Suchi moved into an apartment in the Christodora building, towering over the East Village tenements, and bought a holiday home in Mexico. Iggy had become what few from his era managed to be: a rock 'n' roll survivor. But he had no interest in mellowing out into a toothless MOR money machine. He set out to make a record that leaned harder into The Stooges than anything he'd done since, turning his back on the slick synth sheen of *Blah-Blah-Blah*.

Iggy had it planned: the songs were roughed out, rehearsed in front of the mirror, picturing himself playing them to a crowd. For the band, he kept Beaghen from the previous tour on keyboards, brought in Leigh Foxx on bass, along with ex-Psychedelic Furs drummer Paul Garisto. After hitting it off in the 1985 demo sessions in LA, Steve Jones returned on guitar. The cover design was to be handled by Gary Grimshaw, known for his concert posters for Detroit's Grande Ballroom. And for the video to the album's lead single 'Cold Metal', he requested director Sam Raimi, whose *The Evil Dead* he had loved. Unfortunately, early plans to have Iggy run over by a truck were scrapped in favour of a Spinal Tap-style hair-metal cliché. The album was recorded in New York in April 1988 and hit the shelves two months later. The cover photo was shot by Paul McAlpine, while Grimshaw's design channelled vintage airbrushed art rock posters, colliding mall-punk machismo with retro-futuristic metal kitsch. Even in 1988, it looked dated on arrival. That vibe carries over to the album itself: professionally made, conceptually sharp, aiming for power but landing somewhere between competent and forgettable. *Instinct* has intent and structure, but it never quite catches fire. Expecting another commercial success, A&M were left underwhelmed and considered cutting ties with Iggy. But with a global tour lined up, they held off, hoping the promotion might still give the album a lift.

For an Iggy album that has largely slipped off the radar and rarely inspires treasure hunts, *Instinct* was surprisingly well-received at the time. *Sounds* called it a 'resonant, dignified album' and *Creem* dubbed it 'the hardest, most honest offering he's made in years'. *Rolling Stone* was less convinced, but admitted that 'it takes more than wrong-minded production to keep a good Ig down'. *The Village Voice* was harsher, quipping: 'If Bowie can't save him and Laswell can't save him, maybe he gone.' Yet, it ranked number 48 on *NME*'s year-end list and number 69 on *Kerrang!*'s 100 Greatest Heavy Metal Albums of All Time. As always with Iggy, even when the whole doesn't quite hold, there's still life flickering in the margins and a few gems buried in the dust.

'Cold Metal' (Pop)

From the opening seconds, Iggy reclaims the hard rock edge he felt he'd abandoned on *Blah-Blah-Blah*. Looking back in the *Chicago Tribune* in 1990, he put it plainly:

> As I often do after I work with David, I wanted to make sure I didn't become a producer's singer, just a cherry on the banana split. So I wrote most of the music and tried to make a loud, little rock 'n' roll record. It was me trying to re-create a bit of my past, but I've learned that you should never look back.

A spoiler alert, perhaps, but let's not throw out the baby with the bathwater. Iggy is in fine, tough-guy form, his gnawing stick-it-to-me rock voice front and centre. Jones' guitar is sharp and muscular, the beat lands with punch and purpose. But unlike The Stooges days, where the guitar lashed out with uncompromising snarl, here it sticks to the script: stiff, boxed in by its own rigidity. At first, it feels like a deliberate stylistic choice, in sync with the song's metallic theme. That assumption works in the track's favour, making it hit like a forceful return to Iggy's heavier side. The lyrics hold up, too, paying tribute to industrial America. They open with a stark depiction of his childhood landscape:

> I played tag in the auto graveyard
> I looked up at the radio tower
> Grabbed tit by the railroad tracks
> Concrete poured over steel bridge
> Pondered my fate while they built the interstate

Cold metal defines the skeleton of Iggy's country and runs through his own DNA, having shaped his fate, attitude and music: 'This is the song of my heritage/From the bad to the brutal'. As much a eulogy as a celebration, the lyrics reflect both admiration and disdain for the forces that drive progress and decay. After all, 'It's how we win/And also how we sin'. Iggy's closing 'Better save a tree' exposes the cost of modernity, weighing progress against its consequences.

Musically, subtle variations emerge. The second verse kicks in with a steely clap, a sound that resurfaces in shifting forms throughout this album. Iggy's blatantly hammy 'Yeah, uh-huh' follows his nod to attitude, Beaghen's staccato keyboard jabs hit at 1:57, and at 2:10, guitar and bass mirror Iggy's vocal line on 'how we sin', adding weight to the hook. As the album's lead single, it reached number 37 on *Billboard*'s Album Rock Tracks, scored a Grammy nod for Best Hard Rock/Metal Performance and briefly surfaced in the 1990 sci-fi horror *Hardware*, with Iggy voicing snarky DJ Angry Bob.

'High On You' (Pop)

But hold on: another good song. Where did this notion come from that this record is some dreary, near-impenetrable slog? Sure, it doesn't break new ground, but it seeps in. The pulsing bass and submerged guitar steer the band through the depths of an abandoned swimming pool, while Iggy's hollow, reverb-soaked voice drifts through like a junkie's ghost. Purged of all toxins – well, almost – a refocused Iggy reaches for a new kind of high: human connection. With the weight of simple words, he offers a few lingering lines. 'If I could rule the night, baby, I'd turn it into wine' hints at sacramental transformation. Along with 'Terrorist in my heart, tearing it all apart' and 'Drinking of your soul, baby, and everything I know digs the way your body glows', they teeter on the edge of kitsch, but that's exactly what makes them work. The fusion of darkness, spirituality and the physical feels almost religious in the wake of sobriety. At times, Iggy pushes grandiosity, but every so often, he strikes something seared and fervent, straight from the gut.

'Strong Girl' (Jones, Pop)

The first stumble. This drum-forward, overlong track, with a phoned-in riff stuck in its own chord, recalls the sound of *Electric*, The Cult's hard-hitting record from the year before. Built on iron-clad riffs with a retro bite, macho vocals and a locked-in rhythm section, it echoed across rock radio. With lean, stripped-down production courtesy of Rick Rubin, their platinum-selling album tapped into a new fanbase. On *Instinct*, Iggy seems to be following a similar stylistic blueprint, with Laswell as his Rubin.

Here, Jones steps out of catatonia with a solid solo, though it's slightly overshadowed by Garisto's lumberjack drumming. The brief dropout of the riff at 3:28 offers a welcome breather, but once it kicks back in, we're left enduring nearly a minute and a half of Iggy's vocal fluff. Vocal engineer Martin Bisi recalled the recording sessions in a 2018 interview with *Fear And Loathing Fanzine*:

> Iggy was actually writing most of the lyrics as we were recording, so the informal setting of BC Studio might have been pretty nice for him, rather than a very pro and expensive situation. Iggy generally would walk in, be super nice, but then head straight for the vocal booth and shut the door. He'd sit in there working on lyrics and we couldn't even see him. He'd just tell us to let him know whenever he was needed. Sometimes we would let him be for a while and not bother him.

Maybe they should have let Iggy stew in his booth a little longer because here his lyrics barely move beyond declaring that he needs 'a strong girl' who is 'like an ocean', with a side of grating 'nanana' for good measure. Things spice up a little at the end with a tinny, grainy layer over the riff before the outro breaks the steady 4/4, tumbling through six- and four-beat cycles. The guitar and bass land hard on the downbeats, while the drums shift from pounding quarters to a propulsive eighth-note pulse, cranking up the momentum and tension. A spark of fire after the flood.

'Tom Tom' (Pop)
We're nearly halfway through, and it's starting to feel like the album has already shown its hand. The fourth track picks up right where the last one left off. Blink, and you might miss the transition altogether. Here, let's assume for our own peace of mind that Iggy's tom tom is metaphorical: if he's shut out, he takes his rhythm and walks. The lyrics stay vague, hinting at a hazy love clouded by confusion, distance and melancholy. He ends the song with an 'absolute' truth: despite the city's fury, the cheap distractions and fading memories, everything still circles back to one constant – 'you', whoever or whatever that may be. The trouble is, Iggy doesn't make us care. It's not poorly played or sung, but unbearably flat, drifting along without urgency, resonance or life. After one minute, it feels like you've already been stuck in it for three, and any hope of a shift just drags away. Iggy goes up an octave in the final lines, but the abrupt closing punch is a relief.

'Easy Rider' (Jones, Pop)
1988 was a strong year for heavy guitar music. Guns N' Roses had taken over the world, while new albums by Iron Maiden, Bad Religion, Jane's Addiction, Metallica, Pixies and Sonic Youth hit the shelves. Elsewhere, Rick Astley was inescapable, Public Enemy fully broke through and R.E.M. were set to reach a wider audience. In some overlooked corner, Iggy Pop put out a song that sounded like it belonged on the soundtrack of a 1969 hippie movie.

Structurally, it's as conventional as they come. Jones' brief solo interludes are tame and uninspired. And while Garisto gets the green light to unleash his crashes, Laswell tucks them away where they barely register. Yet, the track injects a welcome jolt as the closer of side one. Jones' chugging, with Foxx's bass snapping at its heels, gives the song a throttle kick. Organ sustain offers a welcome tonal contrast, lifting the mix with a touch of harmonic colour. The surging pace barrels into the rip-roaring chorus, where Iggy, in full raucous mode, drags out the title with raw abandon. You can almost feel the Ape Hanger beneath you and smell the rubber burning on endless asphalt stretches. But this isn't a triumphant road trip; it's a desperate attempt to outrun something that won't let go:

Broken people all around
Old guarantee that pulls you down
You need a way out, you need a ride
'Cause where you are is suicide

From here, Iggy paints a hallucinatory mix of spiritual visions, physical desire and restless searching: 'I wanna find myself in you/You wanna find yourself, too'. The *Easy Rider* reference feels ironic; where the film stood for freedom and rebellion, Iggy suggests disillusionment, longing and the creeping doubt that escape is even possible. Bluntly macho and a little cheesy, but within the tried-and-true power rock lane, it delivers. A ride that makes for one hell of a live track, too.

'Power & Freedom' (Jones, Pop)
By now, it's clear. The production of *Instinct* carries a clinical, impersonal layer that lacks the warmth, depth and natural dynamics that could have given the music heart to truly resonate. This is a missed opportunity for Laswell, as the setup promised much more. Iggy told MuchMusic in 1988:

> It's a good little band. I took a small rehearsal space in the Chelsea area of New York, where we'd just play together every day for a month. Not trying to perfect things or listen in stereo, just playing. We really were a band by the time we went to the studio, and when we cut the stuff, all of it was done live. If we wanted to improve something later, we'd improve it, but everything on this album has a live track where five people played music at once, in the same room, at the same time.

Despite the live approach, the recording feels distant, more like a programmed session than a band in full flight. The guitars slice sharply through the spectrum but never truly ignite. The drums are precise and uniform, but their attack and decay lack nuance, making them sound more mechanical than organic, while the bass and keyboards often remain indistinct. Together, they lie beneath a surgical drape. There is hardly any space for spontaneity or release, reinforcing the cold, almost sterile listening experience.

The opener of side two suffers from the same malaise. Iggy sounds strong, but the track is a generic rock workout with no real impact. The band plays with rigid precision, but it works against the song rather than for it, stripping away the subtle fluctuations in timing and interaction that make music feel alive. If nothing else, the lyrics carry more weight, striking a broad, rebellious tone. 'You want power, you want freedom' reads as a universal battle cry. 'Freedom is another loaded concept. I wanted to write about it at the level of the individual, not politically', Iggy told *The Gavin Report* in 1988.

Given his newly hard-drug-free status, it's tempting to hear it as a reflection on his own fight to stay afloat. Now sober and sharper, he seems to sing of reclaiming autonomy over his body and mind. But reality is unforgiving: 'Nobody cool will save ya'. Even with a clear head, he's on his own.

'Lowdown' (Pop)

Laswell described Iggy's voice as a 'mutant Frank Sinatra' in Ambrose's *Gimme Danger*, adding that 'down at the low end of his voice he definitely had a very real sound'. If anyone ever wondered what Sinatra crooning over the metallic grind of an ex-Sex Pistol might sound like, this track offers a decent idea. Over some slightly corny and dated keyboard touches, as much then as now, Iggy sings in his deepest baritone, delivering lines with a restrained, matter-of-fact detachment: 'I don't want to throw away my time/ Playing games I don't respect or like'. On the early takes, he sang it a full octave higher in a standard rock voice, but quickly decided it sounded dull, so he dropped it to a much lower pitch instead. He only lifts his voice three times throughout the song, and that restraint makes it all the more infectious.

Though fairly plodding, the track works as one of the album's better grooves, carried by a subtly minor feel and a weary sense of melancholy. Iggy acknowledges the walls he has built and the love he has driven away, his own defences and fears leading him deeper into the void he has come to inhabit. His rejection of forced happiness and craving for the smallest sliver of comfort reflect a quiet exhaustion: 'All I really want's a cup of tea/To feel a warmth inside of me'. The repeated 'There's a hole in my heart, I'm lowdown' reinforces the song's sense of defeat, as if he is stuck in this emptiness with no way out.

'Instinct' (Pop)

Chugging chords, a searing slide, then drums and bass slam in. Two power chords, a second slide, and the pace locks in for Iggy's commanding vocal melody. Shifting between restraint and sweeping power, he weighs survival against confinement, as if forced to choose between resistance and a world that seeks to tame him. Instinct is his lifeline, an unstoppable force driving him forward. After laying the groundwork with corruption and the fight to break free, the second verse paints a contrast between decay and privilege:

> I have seen the sludgy beach
> And the poisoned river
> I have met the lordly rich
> They're just getting stiffer
> This whole place is like a maze
> Or like some Medusa
> Let me out I can't accept
> A second-rate life story

One wrong step and you're caught in a system designed to keep you in line. But Iggy refuses to surrender to its deception and control: 'Instinct keeps me running/Running 'cause I don't believe it'. No solos in the instrumental breaks, just seamless riffing, mirroring the song's central theme. It clocks in at over four minutes but feels shorter, kept taut by its relentless pulse. A forceful, surging track that holds its ground better alone than lost in the album's sea of sonic sameness.

'Tuff Baby' (Pop)
Though Iggy's hardest album since The Stooges, their punk abandon is reined in. His pop instincts are left behind, and there's none of the brooding experimentation of *The Idiot* or the offbeat artiness of *Zombie Birdhouse*. The result is an album unlikely to hook fans of his earlier work. At the same time, with little to offer musically for metalheads, it won't win them over either. This track perfectly illustrates the different pillars it's caught between, without adding anything new.

It recalls ZZ Top but desperately needs one of their hook-laden choruses from their golden run of singles. Iggy's repetitive 'I love you, tuff baby' just doesn't cut it. At best, it could serve as a pre-chorus to an actual soaring payoff, but after the first half-hearted refrain, the track slumps back into the same rut. There is no bridge, no middle eight, just Jones and Iggy trading lines in plodding verses, a love letter to both Tuff Baby's looks and resilience. Jones delivers his longest solo on the album: competent, but utterly devoid of goosebumps, while Iggy sounds like he doesn't believe in the song himself. In a last-ditch attempt at variation, there is at least some play with dynamics. The third verse is eased into a laid-back groove, but the song then limps on for another minute of repetition, adding nothing of substance. There's a fun wink to Morrison's 'Cars Hiss By My Window' in Iggy's 'insect cars', but this time, the journey never gets going.

'Squarehead' (Jones, Pop)
The band and production sound unshackled in this closing number, delivering a dose of good old revved-up rock 'n' roll. Jones rips into his strongest solo so far, and for once, there's a looseness that makes this freewheeling piece of silliness downright infectious. On his favourite track of the album, Iggy sounds far more at home, as if shaking off a weight he had been carrying all along. This is him at his most playful and defiant: laughing, snoring, barking and shouting his way through a madcap list of everything he's willing to endure, so long as he doesn't have to be a squarehead:

> You can kick me out of a real good jive
> You can use my friendship like a doorknob
> You can make me super styrofoam
> You can make me feel all alone
> You can stuff hamburger in my head
> But I ain't gonna be no squarehead

The imagery is absurd yet oddly precise. Only Iggy would compare friendship to a doorknob, something everyone grabs without a second thought. With effortless simplicity, the song unfolds as a string of near-dadaist one-liners railing against peer pressure, consumer culture and empty glamour. If this freed-up band approach and punk litany were a late addition, a rare moment of letting go after the formulaic sessions, they should've kept the studio booked for another month.

Brick By Brick (1990)

Personnel:
Iggy Pop: vocals, guitar
Waddy Wachtel: guitar
Charley Drayton, Duff McKagan, Chuck Domanico: bass
Slash: guitar
Jamie Muhoberac: keyboards, piano, organ
Kenny Aronoff: drums
David Lindley: guitar, strings and assorted instruments
David McMurray: saxophone
Kate Pierson, John Hiatt: duet vocals
Sweet Pea Atkinson, Sir Harry Bowens, Donald Ray Mitchell, Alex Brown, Scott Hackwith, Dale Lavi, The Leeching Delinquents: backing vocals
Recorded at Ocean Way and Hollywood Sound Studios, Hollywood, California, between February and March 1990
Producer: Don Was
Release date: July 1990
Label: Virgin
Chart places: US: 90, UK: 50, Aus: 81, Can: 83
Running time: 54:09

Bleached and tousled in a sleeveless leather vest, Iggy hit the road just six weeks after *Instinct* dropped, tearing across the globe until mid-February 1989. Seemingly smaller than ever in his lean frame and hair-metal roadie getup, he still radiated menace and intent. The tour took him across five continents and 20 countries, including debut shows in Brazil and Argentina. The band featured Beaghen and Garisto from *Instinct*, Hanoi Rocks wild card Andy McCoy on guitar and U.K. Subs bassist Alvin Gibbs. Iggy was feral onstage: hurling himself into the crowd, launching off the drum riser, tearing muscles, barking orders, spitting insults and ripping through the *Instinct* set faster, harder and meaner than on record. A live recording from 19 July 1988 at The Channel in Boston captures him with fire in his veins, roaring back to his hard rock roots.

Back in the US, after being pushed out by A&M following *Instinct*'s underwhelming commercial performance, Iggy took a role alongside Johnny Depp in *Cry-Baby*, recorded 'Love Transfusion' for Wes Craven's *Shocker*, reclaimed the rights to his RCA catalogue and signed an unusual deal with Virgin Records: part reissue arrangement, part new recording contract. Virgin gave him artistic freedom, but it came with a clear message: blow it this time, and the runway might be gone for good. The label understood that getting the right people around him was key to making a strong Iggy Pop album. Enter Don Was: Detroit native, founder of Was (Not Was), fresh off an Emmy win for producing Bonnie Raitt's *Nick Of Time* and a lifelong Stooges fan. He and Iggy had hit it off while recording 'Livin' On The Edge

Of The Night' for Ridley Scott's *Black Rain*, and now he was trusted to steer the next chapter. He encouraged Iggy to tap into his reflective, sharp-minded, more intellectual side. Iggy responded with a batch of new songs written on acoustic guitar, tackling America, politics, the music business, urban life and the fight for self-determination. Was told *Performing Songwriter* in 2014:

> On *Brick*, all his personalities come out in those songs. He'll say something really naïve and optimistic, then follow it with something that shows he's not naïve at all, that he's actually well read. All these sides blend in a way that's unique to him.

Sessions began at LA's Ocean Way Studios in February 1990, in an atmosphere of sharp-edged professionalism. Riding a wave of acclaim, Was had assembled an elite group of session players with credits spanning decades of iconic records. Faced with that level of craftsmanship, it was a bold move for Iggy to pick up the guitar himself. He did so at Was' request, on what amounted to Iggy's 'Hollywood album': precision-built, studio-slick and featuring contributions from Slash and Duff McKagan of Guns N' Roses, Kate Pierson of The B-52's and John Hiatt. Also present was his son Eric, now in his early 20s. After sampling a little too much of urban wildlife as a teenager, he was knocking around the LA rock scene as an aspiring artist. Through him, Iggy tapped into a new circle of younger musicians, some of whom would join the upcoming tour, with Eric part of his inner crew.

The cover art was created by illustrator Charles Burns, who had first seen Iggy live on *The Idiot Tour* and had been a fan ever since. Burns produced a dense visual rendering of the lyrics: brick buildings, a claustrophobic street, a starry night over the city. Tucked into the scene are nods to specific tracks, including the joint from 'Pussy Power', the grinning bug from 'I Won't Crap Out' and the cartoon cat from 'Neon Forest'. The beehived woman was loosely inspired by Pierson.

Released that summer, *Brick By Brick* marked Iggy's commercial comeback, landing just as rock was turning away from polished arena excess towards louder guitars and a grittier, more muscular sound. His jagged vocals, confrontational lyrics and guitar-driven edge slotted neatly into the rising alternative ethos. The timing aligned with the rise of modern rock radio and *Billboard*'s Modern Rock Tracks chart, where 'Home' hit number two and 'Candy' reached number five. Lollapalooza would launch the next summer, signalling the rise of the Alternative Nation: a movement that hailed Iggy as a firebrand forefather still burning onstage, as confirmed by his tour across the UK, North America and Europe. The blistering concert film *Kiss My Blood*, directed by Tim Pope, captured him in optima forma, both literally and figuratively, and reaffirmed his reputation as a live force. His role in *Cry-Baby*, a spot on *Shannon's Deal*, and appearances on Arsenio, Letterman and Stern boosted his profile, while his Farm Aid IV performance reinforced his standing in the rock scene at the start of the decade.

The album was well received by critics. *Rolling Stone* gave it four stars and called it 'a strong album', the *LA Times* deemed it 'a blast', *NME* hailed it as 'a knock-out' and the *Chicago Tribune* described it as 'his best album in a decade'. It reached number 26 in *The Village Voice*'s 1990 Pazz & Jop Critics Poll, reflecting its wide critical appeal. It became Iggy's most successful release since *Blah-Blah-Blah* and his first gold record in the US, with over 500,000 copies sold. It reached number 90 on the *Billboard* 200 and stayed on the chart for 37 weeks. 'Candy' peaked at number 67 in the UK and reached number 28 on the *Billboard* Hot 100, becoming Iggy's first top 40 hit in the US.

Brick By Brick is a gutsy release that cast Iggy in a new light: strong vocals, purposeful lyrics, punchy rock songs and semi-acoustic tracks with measured weight and texture. The production is crisp, expansive and deliberate, but still pulses with urban grit. Yet, it's precisely that accessibility and studio finish that hold it back from being a truly great album. With less sheen and a tighter tracklist, it might have come heartbreakingly close.

'Home' (Pop)

A lean and lethal start. Mean, clean and dynamic, the drumming punches through stop-start riffs as Slash's lead guitar snarls and flares. Iggy, credited on guitar for the first time, adds to the song's bite. It charges forward, packed with ferocity, offering more than just a straight-ahead rock song: 'Home' is about hearth and survival.

Since Iggy wrote 'Street Crazies' in 1982, the homelessness crisis in cities like New York and LA not only persisted, but in many ways had worsened by the late 1980s, as economic shifts and policy failures made conditions even more dire. The song walks the tightrope between defiance and dread, staking a claim while fearing it will be ripped away. Iggy's delivery is bold and eager, but the lyrics betray a deeper truth: having a home isn't a privilege, it's a lifeline. As Iggy put it five years later in *Plazm* magazine:

> You've got a geezer singing a hard rock song in a sort of Eddie Cochran genre. But instead of singing about my new '39 Ford and this chick I want to pick up, I'm singing about trying to build myself a solid shelter so that I don't end up homeless. Which is very scary and realistic subject matter.

At first, he worried the topic might be too bleak or boring for a rock song. That doubt didn't last long. The crowd's reaction, especially from teenagers, took him by surprise. It made him wonder whether they, too, felt unmoored, unsure of where they belonged, or anxious about how they'd get by. 'Or maybe,' he shrugged, 'they just know it from MTV.' Either way, these four minutes hit harder than *Instinct* did in 44.

'Main Street Eyes' (Pop)
A wry call to stay true in a world obsessed with the fake. Swapping the opener's harder punch for a country-tinged blend of roots rock, with violin and mandolin, Iggy keeps his lyrical edge sharp. Like Lou Reed on *New York*, the song pairs disillusionment with a stark view of America's decay. Iggy skewers modern artifice, even echoing Reed's vocal style on 'I saw a kitten squashed in the street/I read about a plastic surgeon and his art collection', juxtaposing innocence and luxury in a commodified world. With a quick dig at 'phony rock and roll', the song leans into Main Street values, as Iggy seeks self-respect over ambition. The stripped-back arrangement spotlights his gravelly delivery, pressing weight onto the tension beneath. It's a love letter to those who reject shallow status and embrace authenticity.

'I Won't Crap Out' (Pop)
Another anthem of defiance, yet this one packs more punch. A blast of electric guitar and drums gives way to acoustic strums from Wachtel and Iggy himself, with slide guitar and bouzouki adding colour. Iggy delivers an abrasive declaration of resilience, snapping: 'If you want to stir up real mud, you had better pay with real blood', a line that demands authenticity and commitment. Another jab at commercialism ('And the material singers will fade into dust, like forgotten merchants of disgust') lands at the end, sharpening the song's rejection of shallow artistry. The recurring phrase 'If I don't crap out' sets conditions for a better life, while 'No, I won't crap out' strikes as a defiant stand – part boxer, part survivor – hitting back at life's blows. This reinforces the tone set by the album's opening tracks, where Iggy's mantra rings loud and clear: nothing worth having comes easy. Themes of survival and social critique run throughout, binding idealistic aspirations to harsh truths.

The final 47 seconds hint at the album's untapped potential, had Iggy broken free from its AOR-tailored restraint. At 3:15, the drums and guitars surge, but it's Iggy's fiery, briefly distorted blast as he spits out ''Cause we wanna LIVE, not like a fucking dead fucker' that hits the apex. One of the album's finest moments.

'Candy' (Pop)
Often cited as one of the most iconic duets in popular music, this mainstream-friendly track emerges from a history marked by profound tragedy. In 1970, 23-year-old Iggy met Betsy Mickelsen, a 14-year-old from Ann Arbor, known for her intelligence, street smarts and striking presence. 'I'd never seen anything like her', Iggy recalled in *Please Kill Me*. Legally unable to take her across state lines, he stayed with her family. The relationship quickly unravelled: Iggy, addicted to heroin, introduced her to drugs, cheated on her and left her pregnant. An abortion followed. Not long after, she witnessed him robbing a friend's empty house. After a year, it

ended, and Betsy returned to her parents, devastated. In *Open Up And Bleed*, Trynka notes that she died young from liver disease. She reportedly called Iggy 'the love of her life', while her parents harboured 'immortal resentment' towards him.

Betsy lingered in Iggy's mind, resurfacing in songs like 'I'm Sick Of You', 'Scene Of The Crime', 'Dog Food' and 'Winners & Losers', where he laments that his 'true fine love' had died. He had begun working on 'Candy' as early as 1985, but returned to it in earnest in 1989, while filming *Cry-Baby*. He told the *Pittsburgh Post-Gazette* the following year:

> The song refers back to a key girl in my life, my teenage girlfriend Betsy. I was looking back on my relationship with her, and I thought: 'Let's be fair. Let the girl have her say.' I wanted a girl who would sing with a small-town voice, and Kate has a little twang in her voice that sounds slightly rural and naive.

Initially offered to Chrissie Hynde, the song went to Pierson, who voiced Betsy's side in this lush torch-pop duet, blending regret with bittersweet memory. 'Candy' gained radio and MTV airplay, becoming Iggy's biggest mainstream success and his only solo single to reach the *Billboard* Hot 100, where it peaked at number 28. Yet, its ties to Betsy's tragic story and the circumstances of their relationship cast a sombre shadow over its legacy.

'Butt Town' (Pop)

After sharing a bill with Guns N' Roses in 1988, Iggy quickly hit it off with the era's hottest guitarist. A year later, Slash called Iggy to LA on 24 hours' notice for a benefit gig, sealing their friendship. Now, Slash returned the favour, playing on four tracks and proud to be there. 'If you're into this whole rock and roll trip, it's hard not to be aware of Iggy's influence', he told *Guitar World* in 1990. 'We fit together, attitude and style-wise, pretty well.' One of rock's greatest guitarists, Slash delivers precision, soulful bends and crisp articulation. Even so, his pairing with Iggy sparks less fire than expected. A blues player at heart, he elevates the album's opener, but on this weaker composition, even he seems unsure where to take it. The cluttered production tosses out all its generic ingredients in 30 seconds, stretching the next three minutes. And yet the lyrics, too often dismissed as brainless drivel, cut sharp. While the fixation on butt earned high praise from Beavis and Butt-Head ('This song has the best lyrics I've ever heard'), it offers more: a tongue-in-cheek, backlot-baked caricature of a city where dreams are bought and dignity is negotiable. Its opening lines waste no time setting the scene:

> The cops are well-groomed with muscled physiques
> In Butt Town
> Their tan uniforms are tailored in chic

In Butt Town
Any young Black male who walks down the street
Is going to get stopped by a car full of meat
But the girl with the hair flies by in her underwear
She's done nothing so far to deserve that car

From here, the song skewers showbiz's churn-and-burn cycle, built on disposable talent and an economy of flesh. It could be LA, Vegas or any mirage where opportunity quickly turns into a gilded trap. Or, as the album's sleeve notes put it: 'We all live in Butt Town.' The city chews people up and spits them out, while Iggy straddles the line between critic and casualty, sneering at Butt Town even as it pulls him in. By the time he's gleefully chanting about shaking his butt, the point is clear: you either play the game or get played.

'The Undefeated' (Pop)
In his ironic take on heartland rock, Iggy dissects the disillusionment of privilege and skewers the arrogance of entitlement. We meet someone raised in affluence, every need met, yet trapped in a 'giant jail' of privilege. The refrains echo a false sense of invincibility born from this comfort, turning into a cynical, self-deprecating brag:

We're the undefeated
We got what they want
We're so bored and spoiled
Life is just a bag of pot

We're the undefeated
TV in the shade
Girls at all our parties
We have really got it made

Our protagonist contrasts his stagnant ease with the 'real mean world outside', where struggle breeds growth and purpose, exposing his yearning for meaning and desire to escape his cushioned existence. It's a succinct and witty piece of writing.

As a song, it's a straightforward roots rocker with a spirited chorus by an impromptu group of studio hangers-on dubbed The Leeching Delinquents, including Iggy's son Eric. While a vibrant piano adds sparkling accents to the steady strum of acoustic guitars, it is Aronoff's drumming that elevates the track immensely. A longtime John Mellencamp collaborator, he delivers a masterful performance packed with ghost notes, subtle accents and inventive fills: a true tour de force of percussive brilliance. What's more, the hammering buildup, with Iggy's charged release at 3:18 driving the final salvo of choruses, is utterly irresistible. After wrapping the track, Iggy indulged in some cocaine off the mixing desk before crashing a Debbie Harry gig to co-perform 'I Wanna Be Your Dog'. Here we go!

'Moonlight Lady' (Pop)

Another pristine Was production, with Iggy's acoustic guitar chiming and Lindley's bouzouki steel strings weaving in an extra shimmer to the mix. At 0:51, a warm acoustic bass joins in, slipping in a subtle slide right at the 2:00 mark, filling the open space. Sparse, understated keyboard chords complete the romantic night scene, as Iggy croons a bittersweet serenade to his Moonlight Lady in a tender melody. In mood and delivery, it is the antithesis of 'Sister Midnight', though just as finely crafted within its own dreamlike realm.

Like most songs on the album, Iggy first wrote it on an acoustic guitar. In its early version, it was called 'I Am', with much flatter lyrics: 'Who's gonna comfort your mind? I am'. He later reshaped it into a subtler surrender to love, unexpected but embraced: 'I didn't plan it with you/But now we're here we might as well accept it'. It works as a romantic ode, expressing deep affection and a sense of inevitability. Yet, beneath the tenderness lies a quiet tension of someone grappling with commitment, balancing devotion and doubt. Iggy navigates intimacy not with poetic grandeur, but with the knowing, slightly melancholic honesty of someone who has learned that even the best intentions can't promise forever. The moonlight casts everything in a soft glow, blurring hesitation and certainty.

'Something Wild' (Hiatt)

Traced with Iggy's punk blood, the album dips into the sound John Hiatt had mastered: no-frills, blues-streaked roots rock, too rugged for country yet too grounded for alternative. This made him a fitting, if incidental, addition to the lineup of celebrity cameos during the sessions. Originally penned for his album *Stolen Moments*, recorded around the same time at Ocean Way as *Brick By Brick*, this song didn't make his final tracklist. Instead, he handed it to Iggy and lent his backing vocals, while recording engineer Ed Cherney was officially credited as the 'annoying vocal whine'.

It's a well-crafted piece of songwriting, built like a tool shed: practical, but conventional all the same. Wachtel's guitar sits low in the mix, taking a backseat to Iggy's voice, his acoustic strums and Aronoff's drumming. It takes the edge off a song that, at its core, is meant to hit hard: driven, urgent and tinged with paranoia. The lyrics wrestle with the tension between desire and untamed impulses ('A hungry wolf, an angry child, or something wild'), always skirting the edge of control and abandon. Hiatt released his own version on *Perfectly Good Guitar* three years later. Surprisingly, it's Hiatt, not Iggy, who kicks off the song with wolf cries. Personal taste in voice and delivery aside, Hiatt's take is the stronger cut: wilder, more commanding and enlivened by a more dynamic arrangement. Next to it, Iggy's version feels like an admirable demo.

'Neon Forest' (Pop)

The intro pulls you in, no questions asked. Iggy counts in, and the groove ignites on launch. Here we find those traces of Iggy's punk roots, their edges smoothed into a sleeker alternative rock track. Iggy's muscular chugging pairs with Wachtel's guitar, which echoes his vocal refrain while charging through a grinding mid-tempo beat. Three Was (Not Was) vocalists provide backing, a favour Iggy returned that same year on 'Elvis' Rolls Royce' from *Are You Okay?* The song has its flaws, with a 'dad rock' vibe and a seven-minute runtime that might test patience, but the substance holds up. It wouldn't be out of place on *Instinct*, but here the production and playing feel more organic, and Iggy's message bites harder.

A direct strike at the American Dream, he skewers its numb, warped and self-destructive state: 'America takes drugs in psychic defence'. In 1981, Iggy had surprised and irked many by endorsing Reagan: 'I've been waiting for someone who could communicate the joys of liberty as compared to the joys of equality', he told *ZigZag*. That year on MTV, he declared: 'My views are very right-wing. I'm somewhere right of Reagan, into a sort of hedonistic conservatism.' But as the decade wore on, so did his disillusionment with America's social, economic and cultural decline. By 1992, he voted for Clinton and grew increasingly sceptical of politicians across the board, settling into an independent stance he has held ever since. This track reflects his alienation from a society chasing hollow success, taking a scathing jab at the phoniness and excess of the Reagan years: 'You can join the in crowd for being a whore'. The neon forest is a lurid, artificial refuge, a place where life flickers like a screen and feels increasingly unreal. Here, 'To be a total phony is the winning design' and self-worth is transactional: 'Have you got any money?/Are you anybody?' In a way, the track was ahead of its time, setting the stage for grunge to rise and rebel.

'Starry Night' (Pop)

Some Caribbean-tinged cosmic relativism from Iggy: stars as silent witnesses to human triviality. The acoustically picked demo presents Iggy in a far more subdued state, with no indication that this would later emerge as a lightly ska-kissed, peppy pop song. Was' influence seems likely, given his prior cross-genre experiments with Bonnie Raitt, The B-52's and the eclectic blend of funk, pop and R&B in his own band, Was (Not Was). With Iggy on acoustic guitar, Lindley on electric guitar and slide, Muhoberac's organ and the backing vocalists from 'Neon Forest' once again in place, 'Starry Night' comes across as both studio-smooth and palatable. Though hardly recognisable as an Iggy Pop track, he sounds like he's enjoying himself, and his blunt, dismissive lyrics remain in step with the rest of the album:

I don't care about your city
Or your fat income
I don't care about your Vanity Fair
Or your fucking sitcom

Iggy expresses his disdain for materialism, shallow media, posturing and, while he's at it, the illusion of human importance. He introduces the desert as the city's counterpoint, a place free of noise, where the stars are fully visible, restoring a sense of scale:

Which country is the strongest?
Who plays the best guitar?
Who fucking cares
Under the stars

A flippant swerve between two of the album's hardest-hitting tracks. Nihilism with a touch of enlightenment. Yes, everything is meaningless, but that can be liberating in itself.

'Pussy Power' (Pop)
Remember when two music titans, Michael Jackson and Stevie Wonder, teamed up for *Bad* (1987), only to deliver the forgettable, self-indulgent 'Just Good Friends'? Well, in this twisted parallel two years later, something equally uninspired happens: two rock icons collide, but instead of magic, we get a crude display of Slash's guitar wankery and Iggy locked into pussy power. Although the grave-toned voices are a welcome touch, the song itself is the rock counterpart to the *Bad* trifle, equally devoid of memorability. For his third spin with Iggy, Slash contributes to a track adding absolutely nothing to an album that, by this point, is beginning to feel a little drawn out. The CD era encouraged longer albums, but not every track justified the extra runtime. Frankly, its absence would've hurt no one.

'My Baby Wants To Rock & Roll' (Pop, Slash)
This last go-around between Iggy and Slash might as well be called 'My Baby Wants To State The Obvious', with Slash earning a co-writing credit for rearranging the metal-edged music on the spot. It's a by-the-numbers rocker about living fast and loud that barely expands beyond its own title. The kind of track you forget before it even ends, despite some unhinged Iggy bellowing near the end. Like 'Pussy Power', McKagan handles bass duties here. 'That was a great experience,' he told *Revolver* in 2008. 'Playing with Iggy pulled me back in for a while and reminded me of what I love about music.' Acoustic demo versions of both 'My Baby Wants To Rock & Roll' and 'Pussy Power', included on the 'Candy' single, are just as lifeless as you'd fear.

'Brick By Brick' (Pop)

On Danish TV in 1990, Iggy remarked that while his status afforded him a certain privilege, he was keenly aware that many people were treated unfairly. He resented how, all too often, the worst people reaped the greatest rewards. In the title song, he explained, he tried to create his own frame of reference, building a world where things aligned with his vision:

I wanna build a house, where an ad don't scream
I wanna live in peace, quietly
I wanna have a place of love and safety
People oughta live how and where they want
People oughta have respect in front
People oughta get along pretty okay
So get off my dick
I'm building it, brick by brick

Tying the album's intended final track back to its opener, Iggy's house is more than just a physical space. It is a mental and emotional refuge, a place where he can exist without compromise, in a world where strength means integrity rather than power. Iggy plays acoustic guitar alongside Wachtel, who adds subtle electric touches in the choruses, and Muhoberac, whose sustained keyboard tones emerge near the end. The stripped-back arrangement proved just as effective when fleshed out on stage. A heartfelt, convincing take can be found on *Kiss My Blood*, filmed during the *Brick By Brick Tour*. The album itself lives up to its name: built from the ground up, with a lineup of top-tier session musicians, a seasoned producer, celebrity contributions, sharp lyrics and a well-balanced mix of styles, all converging under Iggy's commanding vocals. As he summed it up that year in a Raw & Uncut interview: 'A lot of thought went into this album. I'm really proud of it.'

'Livin' On The Edge Of The Night' (Rifkin, Rackin)

Originally a bonus track, this song has since become the definitive closer of *Brick By Brick*, slightly diminishing the impact of the title track. Released as a single from the 1989 neo-noir *Black Rain* soundtrack, it gained some airplay but achieved little success. To capitalise on the film's exposure, Virgin tacked it onto Iggy's new album and even shot a minimalist video with a slick, suit-clad Iggy, an image that has since faded from collective memory. Another Don Was production, the track taps into the polished radio-rock of the late 1980s, while its lyrics sketch an urban scene straight out of a Springsteen small-town drama ('You went off the river/Smokestacks fade to black'). Iggy's weary, everyman delivery adds to this, bringing a similarly introspective tone to the Boss' work of the era. Its brief appearance in *Black Rain* undercut its perfect fit for the film, leaving Iggy disappointed. He wasn't wrong: it deserved more attention.

American Caesar (1993)

Personnel:
Iggy Pop: vocals, guitar
Eric Schermerhorn: guitar
Malcolm Burn: guitar, keyboards, harmonica
Hal Cragin: bass
Larry Mullins: drums, percussion
Jay Joyce: guitar on 'Wild America', 'Mixin' The Colors'
Bill Dillon: 'atmospheric' guitar on 'Mixin' The Colors'
Darryl Johnson: percussion on 'Mixin' The Colors'
Henry Rollins: backing vocals on 'Wild America'
Katell Keineg: backing vocals on 'Mixin' The Colors'
Lisa Germano: backing vocals on 'Beside You'
Recorded at Kingsway Studio, New Orleans, in October 1992 and at Bearsville Studios, New York, in February 1993
Producer: Malcolm Burn
Release date: September 1993
Label: Virgin
Chart places: US: did not chart, UK: 43, Aus: 29
Running time: 71:32

Although every label that signed him had sensed major commercial potential, by the early 1990s, even the most hopeful observers had stopped pretending Iggy would ever break into the mainstream. However successful *Brick By Brick* may have been by Iggy's standards, it came nowhere near the multi-million sales *Nevermind* or *Blood Sugar Sex Magik* would soon rack up. His relentless touring had earned him a loyal fanbase, but it was a far cry from the sold-out stadium runs of The Stones, Springsteen or Guns N' Roses. Even Bowie, who had alienated his mainstream audience with the trashy Tin Machine, grossed over $20 million in the US alone with his *Sound+Vision Tour* in 1990. Iggy's own choices hadn't helped: as before, when success had started to take on a professional sheen, he quickly grew tired of the path he was on. Iggy told *Clash* magazine in 2010:

> I'd done pretty well with *Brick By Brick* and *Blah-Blah-Blah*, and I'd lined up a lot of apples in a certain way, but that sort of professionalism – that professional West Coast type of American career that I was beginning to put together – was just a drag. I didn't wanna do 'Candy' live on stage; I thought, 'Maybe I'll get some kid who can play 'Raw Power'.'

That kid was guitarist Eric Schermerhorn, who had just come off the road with Tin Machine. He brought in bassist Hal Cragin, with whom he'd worked in They Might Be Giants, while drummer and longtime Iggy fan Larry Mullins completed the lineup. Their baptism of fire was a big one: in August 1992,

Iggy took his new band to Buenos Aires for four lucrative concerts. On the first night, punks spat at him in a confrontational display of respect. By the next evening, their tribute had softened: they threw flowers instead.

In the months leading up to the Argentina gigs, Iggy and Schermerhorn had already started writing and recording song ideas in New York, living within walking distance of each other in Manhattan. In early 1993, the band played a short run of shows in New Zealand and Australia, previewing songs that would later appear on Iggy's next album. Tired of artists using hollow political posturing to connect with audiences, Iggy believed he could offer something more honest and continued exploring American social themes, blending them with personal reflections on loneliness, hatred, jealousy, love and drugs. Casting himself as a Stars 'n' Stripes Commander-in-Collapse drew on a hefty dose of historical reflection. In a 1995 essay for *Classics Ireland*, Iggy wrote:

> In 1982, horrified by the meanness, tedium and depravity of my existence as I toured the American South playing rock 'n' roll music and going crazy in public, I purchased an abridged copy of *The Decline And Fall Of The Roman Empire*. The grandeur of the subject appealed to me, as did the cameo illustration of Edward Gibbon, the author, on the front cover. He looked like a heavy dude. Being in a political business, I had long made a habit of reading biographies of wilful characters – Hitler, Churchill, MacArthur, Brando – with large profiles, and I also enjoyed books on war and political intrigue, as I could relate the action to my own situation in the music business, which is not about music at all, but is a kind of religion-rental.

To bring that vision to life, a new producer was brought in: Malcolm Burn, a former protégé of Daniel Lanois, had made his name working on albums by The Neville Brothers and Bob Dylan before stepping out on his own. In addition to his contributions on guitar, keyboards and harmonica, the sessions welcomed a loose circle of guest players, including Jay Joyce, Bill Dillon, Henry Rollins and Lisa Germano. Work took place at Lanois' Kingsway Studios, a grand 19th-century mansion in New Orleans' French Quarter, with wrought-iron balconies and Creole flourishes. Additional recording followed at Bearsville Studios in Woodstock, New York.

On the finished record, the star-glossed Sunset Strip haze of *Brick* gave way to a seedy inner-city zeitgeist montage, as if captured on a grainy early-1990s camcorder. The grimy cover photo, shot by Stephen Stickler, shows a cadaverous Iggy with his arms tucked behind his back like a defiant prisoner awaiting judgement, staring down the camera with a death-row glare. Printed on the CD itself was a handwritten message from McCaesar himself, including the line: 'I tried to make this album as good as I could with no imitations of other people and no formula shit.' Critics agreed wholeheartedly. *Rolling Stone* stated: 'The protopunk rocker reclaims the slashing, psychedelic-tinged grunge rock he helped pioneer' and *Melody Maker* called it 'a broad, bold masterpiece.' *Stereo Review* declared: 'Iggy is definitely back, the noblest punk of them all', while *Select* put it plainly: 'Better than ever.' For a moment, it seemed like Iggy had finally broken into the big league. He hadn't. The album didn't even make the *Billboard* 200. Lead single 'Wild America' reached number 25 on the Modern Rock Tracks chart, but missed the Hot 100 and peaked at only number 63 in the UK. Follow-up single 'Beside You' barely scraped into the UK top 50 and didn't chart at all in the US. *American Caesar* drowned between waves. It was released too late to ride the grunge explosion, too early to catch the pop-punk revival led by Green Day and The Offspring, and had no place in the rising tide of West Coast hip-hop. Iggy seemed unfazed. Even his manager at the time, Art Collins, told *The Washington Post* in 1993: 'If people acknowledge that he does credible work, then he's totally happy. He doesn't have to play the stadiums, he doesn't have to make millions of dollars.' In hindsight, the album occupies a quiet corner of Iggy's catalogue, respected but seldom revisited. Iggy rarely looked back either: only 'Wild America' and 'Louie Louie' occasionally resurfaced in his setlists after 2004.

Sprawling, confrontational and occasionally grating, *American Caesar* is no easy ride. Yet, it radiates urgency and force, blending grunge, country, blues and alt-rock into a punked-up rock 'n' roll arsenal. Iggy sounds wired and unrelenting, lyrically volatile and socially locked in. With a ferocious band behind him, he delivered one of the fiercest records of his career.

'Character' (Pop, Schermerhorn)

Iggy Pop's tenth studio album opens with 30 seconds of feedback drone and traffic noise, shifting into gently picked acoustic guitars that complete the minute-long prelude. In the background, barely audible, Iggy's radio-filtered voice delivers a short monologue: a no-frills ode to 'character', blunt Iggy style. Perhaps reflecting on The Stooges or other former bandmates rarely too occupied to say yes to a fix, he says:

Well, I'll tell you
One good thing at least about some
Of these junkies was
They had some character
They may have driven me nuts
Sometimes and screwed up
But at least when they played
The damn guitar they'd play it
Like they meant it
These white bread boys nowadays
Knowin' all the score
Don't even know how to puke

It sets the stage for the album's new recruits to step up, turning Iggy's lyrical ammo into the sonic charge of a crazed Roman legion.

'Wild America' (Pop, Schermerhorn)
The 'real' opener channels Stooges-style ruggedness with a scathing critique of modern America, building on *Brick By Brick* but with dirtier, more invigorating roughness from the start. Iggy pulls us into a night of revelry: 'One night out in LA, I met a Mexicana/With a butchy girlfriend who I thought was a man'. Encounters in bustling alleys unfold, painting a seedy picture: 'Now I'm in a black car with my Mexicana/She's got methedrine but I want marijuana'. These escapades lead to a scalding indictment of greed and privilege later in the song:

They got all kinds of fuckin' stuff
They got everything you could imagine
They're so god dammed spoiled
They're poisoned inside
They judge a man by what he's got
And they wanta have more and more
More power, more freedom
Taller kids, longer lives, everything

This build crescendos into absurdity and darkness with 'Bigger houses, slaves', a cynical, lacerating reflection on the deeply rooted racist undercurrents in American society. Reprising Kurtz's infamous words from Conrad's *Heart Of Darkness*, the repeated 'Exterminate the brutes' ties the critique to themes of madness, brutality and tyranny. Iggy briefly spotlights guest vocalist Henry Rollins, whose patriotism adds to the irony, while Iggy's own juvenile 'Iggy, you have got a biggy' throws some levity into the song's darker tones. Co-written by Schermerhorn and based on his jagged, searing hook, the track rips with unrelenting intensity. Mullins' drums hit with fiery abandon, recalling Sales' explosive work on *Lust For Life*. With this abrasive sound, the track gnashes at both fascination and disgust with an American culture thriving on opulence and rot. It stands as an ever-topical, powerfully unsettling manifesto.

'Mixin' The Colors' (Pop)
This heartfelt track, also released in Spanish as a B-side to 'Louie Louie', tackles one of humanity's oldest divides: race. It unfolds over a steady, trance-like blues groove, carved in history, anchored by a snare that hits like a nail gun. 'All across the continents, everywhere a soul is sent/A new mix of the races is takin' place' introduces Iggy's commentary on a world in flux. Boundaries dissolve and new identities emerge, glimpsed 'on your MTV', still a cultural barometer at the time. 'It's what Hitler didn't like, and it makes a

pretty sight' carries a touch of childlike naivety, but Iggy's no-nonsense honesty allows him to pull it off. 'Some they don't like it, but me I don't mind', he notes, celebrating the vibrant spread of diversity: 'In every city they're mixing the colors/Different shades for the whole countryside'. With 'I like the kids with the opened-up faces/I like the kids with the ways of their own', he adds a personal touch to this socially conscious, uplifting song. With a hint of Anthony Kiedis in his voice, Iggy champions change and unity in the hopeful refrain: 'If you leave the hate alone tonight/Music's gonna get you home tonight'. Rapid hand percussion and harmonica bring a splash of colour from rock's roots, while Katell Keineg's backing vocals lend understated warmth to this melodic track that lingers with infectious charm.

'Jealousy' (Pop)

After catching himself in a moment of jealousy, Iggy took a direct approach and wrote a straightforward song about it. It was one of over 100 songs he wrote during a creative surge following the *Brick By Brick Tour*, armed with a pencil, paper and a cheap acoustic guitar. One night, in the intimate setting of the faded grand mansion studio, the song resurfaced and simply poured out, marking the first time Iggy ever heard it amplified. This soul-baring moment, where emotion and circumstance collided unexpectedly, found its way onto the album, much to Iggy's own surprise. Burn's fingerprints are all over the production, echoing his atmospheric and spacious style. He allows the instruments to breathe within the texture, resulting in a dreamy, almost cinematic quality.

Essentially an acoustic, low-slung burner, it coils with ominous, creeping tension. Smouldering and shadowy, the song mirrors jealousy's slow approach through the veiled night, unseen but already palpable. Iggy's blood boils with envy, stoked by a wealthy musician with a big hit and his aristocratic girlfriend. 'When I look at blue blood, I want to make it mud/And tear that difference down, rock an' roll is how' Iggy sings with subdued spite, almost matter-of-factly. Few lines sum him up better. The track wouldn't feel out of place on Johnny Cash's *American Recordings*, but it carves out its own unique place here. Much like the album as a whole, it runs a bit long, but it also reinforces Iggy's continuing strong songwriting streak, reignited with his previous record.

'Hate' (Pop)

At almost seven minutes, this track stands as a cornerstone, due in no small part to Mullins' phenomenal drumming. The dry, forceful snare hits crack with spite, while the ride cymbal shimmers above, balancing power and finesse through commanding, agile patterns. After the first refrain, the toms erupt in triplets and a flurry of snappy fills lands with attitude, each as expressive as it is deliberate. The guitars fight valiantly against this percussive onslaught, unleashing power chords, dissonant ambience, sticky hooks and snarling menace. In the final two minutes, the track spirals into string-bashing chaos, pure sonic havoc, teetering on the brink of detonation. It's almost enough to make you forget Iggy's unfiltered tirade of anger and frustration. From the opening lines, his attack feels personal, but the venom doesn't stop at individuals; it targets larger phenomena:

> The mean stupidity of what he says
> The millions who admire it and they spread
> And all I wanta feel is just them dead
> And have to eat the things they did and said

In these lines, Iggy takes aim at groupthink and glorified ignorance. The 'he' remains ambiguous: it might point to a populist 'Caesar', symbolise broader societal forces or even reflect hate within Iggy himself. 'I wanted to sing about that because that's something I feel a lot. Not a day goes by without me feeling that', he told *Plazm* magazine in 1995. While condemning the toxic grip of collective stupidity, the recurring 'These are the ways I feed my hate' highlights anger as a self-fuelling cycle. Then comes the twist: 'Why am I afraid?' This sudden, vulnerable shift lays bare a contrast between aggression and introspection that deepens the song, exposing hate as a symptom of something larger. It's a destructive, painfully honest reflection on the corrosive consequences of deeply rooted and suppressed emotions.

'It's Our Love' (Pop)

The grim wino on the album cover sets up many expectations, none of which align with what we're served here. Occasionally, when Iggy strips away his irreverence, grit, irony and humour, we're prompted to stretch our open-mindedness. Here, in a syrupy croon, he offers a steadfast ode to unbreakable love forged in the margins, framed by isolation and hardship. It's a one-dimensional declaration, briefly salvaged by flickers of evocative imagery ('A cold hotel room full of trouble/Beside a blinking traffic light/On all night'). Inspired by his wife Suchi – credited on the album as 'spiritual advisor to Mr. Pop' – the ballad takes itself so seriously it seals off any angle for deeper engagement. The repetition of 'An' there ain't nobody gonna take it/There ain't nobody who's gonna break it' drives home the theme, but the lack of emotional complexity and missed opportunities for deeper storytelling leave the sentiment flat. Despite its sincerity, the song's earnestness walks a fine line between affecting and heavy-handed, at times edging into corniness. Thankfully, the hazy atmosphere and instrumentation with ethereal string textures, shimmering acoustic strums and wiry, squeaky guitar flares offer a saving grace. Beautifully produced and elegantly arranged, the track's rising intensity lends it a sense of purpose that carries it through. Still, with this song, the mock sticker on the album cover – 'This is an Iggy Pop record' – feels less like branding and more like reassurance for anyone wondering if they've got the wrong artist.

'Plastic & Concrete' (Pop)

Credit where it's due, Iggy's love detour is yanked into sharper focus by the brutal reality check that crashes in right after. Cutting through a manic punk assault of guitars and a breakneck rhythm crew, he stirs up a dystopian world trapped in artificiality, severed from organic connection. 'The country is covered in concrete and plastic', Iggy remarked about the US on *Music Box* in 1986, proving that some song ideas take time to fester. 'There's no room for imagination anymore', he added. The repeated phrase 'plastic and concrete' captures not just the physical backbone of modern societies but also the personal suffocation and isolation they breed: 'I'm a nightmare child, stuck on my own knife'. Tying into the thread of America's decay, Iggy turns a simple sandwich into a rotten metaphor: 'The salad on my outside/Is made of suicide'. Even the deli worker squirting the mayonnaise is just a cog in a meaningless machine, doomed to a 'one-way ride'. This is jagged, confrontational commentary, fronted by a frantic Iggy and a band slicing with broken edges. Yet, on an album stacked with bleak and biting tracks, this one lands closer to filler than distinction.

'Fucking Alone' (Pop, Schermerhorn)

On the Dutch radio show *Villa 65* in 1993, Iggy delved into the origin of this reflective, understated piece. He recounted an evening at a metal bar where he abstained from casual sex and drugs, choosing instead to maintain focus on his creative work. The next morning, observing the college-aged crowd in downtown Manhattan, Iggy mused on how people navigate identity, sizing each other up by looks and actions. 'It's a 24-hour travelogue of life in my neighbourhood', he remarked, describing the track as a meditation on self-discovery and authenticity. With urban cues of coffee beans, hideaways, love boutiques and metal rap, the lyrics create a vibrant kaleidoscope of city life set to rhythmic phrasing. Through acute observations of others ('shave-haired girl with a dog/Dressin' cool not too new'), Iggy expresses a collective yearning for purpose and connection:

> Everybody is in a dream
> Of what they want and who they need
> To feel all right to be alive
> To wipe out words that they despise
> From a thunder brain
> That's quick to pain
> And only once to live again

The organic, percussion-infused, downbeat groove carries the fragmented yet flowing lyrics, echoing the free-spirited influence of Beat poetry. Iggy's newly adapted vocal style on this album is characterised by elongated words delivered with a nasal resonance and a slightly twangy placement. Its abrasive tone occasionally grates, sometimes undermining the integrity of the songs. On this track, however, that delivery sharpens the refrain's bluntness, channelling the unfiltered despair of solitude.

'Highway Song' (Pop)
Iggy goes full electric Johnny Cash here, locking into that signature no-frills boom-chicka-boom rhythm with spot-on strumming. At first, it seems an unlikely fit. But on an album that grapples with Iggy's complex ties to his homeland – its flaws, contradictions and his place within it – a touch of 'homeless' country feels like a natural addition. Iggy's voice even takes on a rockabilly tinge, while the snare taps out a swinging groove. This rollicking journey is further powered by straight bass runs and an open tom, delivering a resonant thud with every beat. Iggy, the asphalt outlaw, navigates the road as both an escape and a battleground, wrestling with his demons while carving out a space to live on his own terms. The pressure and anxiety pushing him forward simply surface in 'I'm an ordinary man/With a time bomb in my hand'. Addicted to the highway, he embraces it as both a means of survival and a rejection of societal norms, despite the pain and uncertainty it brings: 'Nothin' gonna take my road away/Nothin' gonna take my road outta my heart'.

'Beside You' (Pop, Jones)
Although Iggy had favoured 'Louie Louie', it was this reworked track from the 1985 sessions with Steve Jones in LA that became the album's second single. With Virgin pushing for a hit, Iggy re-recorded this straightforward love song as a late addition to the album. While it's a refined version, he stays relatively faithful to the demo, adding the voice of Lisa Germano, who at the time was still playing in John Mellencamp's band. A textbook 1990s alt-rock ballad with all the signature elements: an arpeggio intro over rimshots, a sudden shift to a big chorus with heavier drums and guitars, and a middle eight that briefly diversifies before the final repetitive choruses fade. Fully in 'Candy' mode, Iggy drops his off-kilter, dissonant phrasing for a smoother delivery, likely aiming for similar commercial success with this longing-filled counterpart. The black-and-white video shows Iggy alone in a bleak, dystopian setting, seeking connection with Germano through a video link. They also mimed it on *Top Of The Pops*, in a performance as forgettable as it was unambitious. Even so, despite its conventionality and lack of edge, it's an instant sing-along with a charming track appeal.

'Sickness' (Pop)
Charles Thompson, better known as Black Francis of The Pixies, named *New Values* one of his favourite albums in a 2014 interview with *The Quietus*, adding that he had bought *Lust For Life* around 20 times. In a 2004 *Spin* article, he cited Iggy as an influence in choosing a stage name: 'If it's good

enough for Iggy Pop, it's good enough for me.' In a 2021 *Goldmine* feature, Pixies guitarist Joey Santiago called *Fun House* one of the ten most influential albums on his playing. In a 1993 *Rolling Stone* interview, Kurt Cobain admitted that 'Smells Like Teen Spirit' was his attempt at 'trying to rip off The Pixies.' When compiling a list of his 50 favourite albums in his published journal, Cobain placed The Pixies' *Surfer Rosa* second, just behind *Raw Power*.

This circle of influence tightens in this late addition to the album, where the echoes of both The Pixies and Nirvana are clearly felt. The coiling guitar line cutting through the crude ascending riff forms a mangled hybrid of their sound, triggering Iggy to unleash his torment over a soul-devouring sickness. Caught in a vicious cycle of desire, self-destruction and confusion, love has been perverted into something suffocating and destructive. The lyrics may even hint at a narrator whose sickened desire crosses disturbing lines, with the title underscoring the feverish, distorted nature of his craving. It's hard to imagine it getting darker, so perhaps it's time to move on to a lighter, sillier song.

'Boogie Boy' (Pop)

Before we watched Iggy enjoy some BBQ prawns over a chat with long-time Stooges fan Anthony Bourdain on his show *Parts Unknown* in 2015, the answer to the burning question, 'What does Iggy like to eat?' came from this one-take, high-energy track. 'I like to eat spaghetti with tomato sauce/I like to eat clams with Spanish moss', he enlightens us, trading call-and-response lines with the guitar in a punk rock 'n' rolla-fuelled romp so raucous you can almost smell the sweat and steam coming off the band. As often, Iggy balances the album's weightier lyrical content with some straight-up, hard-hitting absurdity. There's not much to unpack in 'I like to go down to mashed-potato town/'Cause that's where a boogie boy can get down'. Silly and enjoyable in delivery, though the album wouldn't have lost any of its punch if this one hadn't made the cut.

'Perforation Problems' (Pop)

The impact of grunge, especially Nirvana's earth-shifting *Nevermind*, resonates throughout this album. This song is no exception, marked by slightly off-pitch tones and chorused guitars. Short leads mimic vocal lines, steeped in feedback and dissonance, boosting the song's abrasive punch.

In a paradoxically cheery melody, Iggy takes an unflinching look at his drug past. Although no monk, he was mostly sober at the time, sticking to a glass of wine and the occasional cigarette. In the *Villa 65* radio interview, he shared his stance: 'I don't recommend them. Especially now, it's not a very good era to take drugs in. If I were 20 this year, I wouldn't think it's a good policy.' In 1993, when heroin haunted rock circles, crack ravaged the streets and synthetic highs crept into clubs, overdose deaths had risen to more than three times the levels of the late 1970s, with drug-related crime and homicides also at their peak. Reflecting on young rock stars flirting with heroin, Iggy predicted, 'Yeah, a lot of them will die.' This track, as he then pointed out, is self-explanatory in its message. Harrowing yet cathartic, it scratches at the scars of addiction. 'Stumbling like a dirty slave' and 'I watched my future become my past' reveal the weight of his struggles and wasted opportunities. The recurring 'perforation problems' point to both needle marks and psychic toll. Iggy's confessional 'Now I'm all right but there's still holes' acknowledges that while he has moved forward, the remnants of trauma and addiction remain.

'Social Life' (Pop)

With a calm, lilting vocal melody that has a sing-song quality like a lullaby, Iggy accompanies himself on acoustic guitar, with Schermerhorn's understated strumming joining in. Gentle bass, synthetic strings and chimes, combined with Iggy's close-mic'd vocal, subtly weave together to draw us into the intimacy of this live-in-the-studio, one-take recording.

Speaking to *Plazm* magazine, Iggy noted that the song resonates with anyone working in a big city, particularly in entertainment, advertising or other high-pressure industries where social demands weigh heavily. 'It's just about having to go out when you don't want to, or getting caught up with a crowd you don't really connect with. Going along with things, even when your heart's not in it. A lot of people are in that situation', he explained. The song sketches a reality ruled by materialism and surface-level conformity. 'Maybe you need new tits' nods to beauty pressure without blinking, while 'God-awful art and clothes, plenty of money though' evokes the same hollow glamour at the core of Bret Easton Ellis' *American Psycho*. It all builds to Iggy's final impulse: he'd rather throw a brick through the window. 'That goddamn social life, it's torture dressed as fun' says it all in true Iggy fashion, blunt and to the point.

'Louie Louie' (Berry)

A, D, E minor. The simplest of chord progressions drives one of the world's most iconic and covered rock songs. Written by Richard Berry in 1955 and immortalised by The Kingsmen's 1963 hit, 'Louie Louie' entered Iggy's repertoire as early as 1964 with The Iguanas. The Stooges took several stabs at the track, and a provocative version with improvised lyrics was captured during their chaotic, then-final show in 1974, later released on *Metallic K.O.* Iggy briefly brought it back during the *New Values Tour* in 1979. When Virgin, after hearing the first recordings for the new album, pushed for a hit, he decided it would be ironic to re-record one. Tied to the album, his long-overdue studio version reimagines the party anthem with a wry political twist. Over its indestructible riff, he delivers verses tinged with tongue-in-cheek commentary:

The communist world is fallin' apart
The capitalists are just breakin' hearts
Money is the reason to be
It makes me just wanna sing Louie Louie

The refrain becomes catharsis, offering a sense of salvation or escape from the absurdity of a chaotic world reshaped by the post-Bush and Gorbachev era. Iggy tilts the original's romantic innocence ('a fine little girl is waitin' for me') by following it with 'but I'm as bent as Dostoevsky', a quip that touches on existential despair and *The Idiot*. Schermerhorn tears through nearly a full minute of thrash-happy soloing before Iggy casually runs through a list of global issues – health insurance, homelessness, world peace, AIDS, education – ending with an offhand remark: 'I'm trying to do right, but ... hey!' His closer 'Turn on the news it looks like a movie/It makes me wanna sing Louie Louie' lands somewhere between resignation and a smirk. On the French TV show *Coucou c'est nous!* in 1993, Iggy described it as 'a simple song with charm that everybody treats like trash.' His version does it justice, infusing it with humour, satire and unmistakable personality, elevating it to one of the album's lighter treats. Not a hit, though.

'Caesar' (Pop, Schermerhorn)
Iggy was so absorbed in *The Decline And Fall Of The Roman Empire* that it led to what he later called 'an extemporaneous soliloquy', originally intended as the album's closing track. In his *Classics Ireland* essay, he reflected on the piece:

> It made me laugh my ass off because it was so true. America is Rome. Of course, why shouldn't it be? All of Western life and institutions today are traceable to the Romans and their world. We are all Roman children, for better or worse.

It opens with a grandiose proclamation: 'People of America, I bring you a great army to preserve peace in our empire', instantly bridging ancient Rome with modern America. 'Who are these Christians? What is this strange religion?' pairs Iggy's mocking laughter with a timeless fear of change. Cultural decline, bloated with pageantry and fed by indulgence, coils around the savage command 'Throw them to the lions'. Decadence and exploitation are flaunted in grapes from Sicily and silks from Asia Minor, while a soothsayer's whisper ('Beware the Ides of March') sketches out a crumbling regime. The closing line, 'The empire is tired ... Caesar will rest now', lands as a fitting epitaph for a regime rotting from within. Iggy's theatrical turn as a heartless American leader camps up this experimental curveball: a mix of satirical theatre and dark entertainment.

Amusing and unconventional as it may be, this is not a track for easy listening. Its melodic framework draws on the microtonal scale of traditional

Indonesian music, distinct from Western equal temperament, and hints at the modal contours of classical Indian ragas. Less a song than a structure for improvisation, it unfolds in cyclical patterns: trance-like, with a touch of psychedelia. The sound mutates through effects, punctuated by flashes of bass and scattered percussion. It shares DNA with 'Watching The News', through its offbeat delivery and a similar line ('Who are these people?'), in a shared critique of power and spectacle. As the seven-minute experiment winds down, Iggy breaks character with a crackling sense of glee: 'We got that, right? You see, I could go more for numbers like that on the record.'

'Girls Of N.Y.' (Pop)

A bonus with commitment issues: not included on all versions of the album, but not a traditional bonus track either. Specifically, it was absent from the original US release, but while featured on the Japanese CD release and the original UK vinyl pressing, it is still missing from streaming services. The lyrics, with references to transvestite transformations and various urban subcultures, may have been deemed too controversial for the American market. It's a shame because 'Girls Of N.Y.' offers a compelling, cinematic sketch of New York's diversity, energy and imperfect authenticity, capturing Iggy's spoken observations of people searching, transforming and surviving: 'People from everywhere, Jamaicans, Puerto Ricans, Englishmen, Spaniards, Japanese, Portuguese, Argentines, Norwegians and Swedes/Can't forget me, from Detroit city, yeah!' The persistent 16th-note guitar chime over a solid backbeat gives the track an infectious cadence, intensifying its rhythmic energy as it carries the album to its fade-out. What lingers is the sense of a city waking up, ready to chase another Wild America.

Naughty Little Doggie (1996)

Personnel:
Iggy Pop: vocals, guitar
The Fuckups:
Eric Mesmerize (Eric Schermerhorn): guitar
Hal Wonderful (Hal Cragin): bass, keyboards on 'Shoeshine Girl'
Larry Contrary (Larry Mullins): drums
Additional personnel:
The Mighty Whitey (Whitey Kirst): guitar
Recorded at Track Record, Inc., Hollywood, California, between June and July 1995
Producers: Iggy Pop and Thom Wilson
Release date: March 1996
Label: Virgin
Chart places: US: did not chart, UK: 77, Aus: 83, Can: 46
Running time: 40:05

After more than a hundred dates, the *American Caesar* world tour wrapped in the summer of 1994. The tight four-man unit had powered through an intense year-long stretch of festivals and indoor shows. With the road behind him, Iggy shifted focus to his growing – if rarely praised – on-screen presence. He filmed the campy sci-fi flick *Tank Girl*, then headed to Spain for *Atolladero*, a dystopian western for which he also performed the mariachi-tinged title track. His expanding screen résumé would soon include *Dead Man*, episodes of *The Adventures Of Pete & Pete* and *Star Trek: Deep Space Nine*, and a cameo as himself in *Private Parts*. His most notable role was in *The Crow: City Of Angels*, where he played the villain Curve. For the part he bleached his long hair, a look he kept, with minor variations.

With his road-hardened band, now called The Fuck Ups, Iggy entered the studio in late June 1995 to begin recording his 11th solo album. Producer Thom Wilson had made his name with lean, hard-hitting punk records for bands like T.S.O.L., Dead Kennedys and The Vandals. In the early 1990s, he produced *Ignition* and its multi-million-selling follow-up, *Smash*, by The Offspring, helping to propel punk rock into the mainstream. Both albums were recorded at Track Record in North Hollywood, where Iggy's new project now took shape. To get in the right headspace, he brought *James Brown: Star Time* to the studio each day. He would blast Brown's hyped-up call of 'Are you ready!?' and charge into the sessions with that energy. The goal was simple: a punchy, no-nonsense rock album with two sturdy ballads, built for impact, not ceremony. Speaking to SVT in 1996, Iggy contrasted it with its predecessor:

> The eccentric and strange *American Caesar* – which I like – was basically a rambling, long and obscure political statement on my part. I then got tired of

being so full of shit and political statements, and I made this one, which is short, funny and has lots of sexual longing and a silly title.

The album photography is by David Sims and Anton Corbijn. Corbijn's shot of Iggy, taken during downtime at the 1995 Rock and Roll Hall of Fame concert in Cleveland, appears on the back of the booklet. The cover shows a black-and-white image of Iggy as a battle-worn misfit, looking as if his helmet is doing all the thinking. Repelled by ageing rock stars relying on filters and hollow bluster, Iggy told WDR in 1996: 'I just hate that. I had this picture, and it looked so miserable, this guy protecting himself from all this dreck falling on his head, and I liked it, so I put it out.'

Upon release, the album drew a familiar mix of reactions, converging on a modestly solid Iggy Pop record. The *LA Times* praised its vitality, while *Rolling Stone* declared: 'The fun house is still open for business.' *NME* gave it 6/10, dubbing it Iggy's 'male menopause album'. *The Guardian* called him 'more a showpiece than a real contender', but felt his 'long, dishonourable service' earned him some indulgence. It peaked at number 77 in the UK, number 83 in Australia and failed to enter the *Billboard* 200. The singles 'Heart Is Saved', 'To Belong' and 'I Wanna Live' didn't chart either, eclipsed by a Berlin-era anthem that stole the spotlight and the momentum. Danny Boyle's cinematic adaptation of *Trainspotting* premiered in early 1996 and quickly became a critically acclaimed box office hit. The film placed Iggy's legacy at the heart of its portrayal of heroin addiction and urban alienation, pairing 'Lust For Life' and 'Nightclubbing' with a soundtrack fusing 1970s art glam and 1990s indie. 'Lust For Life' was rereleased as a single and climbed into the UK top 30, placing Iggy in the orbit of a younger crowd attuned to Britpop and retro cool. A new video was made, splicing scenes from the film with studio footage of Iggy dancing alongside Ewen 'Spud' Bremner. Seeing Iggy, well into middle age, lip-syncing a song from 20 years earlier carried a faint air of indignity. To some longtime fans, it felt like the man they'd stuck with through chaos and comebacks was suddenly being hijacked by newcomers – as though the track hadn't been great all along. Cashing in on the renewed attention, Virgin released *Nude & Rude: The Best Of Iggy Pop*, its cover featuring Gerard Malanga's 1971 full-frontal nude portrait, neatly cropped just above the pubic bone.

Beneath the bravado in mid-1990s TV interviews, subtle signs reveal a man grappling with his place as a middle-aged rock icon. Grateful for the renewed appreciation, he remained warm and sharp-witted when Gen X hosts or callers – often half his age – asked him yet again about Bowie, excess or his favourite colour. But behind the charm, a quiet discomfort seeps in: he's been sealed inside a legacy, a career built around an alter ego with its own set of expectations. With sexual innuendo and naughty 'bad boy' energy, he fends off the passage of time, even as the album cover knowingly amplifies it. That ambivalence runs through the album. To offset the weight of being Iggy Pop, of ageing, and of a marriage beginning to unravel, he turned to immediacy and fun, dishing up a rock album free of overthinking. Loud on entry, hollow on replay. The tension it masked would fuel a sharp turn on his next before he entered the new century and eventually embraced the inevitable with style.

'I Wanna Live' (Kirst, Pop)
A jumpstart, wired to the same current as The Stooges' 'Real Cool Time'. A taut riff rips through the right channel, then the drums crackle in, the bass glides underneath and the riff bursts open in stereo as it doubles on the left. It makes for one of the best opening seconds on any Iggy Pop album. The band hit like a garage outfit, but one with miles of experience under its belt, buzzing through their tube amps. Iggy was particularly taken with the drum sound on The Offspring records, and it's immediately clear why. The high-attack kit is close-mic'd, bright, alive and right in your room. With Schermerhorn, co-writer Kirst as a guest and Iggy himself, three guitars churn and crackle. Then Iggy's voice gnaws its way in:

I see my future shuffling
A shakey step at a time
I got no choice but careful
Thank God, I've done my crime
The tools I see on TV
Can't stand it when they fake
A prick's a prick at any age
Why give one a break?

This is Iggy, alright: phoniness is unbearable, no excuses. The primal chorus ('I wanna live/A little bit longer') is repeated like an incantation. That 'little' does some fine-tuned hedging; he's not demanding immortality, just a slight extension. No big ask. Iggy spins the second verse into a street hawker's sales pitch with 'I'm better than a Pepsi/I'm cooler than MTV', while casually landing a deadpan credo: 'I'm deeper than the shit I'm in/An' I don't really give a damn'. The bridge sharpens the tone, swapping self-awareness for something more combative: 'Step up, it's fight time/Kick, scratch and bite time'. Then comes a guitar solo that resists the urge to spiral into noodling, instead locking onto the chorus melody: simple, effective, no wasted motion. 'I Wanna Live' is as much a creed as it is a song. It's about survival in the face of time and circumstance, bottling up Iggy's core: scrappy and unsentimental, always ready for a fight.

'Pussy Walk' (Pop, Schermerhorn)
A big part of Iggy's appeal has always been his autonomy, rebellious streak and instinctive irreverence, combined with a humour-laced, say-it-like-it-is

lyrical approach. But coming from a man nearing 50, who's seen it all and boasts an influential back catalogue most artists wouldn't dare dream of, yet another dive into the temptations and curiosities surrounding pussy starts to feel a bit thin. Pair that with a fixation on young girls 'with their young girl clothes' in 'high schools and Jr. high schools', and things take a blatantly ephebophilic turn. Not that Iggy cares: 'It's a good song, a true song', he said backstage at Loreley Festival in 1996, speaking to WDR. 'True songs generally cause a little ripple. It's somewhere between either people getting angry or giving a little nervous giggle. Some people like it, you know.' Whether you file the lyrics under funny or just plain embarrassing, the track itself, with Schermerhorn's looping and loping bass-doubled riff, snakes into an easy sway that keeps pulling you in. Iggy delivers his naughty obsession with fervour, escalating into what feels like a closing-in sequence straight out of *Invasion Of The Body Snatchers*.

'Innocent World' (Pop)
Nostalgia for youthful days takes centre stage in this track. When talking about his band's summer gigs in 1996, Iggy, then 49, told *Blender*:

> When I play live, a lot of the way I come on and the way the band sound and the whole music is played feels kinda retro. Kind of like what I was doing when I was 21. Why? Because I was *happy* when I was 21!

The carefree image of fun, cars and young love sets the scene, when any dabbling in drugs was just 'a cute little monkey on my back'. Not an age of wisdom, but of impulse: 'We was too young to know what we were doing'. He paints a familiar picture of freedom before adulthood took the shine off things: 'Now I slink around like a killer/The things they say are just a lot of filler'. The album's skeleton crew keeps the framework lean: another rock-solid riff, bass strapped in, and drums played with sharp attack. The sheer joy of playing bursts through, mirroring the rush of those vanished summer days. The instrumental break layers two guitar parts: the lowest – the riff – glides from the left to the right channel, while the higher runs strike in the opposite direction. AllMusic compared the album to *Instinct*, with its similarly hard, direct rock approach, though these subtle details inject movement and playfulness: the kind of nuance too often missing from *Instinct*. It is a tight, catchy, uncomplicated rock song that steers clear of sentimentality. But on an album where everything moves in the same vein, a few weightier tracks might have lifted it higher.

'Knucklehead' (Pop)
In 1974 in Queens, New York, the lanky Jeffrey Hyman co-founded a band with two other misfits bonded by their love for The Stooges, a group everyone else around them despised. After a fourth member joined, they all

adopted the same last name and went on to play 2,263 concerts over 22 years through various lineups. By 2002, they were ranked the second-greatest band of all time by *Spin* and entered the Rock and Roll Hall of Fame in their first year of eligibility. The Ramones became punk's defining blueprint: raw, fast and stripped to the bone. Pounding rhythms, downstroked guitars, absurdist humour and choruses that stuck like bubblegum.

That same no-frills intensity pulses through this album, from its unvarnished sound to its blunt compositions, with barely a breath between tracks. 'Knucklehead' follows suit. It channels The Ramones' spirit, from its hammering chorus to verses that mix observation, absurdity and deadpan wit. Dumbness as a scalpel to carve out something sharp. Over-the-top luxury ('Fancy Apple laptop cost 5 grand/Fresh girl in a T-shirt still looks best'), a rejection of commercial music ('The music sounds like dead ham/The DJ is a con man') and mindless consumption ('Go to the computer and I'm punching/What's this information that I'm munching') all sit alongside power dynamics. The chorus 'I I I want something from you' sums it up: everyone wants something, and you're just a pawn in the game.

The relationship between Iggy and The Ramones was built on deep mutual respect and a direct line to punk history. A year after Joey Ramone's death in 2001, Iggy reflected in *Interview* magazine:

> He makes those vocals sound easy, but it takes quite a bit of skill. Joey was one of the only ones who was able to make something sound pretty but still punk. The more commercial ones today all sound a bit whiny or cute. The Ramones avoided that. I remember Joey expressing his anger when neo-punk first became commercial in the US, with bands like Green Day and The Offspring. He was very, very angry about it, but I don't think he had reason to be. Stuff that isn't cute just isn't meant to be massively commercial. It's not fit for that particular machine, but there are other rewards.

Fittingly, the link between The Stooges, The Ramones and neo-punk comes full circle here with producer Wilson, who helmed the breakthrough albums of one of their most commercially successful heirs. Joey had no issue with Iggy working with Wilson, though he wouldn't have minded a bigger bite of his successors' success.

'To Belong' (Pop)

The first true shift to restraint arrives. A laid-back groove underpins arpeggiated chords, punctuated by choked hits. Iggy delivers the opening verse with quiet composure, singing about a bird with a broken wing. Then, suddenly, his delivery hardens: 'And the only way to go is DEFY'. Though never stated outright, the song seems to grapple with his position as an ageing rock star, boxed into a fixed role by the industry, the audience or even himself. He lunges into the shouted chorus, the band snapping to attention with a forceful shift in dynamics. 'To belong here!' he belts, pushing the top of his range yet sounding strikingly in control. The second verse reinforces the sense of being slowly consumed:

A spider is sitting in a corner
Gonna catch a fly
The web is pulling tight around him
And the fly's I
But all I do is guard my pile
Cause it's my supply

The soft-loud contrast, a hallmark of the Pixies and Nirvana and eventually baked into the alt-rock playbook by Radiohead's 'Creep', makes its 1990s ubiquity felt here, though The Stooges had been pulling that trick long before any of them. That very history has sealed him into a role he can't easily escape. After the second chorus, two solos by Schermerhorn intertwine, weaving together without overpowering each other. Musically, it's the most captivating moment on the album, setting the stage for an extended freak-out that builds towards an ecstatic release, only to be cut short. This isn't an album for drawn-out sections or embellishment. It snaps right back into the chorus, repeated to the bitter end. Iggy's anger adds a touch of sarcasm, as if frustrated by the fact that he still belongs here, even as it drains him: 'I'm giving up my soul to belong'. The song foreshadows a radical shift, a break from the confines of a road-worn rocker stuck in a loop. His next album will be precisely that.

'Keep On Believing' (Pop, Schermerhorn)

The album's shortest track is more groove than song, but as a rhythmic mini-fest, it gets the job done. A snappy, distorted riff tumbles through an undulating eighth-note pattern, while Iggy's melody in the verses mirrors its rise and fall almost beat for beat. In the chorus, he locks into a stretched 4/4 pulse on 'Keep on believing'. The bass weaves deftly around the snare, while the ride cymbal shimmers above in its own loose rhythmic pattern. A tangle of free spirits, but everything falls seamlessly into place.

Iggy kicks off this brisk hymn of longing with a simple contrast that mirrors his life: domesticity versus the urge to move: 'I woke up in the quiet dark/Fed the cat and hit the park'. During his stroll, he encounters the song's muse, wittily framed in a fourfold alliteration: 'Cutest chicest chocolate queen'. The meeting is as quiet as it is intense, and for a moment, he seems to float, untethered from life's gravity: trouble, strength and truth. He urges us, and perhaps himself, to keep on believing. In what? Magical moments? The resilience of a marriage tested by temptation? Or simply in anything that lifts us above the mundane? No time for answers. Just believe.

'Outta My Head' (Pop)
It opens promisingly, with a deadpan drumbeat that stays stoic and unwavering, accompanied by spacious guitars from Iggy and Schermerhorn, the latter occasionally colouring his parts with a wah effect. In just a few lines, Iggy sketches two characters stuck at the bottom of society. The opening line introduces Sally: 'Sally goes 'round the roses every night', taken from The Jaynetts' 1963 hit, a song about sorrow, loss and female loneliness. Here, Sally roams the streets at night, looking for shelter. 'She becomes a target soon as she rise/Somebody wants to cut her down to his size' leaves no doubt she is never out of danger. The pre-chorus isn't an outburst but a flat statement: 'It's a sad bad feeling'. In Lou Reed fashion, Iggy lets the bleakness speak for itself. As if deliberately countering *American Caesar*, the chorus is stripped to a single repeated line, much like the rest of the album, making for easy sing-alongs: 'I'm going out, outta my head'. A free agent of a line, Iggy delivers it with a slight rasp, but it never really bites.

In the second verse, there's Jimmy, possibly a nod to Iggy's drifting days after the collapse of The Stooges, digging through dumpsters, clinging to any way out. 'He knows he's a target, everyone is' lands alongside 'Strangle that rock and roll star, make him eat jizz'. It is a degrading image, a scornful and violent dismantling of one scraping by in the gutter. Iggy lines up the pieces: a meeting, a climax, a cutting remark that could have tied everything together. Instead, the song settles for circling the drain well past the five-minute mark. The final two minutes flirt with a Velvet Underground vibe, but without enough of their hypnotic mayhem to sustain it.

'Shoeshine Girl' (Pop, Schermerhorn)
Unexpectedly for this album, Iggy delivers one of his strongest ballads. A brooding gothic-country piece co-written with Schermerhorn, it leans heavily on his deft acoustic phrasing, with the occasional rattle of the strings, layered over sustained keys, spare bass and brushed drumming.

Originally demoed as 'Spellbound', a far more fitting title, the lyrics play out like a vignette, recounting a fleeting yet captivating encounter with a 'comely goth girl' at an airport. The spellbound pull merges with a cheeky gaze, almost bluntly so: 'Her cleavage I could see/I contemplated both of them/That's how she spellbound me'. She embodies the archetype of the cool outsider: 'It was Lollapalooza day/But she didn't like the groups', making her all the more alluring. Iggy rolls the six syllables of Lollapalooza day smoothly across the bar, playing into the song's easy sway. He is tempted to linger, but someone is waiting for him, pulling him away, leaving only a wistful parting shot:

So if you're dark and lovely
And you see me passing by
A smile I'd appreciate
And a little bit of crime

The cracks in his marriage to Suchi seem to surface in this piece of Americana noir. Years of touring and filming on location had introduced distance and temptation, straining their relationship to the breaking point. By 1997, they would separate, and two years later, their divorce was official.

'Heart Is Saved' (Pop)
A crucial question when evaluating any artistic work is how much weight to give the creator's intent. If Picasso set out to sketch a cat in ten seconds, it would be odd to hear a critic condemning the lines as too hasty. Although reviews upon release leaned towards the positive, a similar disconnect seems to have developed over time, with *Naughty Little Doggie* coming to be dismissed by the echo chamber of music critics, perhaps because expectations of what makes a 'strong' Iggy album have shifted. Philosopher Susan Sontag, in *Against Interpretation*, argued that art doesn't always need to be endlessly analysed; sometimes, its power lies in the immediate experience. That seems to be exactly what Iggy was aiming for. Looking at the album through the lens of Iggy's own intentions, his 1996 description on *Rock Express* proves insightful:

> I wanted a fucking album you could go sit at McDonald's with, listen to it and go, 'Yeah, yeah, bwuh.' Gobble it down, go 'wheee!' then run around and just do whatever you wanted to do, feeling better than you did before. I did not want to make an album where you had to call up, make a reservation, talk to a maître d' and put on a little white shirt.

This track is another fitting snack from the value menu, a punk rock burst that comes closest to the sound of Green Day or The Offspring. Iggy sings about believing his heart was saved by 'a little white cloud'. Circling in self-inflicted fallout, he clings to the idea of salvation, convincing himself: 'And I gotta believe all night and all day/And when I believe my heart is saved'. The band barrel forward one last time in top gear. It won't make Iggy's Best Of collection, but it satisfies a craving when the mood strikes. With this in mind, the whole album showcases his knack for dishing up sharp, tasty and compact songs. Peppy songwriting with uncomplicated earworm choruses. In hindsight, you might think, 'Was that it?', but in the moment, it hits the spot.

'Look Away' (Pop)
The only Iggy Pop song deliberately pulled from streaming services, following backlash for its autobiographical account involving a minor. A 2021 British documentary on sexual abuse in the rock scene aptly borrowed its title from this track. Long before this, Iggy had already addressed the groupie scene in the Stooges track 'She Creatures Of The Hollywood Hills', a tribute to the girls hanging around Sunset Strip.

Musically, 'Look Away' is stripped back: a descending acoustic guitar, complemented by electric accents and restrained drumming, sets a reflective mood, while Iggy's subdued delivery lends it an intimate, diary-like quality. Blending resignation, self-criticism and detachment, he reflects on the lives of Johnny Thunders, guitarist for The New York Dolls and The Heartbreakers, and a young girl named Sable Shields, better known as Sable Starr. Often described as the 'queen of the groupies', Starr was a prominent figure in the early 1970s LA rock scene and became deeply entwined in a toxic relationship with Thunders. She was also a groupie of Iggy, then 23, and many other rock stars of the era. The song opens with Iggy bluntly confessing:

> I slept with Sable when she was 13
> Her parents were too rich to do anything
> She rocked her way around LA
> 'Til a New York Doll carried her away

This confronting opening line provokes immediate unease, crossing ethical and legal boundaries. Iggy neither obscures the truth nor offers justification, laying bare instead the permissive, often exploitative culture of its time. Upon its 1996 release, the lyrics drew little criticism and were largely ignored, overlooked in an era less attuned to power dynamics. However, the rise of #MeToo and a greater focus on abuse and inequality have drastically shifted the context. In 2023, when asked about his feelings on the matter in *The New York Times Magazine*, Iggy replied:

> I don't think that I was really thinking about anything. Except I think most artists, when they're young, pursue beauty when it presents itself. Things were much different in those times in general. Much, much different. That's all I would say about that.

His response reflects the difficulty of revisiting such moments through today's perspective. It underscores the importance of ensuring that acknowledging realities were different is not conflated with excusing or justifying such acts. Recognising historical context is crucial, but the fact that actions were accepted or ignored in the past doesn't mean they should escape scrutiny today. In that light, as explored earlier in this book, should such criticism not aim to educate and contextualise rather than erase? Judging past works solely through a modern lens risks oversimplifying history, ignoring its cultural and social dynamics. If we choose not to face difficult, confronting expressions from the past, how can we understand the conditions that produced them and ensure they are never repeated? How else can we learn and progress?

In the 1970s, Iggy embodied the sexual free-for-all rock 'n' roll lifestyle, integral to his persona and music. In his 1982 anecdotal and inebriated memoir, *I Need More,* co-authored by Anne Wehrer and currently out of print, he insinuates that he had sexual encounters with underage girls multiple times. His confessions, however reprehensible, cast an unflinching light on his mindset, the decadent environment he was part of and the abusive practices within the era's music scene. It reminds us of a predatory culture that still persists and cautions against romanticising the darker chapters of rock history. Whether one condemns Iggy for his actions and revelations, or continues to engage with his music despite them, remains a deeply personal decision.

Avenue B (1999)

Personnel:
Iggy Pop: vocals, guitar, keyboards
Whitey Kirst: guitar
Pete 'Damien' Marshall: guitar
Hal Cragin: bass
Larry Mullins: drums, tabla, vibraphone, treated 808
Lenny Castro: percussion on 'Avenue B', 'Español'
John Medeski: Hammond organ on 'Avenue B', 'Español', 'I Felt The Luxury', Wurlitzer on 'I Felt The Luxury'
Billy Martin: drums on 'Avenue B', 'Español', 'I Felt The Luxury'
Chris Wood: bass on 'Avenue B', 'Español', 'I Felt The Luxury'
Michael Chaves: keyboards on 'Nazi Girlfriend'
Andrew Scheps: loops, mixing on 'Shakin' All Over'
Don Was: guitar on 'Long Distance'
David Mansfield: violin, viola on The Brave excerpts
Recorded at 262 Mott Street and The Theatre, New York City; Teatro, Oxnard, California; Ocean Way No. 3 and The Record Plant, Hollywood, California; Shacklyn Studios and Studio 12A, New York City, between May and June 1998
Producer: Don Was
Release date: September 1999
Label: Virgin
Chart places: US: did not chart, UK: 105
Running time: 49:26

In the late 1990s, an influential music legend with a lifetime of defiance stepped into the studio to record his most introspective album yet. Stark, haunting and critically lauded, it offered a stripped-down reflection on mortality, relationships and impermanence, and earned him three Grammy Awards. He called it *Avenue B*. Except ... he didn't. The album was *Time Out Of Mind,* and it revived Bob Dylan's career, laying the groundwork for a celebrated late run. While Dylan collected his Grammys, Jim Osterberg was in the winter of his 50th year: divorced, alone in his New York apartment and feeling miserable. Four months later, he stepped into the studio to record an Iggy Pop album with the exact same premise, now one lost to time and scorn.

After *Naughty Little Doggie*, Iggy had remixed *Raw Power* to make it louder and more aggressive. He had recorded the EP *Monster Men* for the animated series *Space Goofs*, contributed songs to various compilation albums and recorded the duet 'I'll Be Seeing You' with Françoise Hardy for the *Jazz À Saint-Germain* collection. He also composed the score for *The Brave*, directed by Johnny Depp, and toured across four continents. By the end of 1997, he was spent. In *The New York Times Magazine* in 2023, he recalled:

> I went on that Iggy path with The Stooges, and once you start and you get somewhere, you just go with it. But what happens is, if you do that over and over, it peters out. Finally, it got to a point with *Avenue B*: I was hitting 50 and hitting a wall, and I was fed up. It was a dark feeling. But I always believed that if I did it – whatever *it* was – for real, then an audience was going to be there.

It would become the quietest album of his career to date, in which he laid bare a world of solipsism, selfishness and evasive love, filtered through acoustic confessionals, spoken monologues and jittery jazz backdrops. It was recorded in studios across New York City, Hollywood and Oxnard, with Don Was once again brought in as producer. Iggy told *The San Diego Union-Tribune* in 2001:

> I was trying to make a middle-aged, desperate, sex-collision record. It was also important to me, just as a sort of musical auteur, if you will. I was aware of the importance of rounding out my oeuvre. So I couldn't look in the mirror if I didn't make it personal. Unfortunately, for some people, 'personal' is really dark.

It hit the shops in September 1999, with a cover shot by Jeff Wall taken in Vancouver. It's an arresting frontal portrait of a reptilian-looking divorcé, cheeks sunken, eyes empty but holding. With its stark intimacy and musical restraint, the album marked a bold new artistic turn – one that left most listeners cold. Sales were poor. It charted lower than even *Naughty Little Doggie*, and yet again, the critical response was divided. *Rolling Stone* gave it a lukewarm 2.5 out of 5, noting that Iggy had 'lost his talent for the odd, apt metaphor.' *Spin* slammed the album's 'uncomfortable ballads' and added, 'He just can't sing.' *Q* echoed the disdain, describing it as 'less a cry for help than the artful musings of a horny old man.' Others were more generous: *NME* called it 'overpowering', *Entertainment Weekly* found it 'tasteful' and 'thought-provoking'. *Mojo* ranked it 27th in their Best of 1999 list, describing it as 'audacious' and 'moving'.

There's no shortage of weak spots. The tracklist wavers between intentions, the lyrics occasionally feel underdeveloped and the music could have used abrasive, destabilising, melody-free guitar textures, adding unease and depth. Was keeps it smooth, safe and crisp, where a more unsettling undercurrent might have worked wonders. Yet, for those drawn to the hybrid tension between Iggy Pop and Jim Osterberg, who know something of the wreckage behind him and value an artist who breaks form while preserving integrity, it's a rewarding listen. For others, it might be one to skip.

He took *Avenue B* on the road throughout 1999, performing solo acoustic songs while seated onstage before shifting into full-band rock assaults. *The Guardian* described a London show as 'not engaging, not punk, not deep, just pitiful', until Iggy suddenly launched into the dance of the electrocuted ant to 'Raw Power' and 'Search And Destroy'. Four stars followed. Even praise for transcending punk rock itself. It showed how expectation, knee-jerk judgement and a lack of openness can shut down fresh perspectives. Iggy looks back on the detour with quiet satisfaction, though he would rarely accompany himself acoustically again.

Before the millennium turned, he quit smoking and gave up drugs for good. He left New York for Miami, cycled through a few relationships and was single once more. One afternoon, cruising through South Beach in his oversized cherry-red '68 Cadillac, he met Howard graduate and flight attendant Nina Alu outside a pizza shop. They started dating, moved in together in 2000 and married in 2008. She has travelled with him ever since, packs his bags, cooks his meals and pays his parking tickets. Speaking to *Rolling Stone* in 2003, Nina said:

> I love Iggy Pop, and I respect him, but I don't think I could live with him. But Jim, Jim is sweet and peaceful and romantic; when we're having dinner or making love, that's Jim, and sometimes I'll catch him just looking at the trees and birds. It's endearing and almost childlike, just the way he looks at the world with those big eyes.

The new century wasn't done with Iggy Pop. After the midlife crisis came renewed purpose: The Stooges reunited, and in 2010, they were inducted into the Rock and Roll Hall of Fame. Genre-hopping albums followed, including *Post Pop Depression*, which earned him a Grammy nomination. A Lifetime Achievement Award soon followed for his solo work. But above all, he kept hitting the stage – bare-chested, tireless, undiminished – drawing from a body of work few could match. As he summed it up in *Rolling Stone* in 2007: 'One thing about Iggy – he pays for Jim's life.'

'No Shit' (Pop)

A spoken monologue over a sombre string bed: intimate, stripped of posture. Iggy reflects on ageing and solitude, as books and home become his refuge and fleeting moments start to carry weight. He wants to go out on his own terms, balancing joy and dignity.

> Above all, I didn't want to take any more shit. Not from anybody.

That line could fuel a thousand punk anthems. But here, it's not spat out, not barked over a power chord. In place of bravado, there's resignation. It's not a revelation at 50. It's not even much of a text. It is the opening of *Avenue B*: unguarded, unsentimental, real.

'Nazi Girlfriend' (Pop)

Few things are off-limits in Iggy's lyrics, yet this isn't a song about a literal Nazi. The title implies discipline, severity, control, and shaping a cold power dynamic. A femme fatale, distant and unreadable, even to Iggy. So he sets out to examine her, already in a studying mood:

I wanna fuck her on the floor
Among my books of ancient lore
So I will make a full report
I got a Nazi girlfriend

Whatever grips him, it's not surface markers: not the high heels, not the blonde hair. It is 'the desert in her stare', suggesting mystery, something beyond the physical. Then he undercuts the setup with a line about her perfect butt, which does nothing to reinforce the intrigue or the portrait he sketches. Another hollow claim follows: 'She's independent, she's not dumb'. It states but reveals nothing. Before this, Iggy notes she is no longer the young 'colt' she once was, yet still elegant. Time has left its mark, but 'still she has ways to make me talk'. Unlike the flat claims around it, this line stirs something: it sharpens the title, faintly echoing the image of icy Nazis extracting confessions. More intriguingly, what does she draw out of him, and how? Before we find out, he circles back to the beginning. The act is done, clinically recorded: a full report on a woman who remains both alluring and enigmatic. But why draft a full report if you withhold what matters?

The musical backdrop is minimal: Iggy on acoustic, backed by bass, drifting keys, faintly mixed vibes and toms played with mallets. It suits the cold, submissive tone. But with a piece this bare, the lyrics need to carry the weight. They draw on Iggy's affair with Nico in 1969. Her father had served in the Wehrmacht, and in *Nico: The Life And Lies Of An Icon*, she is quoted calling herself 'a Nazi anarchist junkie', while her third album was titled *Desertshore*. These elements frame an intriguing premise: a man drawn to a woman he can't fully grasp, both fascinated and powerless. Yet 'Nazi Girlfriend' delivers more mood than substance. It lacks tension, evocative detail and lyrical sharpness. The needy opening line lands like an overshare, and what follows does little to deepen it. It hints at plenty, but leaves too much on the table.

'Avenue B' (Pop)
Avenue B was never the postcard version of New York. The East Village had a ragged edge: a place where anarchists, junkies and outcasts shared sidewalks. In the early 1950s, Charlie Parker lived at 151 Avenue B with Chan Berg, just across from Tompkins Square Park. From the 1960s onwards, the area became a flashpoint for squatters, punks and the city's discarded souls. Then came Christodora House: a former settlement house turned luxury condo, towering over a neighbourhood in turmoil. In 1988, the Tompkins Square riots broke out at its doorstep after a police-enforced curfew triggered days of street violence. Helicopters circled. Mounted police charged with batons. The

homeless, artists and radicals fought back, a battleground where 'gentrification' became the new war cry.

Nearly ten years later, in the winter of his 50th year, Iggy Pop sat alone inside Christodora, watching students from his window, their world moving along without him. His marriage was over. The city he once knew was slipping away, leaving him increasingly alienated. Avenue B wasn't just an address, it was a state of mind: cold, isolated, on the verge of collapse. 'I was living in New York and was incredibly exhausted and sad. I sat all night with my books and a black cloak in front of a candle and didn't go out at all', he recalled in 2001 in *Ox-Fanzine*. What started as a depressing acoustic song became something else entirely in the studio, reshaped by Lenny Castro's percussion and the laid-back touch of jazz-fusion trio Medeski, Martin & Wood, with Medeski's Hammond setting the tone. A poignant, bittersweet lament, opening with:

Rapper standing on the corner
Wrappers flying in the wind
Waitress up from Alabama
Can't believe the cold she's in

And me, I'm sitting in my castle
On the verge of a divorce
And if I haven't got a hassle
I'll create my own, of course

Still I gotta live with my feelings
But I know about science too
And fame and death and money
And what they do to you

It's a finely worded glimpse into the stuck soul of a man at the decade's end, staring down middle age. An ageing rock star sensing he needs a jolt: 'I am gonna need a miracle/Tonight on Avenue B'. That shift would come, and the contrast couldn't be starker: from East Village winter to what came next. The groove, a mere wisp of Latin in the percussion, the café haze and the faint promise of somewhere warmer: it's as if the song itself is already pointing him towards Miami.

'Miss Argentina' (Pop)

A vivid yet fragmented portrait of a woman full of contradictions. The muse is Neuquén native Alejandra Carrizo, whom Iggy began dating in 1993 on his second visit to Argentina. He paints her as both alluring and ruthless, confident yet uncertain, free but afraid. The power of the lyrics lies in their ambiguity, rhythm and sharp imagery, with a shifting tone between idealisation and destruction that gives them depth. He captures her fury in 'her voice is Spanish red', turns on a dime in 'She saves my spirit with a humanistic light/She's greedy, lazy and impossible to like' and distils her contradiction into 'Dripping blood with lots of style'. Iggy balances affection with disillusionment, drawn to 'a masterpiece without a frame'. But he is overwhelmed, buried alive 'in love and birth and jealousy and every emotion totally freed, screaming at once'. In the end, all that remains is the quiet realisation that 'Venus is a dangerous game'.

With Iggy on acoustic and his voice close and intimate, Cragin grounding it with low bass and Mullins stretching the tabla's tonal range, the arrangement is hypnotic and ominous. Together, they reflect her elegance, laced with danger. The rhythm section drops out at 2:46, leaving only Iggy and his guitar. It's a well-timed set-up – a familiar trick but effective: when the refrain returns at 3:28, the bass and percussion bring a subtle thrill. A slow burn rather than a grand statement, but one of *Avenue B*'s most compelling moments.

'Afraid To Get Close' (Pop)

The second of three monologues on the album that draw on fragments from Iggy's score to *The Brave*. The film's music supervisor had wanted someone to support Iggy, with a background in film scoring and roots in rock 'n' roll. Composer David Mansfield, who had toured with Dylan in the 1970s, was brought in, contributing violin and viola to Iggy's mostly keyboard-composed score. In *Rolling Stone* in 2023, Mansfield reflected:

> The score just kind of had endless overdubs and got quite amorphous. I don't even know what really came of it. Possibly what I'm credited on could be stuff that came out of those sessions because they were endless. And Iggy was great. He was really cheerful and humble and just wanted to do a good job.

Set against the cinematic sweeps, Iggy delivers a stream-of-consciousness piece, caught somewhere between confessional poetry and a late-night diary spasm. A cat sleeps on his pillow, while he drifts from isolation to self-loathing. At its core is fear: not just of getting close, but of what closeness might cost. 'I think the writing is eating up myself', he mutters before admitting he keeps 'hurting and recycling people over and over again'. It's bleak, tangled and feels more like catharsis than craft.

'Shakin' All Over' (Kidd)

Drum loops started in hip-hop, crept into the underground and alternative scene in the 1980s, and by the mid-1990s, pop and rock acts of all stripes were looping their way into the next millennium. Iggy's cover of the 1960 rock 'n' roll hit by Johnny Kidd & The Pirates credits renowned mix engineer

Andrew Scheps for 'loop stuff'. Mullins' drum part gets run through the machine, re-emerging as the backbone of this energetic, guitar-soaked but otherwise forgettable take. A simple thrill ride: boy meets girl, knees turn to jelly, the whole body signs up. For 1960, 'Shakin' All Over' was fairly bold, especially in the British pop scene. No explicit lyrics, but the way it maps out the body's response to desire ('Shivers down my backbone/I get the shakes in the thighbone') was noticeably more sensual than most hits of the time. Iggy sings it with relish, delivers it with gusto, and within the album's context, it could wink at his renewed bachelor status. But really, it's just another square on the Iggy Bingo Card: throw some levity in with a lighter rock song for good measure.

'Long Distance' (Pop)

Late 1997. Internet calls still ran on dial-up, piggybacking on phone lines with lag, dropouts and voices blurring like letters smudged in rain. Iggy too, not one to sweat a dollar per minute, was still at the mercy of the telephone. A lifeline holding a long-distance relationship together, like a candle flickering in Christodora House as the air grows thinner. On yet another 'cold grey wet December/Shitty, shitty day', the calls have become a ritual to fill a void. As the deepening light seeps into his mind, he's alone with the phone. Again. Dependent on the device just to hear a voice. 'Can this really be my choice?', he wonders. Reflective, sombre, lost in thought, he looks back on love, forward into patterns he cannot break. One fades into the next, a brief entanglement overwriting what came before, never quite taking hold. He dials a young woman, far away, who brightens him for a moment. Maybe this time, it will be different. The warmth on the other end is real, but fleeting. And then, the most unguarded line: 'I'm listening close, and I'm hoping/To learn love, but I don't know how'. The real distance isn't on the line: it's in him.

The writing is pared down and effective, and the music naturally shapes a sonic reflection of its meaning. The TR-808 and synth bass are fittingly used, cold and mechanical, like the distant phone connection itself, echoing empty patterns and the void. The hushed nocturne is carried by Iggy on acoustic and keyboards, with a touch of Was' subtle slide guitar rounding it out. Not one Iggy Pop will be remembered for, but for those who dismissed it the first time, it just might be worth another listen.

'Corruption' (Cragin, Kirst, Pop)

This commercially failed single is one hell of a song. Not just the standout of the album, but a track that might even hold its own among this book's highlights, if not for a weak outro that blunts its impact. But let's focus on its strengths, because this album could use some grit.

The production is pristine and wide, yet in your face with a ragged edge. Mullins' drumming is tight, dry and minimal. Each shot cracks like a whip, the rim occasionally splintering through. Cragin's bayou bassline burrows into your skull, deep and repetitive, crucial to the track's menace. Their groove lays the groundwork for Kirst and Marshall, who shift between dirty, drawn-out chords and chugging along with the pulse. Drifting through the mix, flanged 'whoosh' effects swoop from channel to channel, injecting uneasy motion. There's a churn to it, as if corruption itself rumbles forward like a train with no way off. Iggy kicks in with a series of potent images, sketching a downward spiral as its only destination: sorrow ('teardrops'), greed ('cash'), lost friendships and violence ('bash'). The sonic punctuations ('drip', 'chink', 'end' and 'wack') land on the first three beats of the bar, effectively hammering in an endless, grinding cycle. Iggy's snarling voice is fantastic. When he roars the fatalistic 'Corruptiooon!', his frustration and rage cut straight to the nerve and bone. The second killer verse hits:

From the tick tick tick of your time's up
To the yes yes yes of 'I'll sell'
From the fact fact fact of the soulless
To the pact pact pact with hell

The clock runs out. Power fades. Betrayal and surrender. Babies scream, the youth retch in disgust, the 'righteous' lie and Iggy himself is lost. Then, he bites down and delivers:

Order in the court
Decision to abort
The monkey wants to speak
So speak monkey speak

A pawn, insignificant and ridiculed. A defendant mockingly granted a voice, just for show. Iggy cast as the scapegoat in a divorce trial or a puppet in a corrupt system where the verdict is already written. An inner dialogue: the corrupted part of the self crushing what little resistance is left. The track bleeds, dripping with bile and spit.

'She Called Me Daddy' (Pop)

The idea of Iggy stripping back the rebel persona for honest, vulnerable ruminations on love and loss is compelling. Yet these intermezzos start to resemble barstool monologues no one asked for: a grizzled burnout, muttering about failed relationships, mostly to himself but loud enough to be overheard. Fine for one spin. But how often do you really want to hear it again?

The Brave score is too heavy for Iggy's spoken reflections, fitting better in *Platoon* or *The Pianist* than here. It gives his words an unearned gravitas, undermining them instead of complementing them. The result feels bloated with pretension when the power of his lyrics lies in their directness. Here, he dissects a breakup like a ruthless strategist, shutting her out move by move.

Although the women on the album were composites of real and imagined figures, this track seems grounded in the lead-up to his breakup with Alejandra, laced perhaps with a bitter aftertaste of his divorce from Suchi. First, he didn't hold her hand. Then, he didn't touch her in bed. Then, he wasn't tender with her upsets. 'And still, she didn't go'. He had to push. Now, 'this place is peaceful as a grave', but the silence is suffocating. 'I was always ashamed she read *Cosmopolitan*', he admits, followed by a quiet regret. A self-critical afterthought: 'What did she want that was so bad?' She had her own interests, her own dreams. All she wanted was love and security. 'She called me Daddy', he closes. A tender memory, or was it the nail in the coffin? When mentioning *Cosmopolitan*, Iggy barely holds back his laugh, unlike the others in the room. The decision to keep that take is a nice touch, lightening the weight of the piece and reminding us that a touch of humour is still one of the best remedies for heartache.

'I Felt The Luxury' (Martin, Medeski, Wood, Pop)
Over a backdrop that could have slipped onto Portishead's second album, Iggy delivers a lengthy monologue. The jazzy drum groove is laced with staccato Wurlitzer accents, streaks of Hammond and casual bass runs. His voice is mixed differently than on the other spoken-word tracks: drier, with a faint touch of distortion. Talking about the track and Medeski, Martin & Wood, Iggy recalled in *JazzTimes* in 2012:

> The most successful thing we did was 'I Felt The Luxury'. That was a spoken-word thing I had. I went to their loft, and the four of us sat in a circle, no bigger than where each guy could reach out and touch the other guy. We sat facing each other and played the song with a live vocal, live drums, the works … John was running the recording machine; he'd reach over. It was like that. It was a great experience.

Iggy charts a love affair's descent from passion to burden. A long-resisted temptress becomes an obsession: intoxicating at first, then suffocating. 'I felt the luxury of her' shifts from reverence to resentment as love turns to obligation. Frustration erupts into offhand cruelty. A hospital visit follows, yet no reckoning. In the end, detachment wins: 'So for now I'll say so long/I gotta go do wrong'. What once passed for indulgence fades into a lingering absence, shaded by denial, control and violence.

Iggy's writing here is vivid and ironic, with a sharp edge. 'She had curls like Delilah/And a smile like the sun' wraps betrayal in the guise of warmth, while 'I can piss on a grave while welcoming guests' is a coldly ironic paradox. 'Maybe she'll die/Maybe I'll cry' is tossed off with unnerving ease, striking in its indifference. This sharpness runs through his work, shaping a body of lyrics more layered than often acknowledged. Beneath the nonsense and mock-naivety, Iggy weaves madcap absurdity, wit and critique into something uniquely his. This book set out to shed light on his overlooked role as a lyricist. Sometimes, all it takes is looking past the preconceptions to find the reward.

'Español' (Kirst, Pop)

This track shows Iggy straddling two impulses while making the album. Rather than fully committing to a brooding record in the vein of Nick Cave's *The Boatman's Call* or the autumnal tone of Frank Sinatra's *September Of My Years*, he throws in another bit of silliness. With playful songs set against the heavier, more serious pieces, the album feels less a cohesive statement of style and subject, and more like two EPs stitched together.

Thematically, though, this track brushes up against 'Miss Argentina' and the Spanish-speaking woman in 'Motorcycle', fuelled by his growing command of Spanish. Iggy found warmth and a different way of living not just through the language, but through the culture and its more relaxed social codes. In 1999, he told *Bluecoat* it was 'a balance, an antidote' to the emptiness he felt, 'square and cold, kinda like a fuckin' Häagen-Dazs or something.' Cheekily singing about his self-reinvention as a gringo ditching his old life, picking up the language and drifting into love and freedom, he delivers a breezy, pseudo-adventurous throwaway wrapped in a bossa nova-rock hybrid. Iggy admitted in *JazzTimes* that it was the least successful of the three tracks with Medeski, Martin & Wood, adding: 'But I really like what they do.'

'Motorcycle' (Pop)

In this brief glimpse of fatal attraction, Iggy accompanies himself on acoustic guitar, singing softly over simple chords in G major. 'Motorcycle' captures a romance that vanishes on impact, an illusion already in ashes. She is speed and recklessness, and he knows how this ends: 'a scene I'm playin' in which I die'. She laughs, loves and uses him up. When Iggy sings 'And I'll never fall in love again', it isn't heartbreak, only resignation. The melody drifts, unhurried, like a story with an ending already written. No drama, no crescendo: another ride that didn't last. A bit like this song. It doesn't hurt the album, but it doesn't lift it either, just like the record itself did little to change Iggy's trajectory. Producer Was felt that the album deserved better. In a 2014 *Performing Songwriter* interview, he called it 'a brilliant way of documenting a combination of Jungian mid-life transition issues' and praised Iggy's courage:

> Making an album like this is a brave thing to do in rock 'n' roll. Record companies don't want you to do that; they want you to pretend you're 18. For Iggy, especially, to do something that was intimate when he's got this core audience who expects something else … that's really hard for him. That album didn't sell a lot, and people didn't respond to it the way I felt they should have.

Maybe that was the real fatalism at play: not the songs themselves but the way they were destined to slip by unnoticed.

'Facade' (Pop)

Those first ten seconds. Crank the volume, blast the acoustic 'Motorcycle' and then catch the contrasting, indestructible thrill of an electric guitar plugged straight into an amp. The no-upschmuck chords and Iggy's 'I'm New York scumbag tough' wouldn't feel out of place on Lou Reed's records from before and after *Avenue B*. Both *Set The Twilight Reeling* and *Ecstasy* are a midlife rocker's reflections on relationships, one lit with a bit more optimism than the other. Here, Iggy sings of disillusionment, emotional emptiness and the realisation that love and connection will eventually crumble when built on a facade. No surface can hide what lies beneath: loneliness, uncertainty and the inevitable reckoning with himself.

> So night is falling
> And I'm gettin' tired
> And it's time to get my slippers and books
> Got a sweater and glasses
> And something that passes
> For a way to get by in this world

Iggy Pop fans who wanted to preserve him as a wildman exhibit must have scratched their heads at this passage. But that was the whole point of *Avenue B*: breaking out of the cage. He had already hinted at it on his previous album and in interviews, but here he swings the door wide open. No eternal frenzy, no forced tough-guy stance. 'Facade' fits into a record where Iggy steps away from the rock 'n' roll myth and lays bare age and vulnerability. Two years after its release, Iggy reflected in *The Chronicle*:

> There were people who really appreciated the record because it was a serious piece and because it had some real content there and wrestled with more things. I think there are a lot of different circles of opinion. I think it was Fatboy Slim who mumbled something to me: 'Just rock, because that is what you should be doing.' And I thought, 'Well, you're a DJ. Shut up and have another drink. Who are you?' I think it was a good record. It was a real record.

And so, Iggy Pop reached the end of his 20th-century studio album output. True to his contradictory and occasionally self-sabotaging instincts, he kicked off the new millennium with his loudest and most ferocious record since *Raw Power*. He was ready for yet another round, one he'd call *Beat Em Up*. This wasn't the end.

B-sides & Deep Cuts

Beyond the albums covered in this book, Iggy put out plenty more: soundtrack cuts, one-off singles and, of course, B-sides. Then, there's the mountain of songs he covered live – enough to fill entire setlists with tracks that never saw a studio. In the 21st century, his guest appearances would snowball. By then, musicians had grasped the truth about his voice: you could hand him a drain cleaner manual, let him read it out loud and it would still give your record a jolt of character. This chapter doesn't claim to be the ultimate inventory of Iggy's lesser-known tracks, but as a further dive into his catalogue, it offers a selection of curiosities from his solo years up to 1999 that deserve a closer look.

Party Outtakes (1980)
'I'm The Original One' (Pop, Kral)
'It's My Life' (Atkins, D'Errico)
'Brakes On' (Pop, Kral)
Over the years, several *Party* outtakes surfaced, including on the unofficial 1984 LP *Liquor And Drugs*, released by the Iggy Pop UK Fan Club under the Leisure Records label. The classic bar-band strut 'I'm The Original One' has Iggy in a sandpapered voice, delivering more conviction than anything on the album. A fully formed cover of The Animals' 1965 independence anthem 'It's My Life' also emerged, its sentiment mildly ironic given Arista's interference during the sessions. 'Brakes On', also known as 'Don't Put The Brakes On Tonight' and sometimes played live in 1980, is an exhilarating punk rocker. It includes the line 'I hear a sheep bleat', which Kral, not a native speaker, misheard as something about a bleeding sheep until Iggy set him straight. Swapping in these tracks would've given the album the backbone it lacked. Then again, that wasn't a high bar to clear.

Ric Ocasek Sessions (1983)
'Fire Engine' (Pop, Jourgenson)
'Old Mule Skinner' (Pop)
'Warrior Tribe' (Pop)
In 1983, after *Zombie Birdhouse* flopped and with no label in sight, Iggy teamed up with Ric Ocasek, frontman of The Cars and a renowned producer, at Syncro Sound Studios in Boston. The sessions yielded three tracks, later surfacing in various mixes on bootlegs and compilations. Ministry's Al Jourgensen, who had opened for Iggy in Chicago four years earlier with his band Special Affect, contributed to the sessions and co-wrote 'Fire Engine'. A manic ride, it was first released as a limited-edition single in 2016, then remastered as the 'Ministry Mix' on *Rare Trax* (2022). Its sonic intensity and surreal imagery recall 'Run Like A Villain', but Iggy repeating the title over 40 times before devolving into beeping squawks takes its oddness even further.

In the delightfully odd 'Old Mule Skinner', Iggy draws on Jimmie Rodgers' 1930 country classic 'Mule Skinner Blues', even diving into Rodgers' signature yodel. Over galloping guitar and swirling synths, he reimagines the title's persona as a 'dirty, old, filthy mule skinner' and delivers the gloriously absurd litany: 'Mule skin boots, mule skin cloaks, mule skin rug, mule skin mule', before spiralling into a maddening chant.

'Warrior Tribe' is the standout. Iggy charges through visions of a 'warrior tribe far from home', 'with your bloodline watered down' and a 'warrior brain free at last'. Light on composition but heavy on atmosphere, this distortion-soaked guitarscape with reverb-laden drums strikes as an overlooked goth gem, hitting as hard as Iggy's most forceful solo tracks. A shame the sessions fizzled: they showed real promise.

Repo Man OST – Various (1984)
'Repo Man' (Pop)

The following year, Iggy's career was still in a rough spot when director Alex Cox visited his barren LA apartment and gave him carte blanche to record a song for *Repo Man*, now a cult classic. Grateful for the opportunity, Iggy assembled a supergroup: Steve Jones on guitar, with Blondie's Nigel Harrison and Clem Burke on bass and drums. After days of rehearsals, the initial approach was mostly scrapped at Cherokee Studios, where the band hammered out the song in 20 minutes and recorded it in two takes. Assistant engineer Chas Ferry recalled on Repomanfilm in 2007: 'Everyone looked at Iggy, who said: 'Well, I think that's good enough unless somebody has a problem with it.' Nobody did.'

Before recording his final vocals, Iggy's coke dealer arrived with two grams of fresh product. Iggy carved it into two Cuban cigar-sized lines and snorted them in a single, unflinching hit. He staggered to the mic, his clarity gone, reducing his vocals to garbled mush. After ten minutes of incoherence, engineer Bev Jones called it a night. The next day, clear-headed, Iggy swapped 'I'll make you eat till you vomit' for the surreal 'I'll turn you into a toadstool', completing a ferocious rock juggernaut with fierce vocals over Jones' semitone riffs. Satirising existential frustration, it mirrored the film's anarchic, absurdist themes:

I was a teenage dinosaur
Stoned and obsolete
I didn't get fucked and I didn't get kissed
I got so fucking pissed
Using my head for an ashtray
Now I'll tell you who I am
I'm a repo man

Weaving self-deprecation with stagnation, Iggy captures alienation not just from the world but from oneself. Cynicism and black humour permeate the fragmented imagery, summed up in his biting line, 'I'm looking for the joke with a microscope'. 'I always wanted to write a hot rod motorcycle badass guitar speed-and-death theme', Iggy shared in a *Criterion* feature in 2013, adding that it was inspired by 'The Wild Angels Theme' by Davie Allan & The Arrows. Positioned on the soundtrack alongside West Coast hardcore punk bands like Black Flag and Suicidal Tendencies, the track boosted Iggy's relevance. A fan favourite ever since, this blistering salvo remains essential to both the film and his career.

Steve Jones Sessions (1985)
'Purple Haze' (Hendrix)
'Family Affair' (Stone)
'When Dreaming Fails' (Pop, Jones)
'Warm Female' (Pop, Jones)

Of the demos Iggy and Jones recorded in 1985 in Hancock Park, LA, three made it onto *Blah-Blah-Blah* and one to *American Caesar*. The rest trickled out on scattered compilations.

Iggy's take on 'Purple Haze' bears little resemblance to Hendrix' original. The drum machine turns it into sludge, the groove drags its feet and Iggy comes up with 'I saw a movie about chainsaws/It's fun to live in America', yet it somehow lands as its own oddly likeable little mutt.

His version of Sly & The Family Stone's 'Family Affair' stays closer to the source. The demo was later smoothed into a cocktail-lounge shimmer by Bill Laswell, with overdubs likely added during the 1987 sessions for Ryuichi Sakamoto's *Neo Geo*. Bootsy Collins, who played on those sessions, is also credited on the track. In 2020, with the world in lockdown, Iggy marked his 73rd birthday by offering it as a free download on his website.

The wistful 'When Dreaming Fails' shows how much Iggy's singing had improved by 1985. The track hints at a mid-1980s sophist-pop ballad, shaded with new romantic melancholy and a touch of blues guitar. Jones re-recorded it with new lyrics as 'Raining In My Heart' for his 1987 solo debut *Mercy*.

'Warm Female' appears on some circulating releases as 'Woman Dream' and 'Warm Feeling', almost certainly both mislabelled, as Iggy, in full Billy Idol mode, clearly sings 'warm female'. With lines such as 'She got a blue guitar and a cigarette/And she knows everything in the alphabet', set to Jones' plodding chug-a-chug riff, it's no great loss that this one vanished without a fuss.

Neo Geo – Ryuichi Sakamoto (1987)
'Risky' (Sakamoto, Laswell, Pop)

Between *Blah-Blah-Blah* and *Instinct*, Iggy delivered a subdued yet standout vocal track for *Neo Geo*, co-produced by Laswell, who would go on to produce *Instinct* the following year. Boasting an ensemble that included Sly Dunbar, the refined song blends ambient textures with poetic melancholy.

Iggy stepped in at the last minute, after first choice Peter Gabriel fell through. His lyrics critique modern life's 'corporate dungeon' and the relentless pursuit of 'career, career, acquire, acquire', while contrasting it with a yearning for authenticity and connection, asking: 'What is life without a heart?'

Wes Craven's Shocker OST – Various (1989)
'Love Transfusion' (Cooper, Child, Matetski)
Originally written by Alice Cooper and Bon Jovi producer Desmond Child for Cooper's 1989 *Trash* album, 'Love Transfusion' didn't make the cut. Instead, it landed on the soundtrack for Wes Craven's supernatural slasher *Shocker* that same year. Opening with a harpsichord-like intro that bursts into late-1980s pop metal, the song seizes attention with its blaring saxophone. Strip away the vocals, and it's unmistakably a *Trash* B-side in disguise – no surprise, given it's built on a leftover backing track from those sessions. The wild card is Iggy, whose snarl delivers a theatrically morbid tale of love as lifeblood, with gothic metaphors framing the life-or-death struggle. This castoff may not have been *Trash*-worthy, but it fits *Shocker*'s over-the-top horror aesthetic like a bloody glove: campy, dated and not built to last.

Butt Town EP (1990)
'Foolish Dreams' (Pop)
'Beggar' (Pop)
'The Wind' (Pop)
'Think Alone' (Pop)
'L.A. Blues' (Pop)
A promotional-only CD, the *Butt Town EP* includes the full album version of the title track, plus 'When Dreaming Fails' and nine acoustic demos recorded in the lead-up to *Brick By Brick*. Alongside unplugged takes on 'Butt Town', 'Brick By Brick', 'I Am' and 'Starry Night' – all of which ended up on the album in some form – Iggy appears solo on guitar with 'Foolish Dreams', 'Beggar', 'The Wind', 'Think Alone' and 'L.A. Blues' (not the *Fun House* track). Call it a private rehearsal rather than a compelling singer-songwriter experience. His voice is warm and restrained, and you don't have to be a guitar virtuoso to sell a song. But the tracks themselves simply aren't strong. They lack melody, tension, variation and impact, and the lyrics are no better. Lines such as 'I need some wind/My friend, the wind/'Cause it lets me change', 'Want to be tasting the joy of life' and 'Your burn is in my heart/And I'm feeling too much' don't exactly knock you flat. If you heard this man strumming at a campfire with no idea who he was, you wouldn't guess he'd made much of a dent with his talents. The hastily strummed 'Think Alone' would later resurface, electrified and with new lyrics, as 'Love Bone' during Iggy's 1991 European summer festival sets. It also appeared on the 1995 Skydog release *Wake Up Suckers!!!*, with the acoustic set reissued as *Acoustics KO* in 2007. A few copies of the *Butt Town EP* came with photocopied

artwork, crudely marked in yellow highlighter. A fitting touch for such a scrappy release.

Red Hot + Blue – Various (1990)
'Well, Did You Evah!' (Porter)
Written by Cole Porter for his 1939 musical *DuBarry Was A Lady*, this song is best remembered for its 1956 film version in *High Society*, sung by Bing Crosby and Frank Sinatra. Decades later, the 1990 *Red Hot + Blue* release, a tribute to Porter's music, became the first in a series of all-star collaborative albums benefiting AIDS research. Iggy and Debbie Harry brought the song back to life with a knowingly over-the-top duet that reached number 42 in the UK.

Opening with an intro reminiscent of Bowie's 'Let's Dance', they breeze through it with carefree energy. Their chemistry captures the song's playful spirit in a way no straight-laced rendition could. They ad-lib, ham it up and revel in the absurd, with Iggy name-dropping Pia Zadora and Harry cheekily tweaking the lyrics ('What cocks!'). Together, they inject the banter with gleeful, possibly tipsy mischief before Harry wraps it up with a sharp 'piss off', sending Iggy into giggles. The song's infectious music video, directed by *Repo Man*'s Alex Cox, follows the wonderful duo through Manhattan. It features petting zoo animals, Harry burning lingerie, a nod to Iggy's 'Dog Food', a robbery and – why not – a flying dinosaur.

Freddy's Dead: The Final Nightmare OST – Various (1991)
'Why Was I Born (Freddy's Dead)' (Pop, Kirst)
Panned by critics upon release, the sixth instalment in the *A Nightmare On Elm Street* franchise features this track by Iggy, which plays over the film's best part: the end credits. Director Rachel Talalay, who had worked with Iggy on *Cry-Baby* the year before, invited him to compose a song for the film. 'Don't you fuck with me/'Cause I am bound for bloody glory, the world will know my murder story', Iggy growls in his dug-up zombie's voice. He shifts to a higher pitch in the second half as the track roars into fourth gear, only to lumber back to its weighty beat. Iggy signs off with the rhetorical, 'You really think Freddy's dead?' It breaks no ground and reinvents no wheel, but it delivers good old macho hard rock. Its nomination for a Golden Raspberry Award for Worst Original Song is as ridiculous as believing Freddy was truly dead after this flick.

Arizona Dream OST – Goran Bregović (1993)
'In The Deathcar' (Bregović, Pop)
'TV Screen' (Bregović, Pop)
'Get The Money' (Bregović, Pop)
'This Is A Film' (Bregović, Kusturica)
The soundtrack to the 1993 film *Arizona Dream*, directed by Emir Kusturica and featuring music by Goran Bregović, both of whom were born in Sarajevo,

captivated Iggy with its refreshingly different melodies. He lent his voice to four tracks, writing lyrics for three.

The memorable 'In The Deathcar' blends mariachi, Balkan folk, mandolins and an angelic choir, casting a cinematic desert glow. Over this evocative backdrop, Iggy delivers a restrained sung-spoken vocal, weaving a surreal road tale of life, death and the ride in between. He also slips in yet another weary nod to the corruption of a young woman through a few explicit lines. Taken with the song, he occasionally added it to the *American Caesar Tour* setlist.

'TV Screen' is Iggy Pop in all but composition, centring on his twisted relationship with television. It could have landed on *Blah-Blah-Blah*, if not for the Mark Knopfler-esque guitar break and Balkan chanting. Notably, Iggy's voice, tone and phrasing here closely resemble the singing style he would adopt on his 21st-century albums.

In 'Get The Money', Iggy injects satire into a jagged capitalist critique, covering a 1986 track by Bregović's band Bijelo Dugme. Brass and percussion jolt it to life, while his delivery grows increasingly deranged: 'It's kind of like a fortress, it's kind of like a tomb/Sitting with your money in a near dark room'. Wealth becomes a suffocating prison, its slimy, deceptive power likened to 'a toad', 'a frog' and 'a serpent'. Rather than offering clarity, Iggy throws absurdity in your face and makes chaos compelling.

In 'This Is A Film', a reworking of 'In The Deathcar', Iggy's dry delivery and Kusturica's minimalist lyrics shape a mock-philosophical discourse. 'This is a film about a man and a fish', he intones. Beneath the silliness lies a reflection on human complexity and a Zen-like embrace of simplicity, with the fish's muteness framed as transcendence, inspired by Platonov's *Chevengur*. Like 'In The Deathcar', its melody borrows heavily from Enrico Macias' 'Solenzara'. The theft didn't go unnoticed; Bregović was ordered to pay one million euros in damages for copyright infringement.

Wild America EP (1993)
'Credit Card' (Pop)
'Come Back Tomorrow' (Pop)
'My Angel' (Pop)
'Evil California' (Pop, Adams)

This EP was released ahead of *American Caesar*. In addition to the album cut 'Wild America', it features three outtakes from the *Caesar* sessions. Among them is 'Credit Card', a start-stop punk blitz, opening with the punchy simile: 'Life is like a parking meter, death is like an empty theater'. Driven by a gunfire drum assault and snarling guitars, Iggy wryly quips: 'Everything is really hard, if you ain't got that credit card'. Originally intended for the album, this gleeful ode to capitalist survival brims with unapologetic energy, though its similarity to 'Plastic & Concrete' likely kept it off the final tracklist.

In 'Come Back Tomorrow' a slightly distorted guitar motif rides over a sober mid-tempo beat as Iggy rallies both himself and us listeners to push through life's setbacks: 'I can return, because I swear to/Come back tomorrow, that's what you must do'. At over five minutes, the song overstays its welcome, lacking Iggy's usual snap and spark. Where he typically delivers a clever pun or a sharp, inventive line, this leans closer to an angsty teenager's first songwriting draft. On the bright side, 'Think of the waves, they come back tomorrow' is a bit of advice a shrink could have charged an hour for.

Early 1990s soft alt-rock simplicity defines 'My Angel', a laid-back ballad grounded in a measured rhythm, unhurried strummed guitar and Iggy's low, reflective vocals. It expresses quiet gratitude to an angelic presence. 'I'm a lucky guy just to breathe the air', he muses on a winter's day walk. A whistling outro adds a wistful touch, but while it's good to know Iggy has an angel, this song doesn't quite make it our concern.

'Evil California', a collaboration with Annie Ross & The Low Note Quintet, features mostly spoken vocals from Iggy, with Anthony Coleman on clavinet and synthesiser. A jazzy blues piece, it delves into California's darker corners, aligning with the themes of the 1993 film *Short Cuts*. In addition to its soundtrack, the track appears on the *Wild America* EP and the 'Beside You' single.

Iggy has often expressed admiration for jazz legends like Miles Davis, Jelly Roll Morton and Louis Armstrong. Speaking to *The Quietus* in 2010, he reflected on discovering Davis' *Sketches Of Spain* and *A Tribute To Jack Johnson*, albums that became lasting sources of inspiration. His voice proves remarkably suited to such a setting, and it would take until the turn of the millennium before he fully embraced this jazz-inflected side of himself.

'Beside You' Single (1993)

'Les Amants' (Ringer, Chichin, Pop)

The CD age threw a wrench into the tidy world of simple A- and B-side singles. 'Beside You' appeared in several versions, featuring an acoustic rendition of the song, live recordings of 'Home' and 'Louie Louie' from the 1993 Féile Festival in Ireland and a demo of 'Les Amants' by French art-pop duo Les Rita Mitsouko. On the latter, Iggy lets loose with improvised, raunchy lyrics that could have made Madonna blush, earning some copies a sticker warning of potentially offensive language. It's all set to a rolling 6/8 lilt, laced with the playful swirl of a fairground accordion.

Système D – Les Rita Mitsouko (1993)

'My Love Is Bad' (Ringer, Chichin)

An Iggy-less and therefore less raunchy version of 'Les Amants' appeared on Les Rita Mitsouko's 1993 album *Système D*. However, this album featured a second collaboration: the mysterious, smoky vignette 'My Love Is Bad'. Both Iggy and the duo's singer, Catherine Ringer, switch between French and

English in this push-pull art rock duet. The bilingual structure adds a dynamic layer, reflecting the interplay of perspectives within their volatile chemistry.

Back To The Streets: Celebrating The Music Of Don Covay – Various (1993)
'Sookie Sookie' (Covay, Cropper)
On this all-star tribute, Iggy tackles a 1966 R&B stomper, once covered by Steppenwolf. Backed by Paul Shaffer's band, his version is raucous and to the point: grinding guitar, jagged groove and a breathless, wild vocal delivered with delight. Caught between excitement and possession, his voice pushes the words forward with jittery urgency. The result is a loose, charging salute to Covay's rhythmic core: gritty, giddy, fully committed.

Fast Track To Nowhere – Various (1994)
'C'mon Everybody' (Cochran, Capehart)
First tackled by UFO, Humble Pie and The Sex Pistols, Iggy's take on Eddie Cochran's 1958 rock 'n' roll anthem appears on the soundtrack to the retro-styled *Rebel Highway* series. Backed by the *American Caesar* trio, he tears through a full-throttle rendition, all handclaps and bite. It's both a salute to one of his early heroes and a playful reminder of how instinctively rock 'n' roll pulses through his veins.

Pre-Naughty Little Doggie Sessions (1995)
'Goner' (Pop, Schermerhorn)
'I Don't Really Wanna Know' (Pop, Schermerhorn)
'Saturday Traffic' (Pop, Schermerhorn)
'Untouchable' (Pop, Schermerhorn)
'Blank' (Pop, Schermerhorn)
'Words' (Pop, Schermerhorn)
'Stragglers & Strays' (Pop, Schermerhorn)
Recorded as fast, off-the-cuff ideas between Pop and Schermerhorn in the latter's apartment, these acoustic outtakes offer a glimpse into Iggy's creative process. They are rough sketches, catching songs in their first flickers with the occasional flash of potential, likely to be of interest to completists only.

'Goner' is a lamenting draft, Iggy's unsteady vocals floating over an A minor progression, with a disarmingly melodic chorus. 'Goner in my heart, and all I touch is gold', he sings, though the meaning remains as elusive as the delivery.

'I Don't Really Wanna Know' leans into a bluesy vibe in A major, pairing loose strumming with minimal lyrics. With fragments like 'News is blowing my mind' and 'I don't really wanna know, too late to tell me so', Iggy drifts, almost naggingly, musing on his longing for love. A fleeting improvisation, passing by with just enough shape to suggest something unresolved.

Set in the same key, 'Saturday Traffic' shifts to a more pleasant tone, with handclaps, a shaker and casual hand drumming. The lyrics feel more developed, capturing the bustle of traffic as Iggy revels in watching the girls on the street while brushing off 'big shots' who fail to impress. The song ends with an earnest plea: 'I just need a real good friend, put one near me'.

'Untouchable' takes a darker turn, its sombre E-flat minor chords underscoring Iggy's self-destructive lament over an unattainable love. 'I've emptied myself out, and I've just caved in/I leave my blood at her feet, I destroy myself', he confesses, concluding with: 'That's when I find myself alone'.

'Blank' carries an affecting wistfulness in its small F-sharp major frame, with Iggy whistling between offbeat metaphors about 'going blank'. 'Like a divorcee with nothing in the bank/Like a beetle who's run over by a tank', he sings with traces of defeat and sadness. 'Leave me a marker by the highway/ Give me flowers and a rosary, baby, now I'm going blank' conveys a sorrowful resignation that leads him to question 'They say goodbye, but do they mean it?' With the right touch, this unassuming piece could have become a tender little treasure.

'Words' offers another heartfelt piece revealing potential. Over two interwoven guitars in G major, Iggy offers: 'Sha-la-la no no, it's not over, I love you more than words can say'. His confessions, 'If you can't go through, I feel I failed you' and 'My life's been spent in trance, in pursuit of romance', carry a bittersweet sincerity that lingers in their simplicity.

'Stragglers & Strays' offers an introspective A-flat major country vibe, evoking alienation and loss. Once one of them, Iggy watches the 'stragglers and strays on the six o'clock street', delivering the poignant line: 'All my good wishes go with you tonight, from the pain on your boots to the lips that you bite'. The outro's repeated plea, 'Show me someone who can give me some faith in this hard world', fades into quiet longing.

'Heart Is Saved' Single (1996)

'(Get Up I Feel Like Being A) Sex Machine' (Byrd, Brown, Lenhoff)

For Iggy, James Brown was never just a voice, but the whole package. He has openly credited Brown with shaping his electrifying stage presence and never hidden how deeply he admired him. On his BBC Radio 6 Music show, Iggy laid it on thick: 'Easily the most amazing person who has ever lived. I can die peacefully knowing that I was several times in the general physical presence of James Brown: Soul Brother Number One, Mr. Dynamite.' Included on the 1996 singles of the dusted-off 'Lust For Life' and that year's 'Heart Is Saved', the 'Godfather of Punk' pays homage to the 'Godfather of Soul' with this faithful cover, blending admiration and attitude. But did anyone really need it?

Shaken And Stirred: The David Arnold James Bond Project – Various (1997)

'We Have All The Time In The World' (Barry, David)

Under the direction of British film composer David Arnold, Iggy delivers a moving take on the 1969 James Bond theme made famous by Louis

Armstrong. His phrasing is restrained and elegant, marked by the quiet poise of a late-night lounge singer tiptoeing through the melody, lending the track a fragile sincerity. His Sinatra-esque croon is measured and unforced, hinting at the more introspective style he would embrace with quiet command in the years to come.

'Corruption' Single (1999)
'Hollywood Affair' (Pop, Depp)
'Rock Star Grave' (Pop)

Before his film career took off, Johnny Depp dreamed of rock stardom. He dropped out at 16, played in The Kids, and once opened for Iggy, one of his heroes. On *The Graham Norton Show* in 2016, Depp recalled heckling Iggy – 'Iggy Flop, Piggy Slop' – only for Iggy to lock eyes and deadpan: 'You little turd.' It became one of Depp's favourite memories.

Years later, they reunited for *Cry-Baby* and *Dead Man*, forging a lasting friendship. Besides composing the score for *The Brave*, Iggy appeared in the film as 'Man Eating Bird Leg'. In 1999, Depp joined in on 'Hollywood Affair', one of two B-sides to 'Corruption'. Calling it a song would be generous. It sounds like two friends, half-drunk on a couch, convinced they're making something profound, only to forget it by the time the ashtray's full. Depp wobbles through arpeggiated chords while Iggy sing-speaks half-baked thoughts about an affair with a stripper. Given the chance to record with a musical idol, this is what you come up with? They even performed it on the 1999 TV special *Nightclubbing In Paris*, where Depp also played guitar on 'Nightclubbing' alongside Vanessa Paradis and Chrissie Hynde.

Speaking of Paris: on the stronger 'Rock Star Grave', Iggy takes us to Père Lachaise, where he visits Jim Morrison's grave, strewn with 'cigarette butts and passport photos' and 'letters from children of love and problems'. It's 'the quietest crowd I've ever been in', he observes – a moment of secular awe that reads like a brush with living religion. Things heat up in the final minute, as a tempo shift and rolling drums intensify the mood around Iggy's ghoulish chant, 'It was a rock star grave'. The snappy track didn't make it onto *Avenue B*, likely for tonal reasons, but it could easily have replaced 'Shakin' All Over' or 'Español' without harm. If anything, it resonates with the reflection in 'No Shit', where Iggy considered the circumstances of his own death. As for 'Hollywood Affair', the footnote resurfaced on *Hollywood Goes Wild!*, a 2001 benefit album for the Wildlife Waystation. At least it served some purpose.

Appendix: Outliers

1989 'New York City', *Sonic Temple*, The Cult
1990 'Good Morning Amerika', *Hardware* OST, Simon Boswell
1990 *The Manson Family: An Opera*, John Moran
1991 'Give Peace A Chance', The Peace Choir
1991 'Dance Of The Freaks', *Border Drive-In Theatre*, Raindogs
1991 'Miniskirt Blues', *Look Mom No Head!*, The Cramps
1992 'Daw Da Hiya', *Kirya*, Ofra Haza
1992 'Black Sunshine', *La Sexorcisto: Devil Music Vol.1*, White Zombie
1993 'Sodom', *Wild America* CD EP, French version
1994 'Buckethead's Toy Store', *Giant Robot*, Buckethead
1994 'Post Office Buddy', *Giant Robot*, Buckethead
1996 'Hades, The God Of The Underworld', *Myth: Dreams Of The World*, Various
1996 'Back Door Man', *The Concert For The Rock And Roll Hall Of Fame*, Various
1997 'The Tell-Tale Heart', *Closed On Account Of Rabies: Poems And Tales Of Edgar Allan Poe*, Various
1998 'This World Is Something New To Me', *The Rugrats Movie* OST, Various
1999 'The Western Lands', *Hashisheen: The End Of Law*, Bill Laswell
1999 'A Quick Trip To Alamut', *Hashisheen: The End Of Law*, Bill Laswell
1999 'Aisha', *The Contino Sessions*, Death In Vegas

Inside The Circle: Touring, Writing And Recording With Iggy Pop

This volume in the *On Track...* series closes with a Q&A featuring American guitarist, composer and voiceover artist Eric Schermerhorn. As a musician, he has worked with David Bowie, Ric Ocasek, Richard Butler, The The, They Might Be Giants, Melissa Etheridge, P!nk, Christina Aguilera, Seal, Sheryl Crow and Lucinda Williams. Between 1992 and 1995, he was deeply embedded in Iggy Pop's creative circle, co-writing and performing on two albums and joining the live lineup during the *American Caesar Tour.*

Q: Your career and collaborations as a musician are remarkable by any standard. Let's pick up your story in 1991, when you joined Tin Machine as rhythm guitarist and backing vocalist for their second tour. How did that chapter begin for you?

A: I moved to New York City in 1990 at 29, working studio sessions and playing guitar wherever I could. It was a low point: I arrived with just a guitar and a couple of books. Reeves Gabrels was an old friend from Boston, and we shared a love for adventurous guitarists like Adrian Belew, Robert Fripp, Hendrix and Tommy Bolin. Early in 1991, Reeves asked me to audition for Tin Machine's *It's My Life Tour.* Of course, I said yes. I flew to LA for a weekend and had learned all the songs from the two albums because you never knew what David might ask you to play. I will never forget packing up my gear at the end of the audition when Reeves said, 'Eric, play 'Little Wing' for David.' So I did. I got the gig, and David said, 'I'm really looking forward to working with you', as he shook my hand. That was the moment my life changed.

I had been a huge fan of *Low* and *"Heroes"*. Those records had shaped my life. I told David that once, and he smiled and said they had changed his life, too. He was warm and generous, and his sense of humour was so dry and British. It was my first world tour: incredible travel, beautiful hotels and late-night meals. In every city, artists, musicians and actors would come out to meet David. I am forever grateful to Reeves for making that call. As for backing vocals, I am not a great singer, but my low register worked well, and David liked it, so I would sing below him on certain songs. That was pretty fun.

Q: After the Tin Machine tour ended, how did your connection with Iggy come about? Were you familiar with his music beforehand?

A: At the last gig at the Budokan in Tokyo, David asked me what I was planning to do next. That is just a great example of David looking out for people and being so generous. I mentioned Chrissie Hynde, who was looking for a guitarist at the time. A few weeks later, his manager called and said Chrissie wanted to meet me in London. We spent a day at her house, where she said David had recommended me, but she wanted a band based in London, and I had just moved to New York. About two weeks earlier, I had sent Iggy a cassette of me playing guitar. He lived in the East Village, and I was in Soho, so we were pretty close geographically. When I mentioned that, Chrissie got excited: 'No, you have to play with Iggy. He's the greatest!' So she let me off the hook, even though I love her and would have loved to work with her.

My first meeting with Iggy was at his place on Avenue B. I brought my acoustic because I figured if you can impress someone on acoustic with your sense of time, dynamics and feel, then you are in. In my apartment, I usually just played my Martin D-28, because if it sounds good on acoustic, it will probably sound great on electric. I think he was impressed that I brought an acoustic. Playing at low volume in an apartment with a distortion box can be goofy, especially if you are both used to walls of 4x12 cabinets thundering away.

I was familiar with *The Idiot*, *Lust For Life* and *Fun House*. I love *Fun House*. But I was definitely more of a Bowie fan. Iggy taught me a lot. We used to sit around his apartment and listen to Neu! and CAN, and if he was in a good mood, I would hear great stories about him, David and Eno in Berlin, which is still my favourite era of both of their careers. I always found it interesting walking around Berlin with David, and later with Iggy, because I would hear both sides of their stories about what that city meant to them before the Wall came down.

Q: Before recording *American Caesar*, you joined a four-piece band for a run of shows in Buenos Aires in August 1992. What was that experience like, and what memories from your time on the road with Iggy have stuck with you most?

A: Yes, that was the first gig, Argentina. We were there for a week, playing with The Ramones. As anyone who tours knows, staying in one place for more than two days is not good for your health or mental state. I have a few great memories of Iggy's advice before we went on stage. The best was him saying: 'Do not ever turn down. Do not ever turn your volume down. I do not care what anyone says, the sound man will tell you to turn down, the monitor guy will tell you to turn down, everyone will tell you to turn down. Do not fucking turn down.' I thought, okay, first time in my life a lead singer was not telling the guitar player to turn down.

He also warned us not to drink anything handed to us by other bands, especially the guys in The Ramones, because he thought they might spike the drinks with drugs. I think he still thought it was Detroit in 1969. I do love the guy, and he did look out for us, not like a dad but more like the older brother who had run away before you were born and you had only heard rumours about.

Generally, in all the Latin countries, be it Spain or South America, the spit flew like rain. I would stand back a few feet while Iggy walked forward with arms outstretched. He once told me I could also jump into the pit and stage-dive. Mmm, no thanks! They want you, not me! Another great memory is from a hot afternoon at a festival in Europe. We were waiting to go on: one hour late, two hours late, three hours late, just sitting backstage, drinking in the heat. I had these beautiful new suede pants on, and I was just about to get up and go to the bathroom when the promoter ran back and shouted: 'Now! Hurry! Get on stage now!' I told Iggy I needed to use the bathroom, and he looked at me with a deadpan expression and said, 'Just pee in your pants.' I laughed and ran to the toilet, but he was dead serious.

Q: How did the writing for*American Caesar* first take shape?

A: The songs for *American Caesar* started when I first met Iggy in May 1992 in New York City. Most of those were written on an acoustic guitar either at my apartment or his. I had a ton of music for him: riffs and songs, chord changes. The material happened right away, which was before we went to Argentina, and we kept working on it right up until we recorded the album in New Orleans that fall. I think one thing we had in common was not to sweat the small stuff. If it feels good, go with it. That doesn't work for everyone, but with him, it's all instinct. Work fast, and if it becomes laborious or tedious, move on. He was fearless and never afraid to fail. We never did more than two takes in the studio, and no fixes.

Q: What do you remember about the day-to-day rhythm of writing together?

A: Iggy was really easy to write with. You got an immediate reaction from him if he felt he could actually sing over the ideas. He was really fast with lyrics, and many times we got a bunch of songs done pretty quickly. I recorded everything on cassette and later on a half-inch 8-track reel-to-reel recorder in my apartment on Christopher Street. I remember one time we were looking out the window when Lou Reed walked by with Laurie Anderson. Iggy told me his relationship with Lou had never been very good. That's what I loved about him: he was always so honest and forthcoming about his relationships.

One time, we were playing guitar so loud that my elderly German neighbour started pounding on the door. Iggy answered it and apologised profusely. During the sessions, he would drink half a beer and smoke half a cigarette, and we'd usually work from 1 to 4 pm, then walk around the West Village and get dinner. I probably saw him every day, honestly, for two years. We went to crazy experimental theatre on Wooster Street, and he always called me to go see bands. I remember we saw My Bloody Valentine, and it blew our minds. Another great moment was going to a nice restaurant one night, red wine and steak, and within minutes, he was eating the steak with his hands and hitting on the waitress after half a glass of wine ... Imagine the old days?

Q: How did Iggy respond to your musical ideas in those early sessions?

A: Iggy was pretty primal and went with his gut as I would play ideas for him. He would really furrow his brow and listen critically, and take every idea very seriously, which I loved. He had that base approach to life, but he was also very studious and serious ... a real dichotomy, which I'm sure made a big impression on David. He would come by my apartment around noon-ish, and we would get to work. He had a very strong, concentrated work ethic, very focused. We were together to come up with material, hang out, listen to music and eat lunch, but only after we were productive. I liked that very much. It didn't drag on aimlessly for hours.

Q: Is there a song from that period that stands out to you, whether because of how it came together or how you look back on it now?

A: I think a place we met musically was in the drone music of Indian ragas and, for sure, gamelan music from Java and Bali. I worked in a record store in Boston in the early 1980s, where I was exposed on a daily basis to the most out, experimental and avant-garde music. So when Iggy played me the *New Grass* album by Albert Ayler, I got it. That was one of his favourites, along with Coltrane. As I mentioned, we also listened to a lot of Neu!. I think all that led to the relenting drone of 'Caesar' at the end of *American Caesar*. Now that was a good example of him and me jamming and of the stream-of-consciousness verbal riffing that really is his genius. I really like that track.

I also really like that little acoustic intro we did for 'Wild America'. I love how it leads into that bitchin' riff. I always wished we recorded 'Goner' with the band, but Iggy had the habit of second-guessing music as we got to the end of the process, if it didn't fit his idea of what his fans were possibly expecting from him. Nothing could be too sophisticated. That's what ultimately frustrated me and led me to quit in 1995. He was so angry and told me nobody ever quits him! Ha! I had to.

Q: Before you left, you recorded *Naughty Little Doggie* and co-wrote songs with Iggy once more. On a track like 'To Belong', did he follow a clear method, or did things evolve from song to song?

A: Most of the time, we recorded live with no overdubs because Iggy has no patience for overdubs or trickery. We recorded the track in LA, and I used my '57 Les Paul Junior into a Matchless Clubman amp. I did one overdub; that's usually all he would give anybody if you were lucky. You had to get it in the first take, so it's kind of a cool idea to have two solos going at once. It's been done before, but I also threw in some of those Indian bends that he loved. You have to remember he came up before the British Invasion and loved Link Wray, Chuck Berry and Johnny 'Guitar' Watson. Those guys recorded pretty much everything in one take, and if it wasn't feeling right, you simply moved on to the next song. That was really Iggy's method. If you play it too much, you'd beat it to death and it loses any of its original spark.

The other interesting thing with Iggy is that he picks the best take by his lead vocal, which could seem pretty wacky or unorthodox at first. But at the end of the day, who cares if the drummer's dragging or the guitar is out of tune? It really can and should be the vocal delivery. Why not?

Q: Was there something about Iggy's inner world or outlook that resonated with you beyond chords and riffs?

A: I remember on the road, he was reading *The History Of The Decline And Fall Of The Roman Empire*. Quite a tome. But then again, it was the *American Caesar Tour*! He would sit in the back of the bus reading, with his glasses down his nose like a college professor. The fact that he was selling his public persona as the runaway son of the nuclear A-bomb was one thing, but when he was just Jim O., a Midwestern guy hungry for knowledge and ideas, that made me love him even more. All my heroes in music had a thirst for art, film, history, poetry and more. They would synthesise it and make it their own. Iggy was a sponge, just like David.

Q: What are some of your favourite Iggy Pop songs? Whether you played them on stage or simply loved them as a fan.

A: I always liked 'Dum Dum Boys'. We used to do that in rehearsal. My favourite to play live was 'Loose'. But lyrically, 'Raw Power' kind of nails the nihilism and alienation of post-war American youth. Brilliant song. On another note, we did attempt a version of Joni Mitchell's 'Big Yellow Taxi'. We recorded it, but I've no idea what became of it. We all love Joni, and so does Iggy.

Q: Iggy has influenced generations of musicians and artists, from punk pioneers to modern icons. What stayed with you most about Iggy as an artist, looking back on your time together?

A: I think his genius is his very American ability to improvise and create on the spur of the moment. I saw him write lyrics and tap into this many times as I played guitar. He never overthought it, but just let it pour out and edited later if it needed that. Nothing with him was artifice, or put through an 'is this cool' filter. He really was always naked to the world. But he is also the guy who never gives up. He's on the ropes, getting beaten, but he always perseveres. He told me when I started playing with him that *Raw Power* was in the cut-out bin within weeks of its release. Nobody cared, and nobody wanted it. The Stooges never really toured. It was not glorious at all. There were no rehab centres back then. It was jail time to clean up. He is a survivor.

Selected Bibliography

Adams, R., *The Complete Iggy Pop* (Reynolds & Hearn, 2006)

Armstrong, K., *Absolute Beginner: Memoirs Of The World's Best Least-Known Guitarist* (Jawbone Press, 2023)

Ambrose, J., *Gimme Danger: The Story Of Iggy Pop* (Omnibus Press, 2004)

Buckley, D., *Strange Fascination* (Virgin Books, 1999)

Clerc, B., *David Bowie: All The Songs* (Running Press Adult, 2022)

Gold, J., *Total Chaos: The Story Of The Stooges, As Told By Iggy* (Third Man Books, 2016)

Gibbs, A., *Some Weird Sin: On Tour With Iggy Pop* (Helter Skelter Publishing, 1996)

Hagler, T., *We Could Be: Bowie And His Heroes* (Octopus Publishing Group, 2021)

Harry, D., *Face It* (HarperCollins, 2019)

Jones, D., *David Bowie: A Life* (Windmill Books, 2017)

Kent, N., *The Dark Stuff: Selected Writings On Rock Music* (DaCapo Press, 2002)

Matheu, R., *The Stooges: The Authorized And Illustrated Story* (Harry N. Abrams, 2009)

McCain, G., McNeil, L., *Please Kill Me: The Uncensored Oral History Of Punk* (Grove Press, 1996)

McKenna, K., *Book Of Changes* (Fantagraphics Books, 2001)

Nilsen, P., Sherman, D., *The Wild One: The True Story Of Iggy Pop* (Omnibus Press, 1988)

O'Leary, C., *Ashes To Ashes* (Repeater Books, 2019)

Pegg, N., *The Complete David Bowie* (Titan Books, 2016)

Rodgers, N., *Le Freak* (Spiegel & Grau, 2011)

Rüther, T., *Heroes: David Bowie And Berlin* (Reaktion Books, 2014)

Seabrook, T. J., *Bowie In Berlin: A New Career In A New Town* (Jawbone Press, 2008)

Soligny, J., *David Bowie Rainbowman 1967–1980* (Monoray, 2023)

Stein, C., *Under A Rock* (Corsair, 2024)

Thompson, D., *Your Pretty Face Is Going To Hell: The Dangerous Glitter Of David Bowie, Iggy Pop And Lou Reed* (Backbeat Books, 2009)

Trynka, P., *Iggy Pop: Open Up And Bleed: A Biography* (Little, Brown, 2007)

Trynka, P., *David Bowie: Starman* (Little, Brown, 2011)

Valentine, G., *New York Rocker: My Life In The Blank Generation With Blondie, Iggy Pop, And Others, 1974-1981* (Ecco, 2006)

Visconti, T., *The Autobiography: Bowie, Bolan And The Brooklyn Boy* (HarperCollins, 2007)

Wilcken, H., *Low* (Bloomsbury Academic, 2005)

Pop, I., *'Til Wrong Feels Right* (Viking, 2019)

In addition to the cited sources – including books, articles, interviews, podcasts, websites, videos and magazines – brief excerpts from song lyrics are quoted for the purposes of commentary, analysis and criticism, in accordance with the fair dealing provisions of UK copyright law. All sources have been cited with care and clarity.

Iggy And The Stooges – on track

Every album, every song

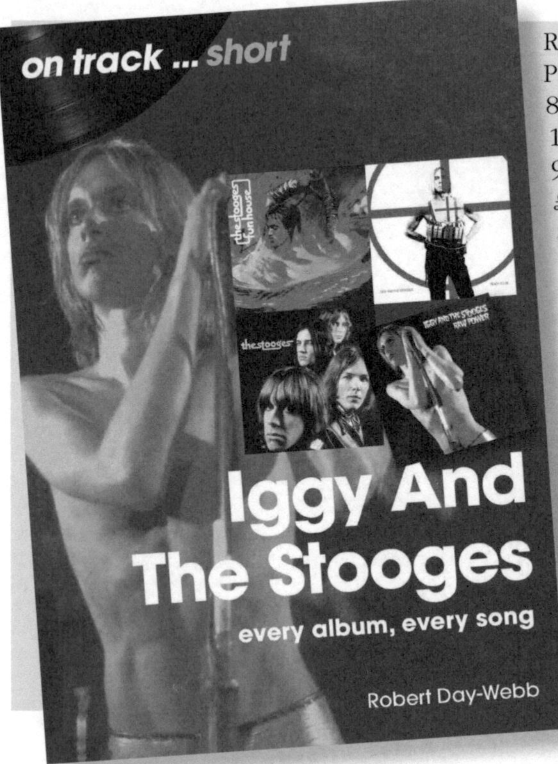

Robert Day Webb
Paperback
88 pages
18 colour photographs
978-1-78951-360-7
£14.99
$19.95

Every album by this notorious proto-punk band.

Exploding onto the late 1960s scene, The Stooges were a bunch of misfit Mid-Western delinquents, and their charismatic frontman, Iggy Pop, was a performer extraordinaire. Confrontational and theatrical, this maniacal entertainer was originally joined by the Asheton brothers, Ron and Scott, and Dave Alexander. This lineup delivered two albums of primal, brutal-sounding rock before fracturing. A fortuitous crossing of paths with David Bowie in 1971, however, led to a creative rebirth with a new guitarist in place, James Williamson and the delivery of a third album of nihilistic ferocity. However, the album bombed, leaving the band to limp on until 1974 before calling it a day.

In 2003, the original trio reunited, once again performing under The Stooges banner. The band toured extensively, finally achieving the respect and adulation that had been lacking the first time around. A new album appeared in 2007 before Ron's passing in 2009. Williamson subsequently returned, enabling the band to continue touring and recording before Scott Asheton passed away in 2014 and the band folded.

The Stooges' music has influenced countless other bands, artists and genres, and this book examines the band's enduring musical legacy by taking a fully comprehensive look at all the group's officially recorded output.

Iggy And The Stooges – on stage
1967-1974

Per Nilsen
Paperback
176 pages
43 colour photographs
978-1-78951-101-6
£16.99
$24.95

Every gig that the band performed in the first phase of their existence.

The Stooges were formed in 1967 in Ann Arbor, outside Detroit. They created three classic albums between 1969 and 1973, *The Stooges*, *Fun House* and *Raw Power*. Despite a lack of commercial success, the band attracted a small, devoted following and laid a musical foundation that would influence generations of artists. The Stooges' performances were unpredictable, with Iggy inciting audiences to react and making it impossible for them to remain complacent. The singer was passionate, fearless and, at times, expressed himself in genuinely frightening ways, performing self-mutilation, stage dives, crowd surfing and rushing into crowds to confront hecklers or spontaneously interacting with audience members who struck his fancy. Iggy tore down the barriers that traditionally existed between audience and performer, forcing the audience to become part of the overall performance. But by 1974, Iggy was locked into an orbit of self-annihilation and drug abuse that ultimately led to the demise of the band in February 1974.

This book explores in depth all the concerts The Stooges played from 1967 to 1974, bringing the live experience to life through eyewitness accounts, press reports and other source materials to present an unprecedented account of the Stooges' performances during this period.

Also available from Sonicbond

On Track series

AC/DC – Chris Sutton 978-1-78952-307-2
Allman Brothers Band – Andrew Wild 978-1-78952-252-5
Tori Amos – Lisa Torem 978-1-78952-142-9
Aphex Twin – Beau Waddell 978-1-78952-267-9
Asia – Peter Braidis 978-1-78952-099-6
Badfinger – Robert Day-Webb 978-1-878952-176-4
Barclay James Harvest – Keith and Monica Domone 978-1-78952-067-5
Beck – Arthur Lizie 978-1-78952-258-7
The Beat, General Public, Fine Young Cannibals – Steve Parry 978-1-78952-274-7
The Beatles 1962-1996 – Alberto Bravin and Andrew Wild 978-1-78952-355-3
The Beatles Solo 1969-1980 – Andrew Wild 978-1-78952-030-9
Blue Oyster Cult – Jacob Holm-Lupo 978-1-78952-007-1
Blur – Matt Bishop 978-178952-164-1
Marc Bolan and T.Rex – Peter Gallagher 978-1-78952-124-5
David Bowie 1964 to 1982 – Carl Ewens 978-1-78952-324-9
David Bowie 1963 to 2016 – Don Klees 978-1-78952-351-5
Kate Bush – Bill Thomas 978-1-78952-097-2
The Byrds – Andy McArthur 978-1-78952-280-8
Camel – Hamish Kuzminski 978-1-78952-040-8
Captain Beefheart – Opher Goodwin 978-1-78952-235-8
Caravan – Andy Boot 978-1-78952-127-6
Cardiacs – Eric Benac 978-1-78952-131-3
Wendy Carlos – Mark Marrington 978-1-78952-331-7
The Carpenters – Paul Tornbohm 978-1-78952-301-0
Nick Cave and The Bad Seeds – Dominic Sanderson 978-1-78952-240-2
Eric Clapton Solo – Andrew Wild 978-1-78952-141-2
The Clash (revised edition) – Nick Assirati 978-1-78952-325-6
Elvis Costello and The Attractions – Georg Purvis 978-1-78952-129-0
Crosby, Stills and Nash – Andrew Wild 978-1-78952-039-2
Creedence Clearwater Revival – Tony Thompson 978-1-78952-237-2
Crowded House – Jon Magidsohn 978-1-78952-292-1
The Damned – Morgan Brown 978-1-78952-136-8
David Bowie 1964 to 1982 – Carl Ewens 978-1-78952-324-9
David Bowie 1964 to 1982 – Carl Ewens 978-1-78952-324-9
Deep Purple and Rainbow 1968-79 – Steve Pilkington 978-1-78952-002-6
Deep Purple from 1984 – Phil Kafcaloudes 978-1-78952-354-6
Depeche Mode – Brian J. Robb 978-1-78952-277-8
Dire Straits – Andrew Wild 978-1-78952-044-6
The Divine Comedy – Alan Draper 978-1-78952-308-9
The Doors – Tony Thompson 978-1-78952-137-5
Dream Theater – Jordan Blum 978-1-78952-050-7

Bob Dylan 1962-1970 – Opher Goodwin 978-1-78952-275-2
Eagles – John Van der Kiste 978-1-78952-260-0
Earth, Wind and Fire – Bud Wilkins 978-1-78952-272-3
Electric Light Orchestra – Barry Delve 978-1-78952-152-8
Emerson Lake and Palmer – Mike Goode 978-1-78952-000-2
Fairport Convention – Kevan Furbank 978-1-78952-051-4
Peter Gabriel – Graeme Scarfe 978-1-78952-138-2
Genesis – Stuart MacFarlane 978-1-78952-005-7
Gentle Giant – Gary Steel 978-1-78952-058-3
Gong – Kevan Furbank 978-1-78952-082-8
Green Day – William E. Spevack 978-1-78952-261-7
Steve Hackett – Geoffrey Feakes 978-1-78952-098-9
Hall and Oates – Ian Abrahams 978-1-78952-167-2
Peter Hammill – Richard Rees Jones 978-1-78952-163-4
Roy Harper – Opher Goodwin 978-1-78952-130-6
Hawkwind (new edition) – Duncan Harris 978-1-78952-290-7
Jimi Hendrix – Emma Stott 978-1-78952-175-7
The Hollies – Andrew Darlington 978-1-78952-159-7
Horslips – Richard James 978-1-78952-263-1
The Human League and The Sheffield Scene – Andrew Darlington 978-1-78952-186-3
Humble Pie –Robert Day-Webb 978-1-78952-2761
Ian Hunter – G. Mick Smith 978-1-78952-304-1
The Incredible String Band – Tim Moon 978-1-78952-107-8
INXS – Manny Grillo 978-1-78952-302-7
Iron Maiden – Steve Pilkington 978-1-78952-061-3
Joe Jackson – Richard James 978-1-78952-189-4
The Jam – Stan Jeffries 978-1-78952-299-0
Jefferson Airplane – Richard Butterworth 978-1-78952-143-6
Jethro Tull – Jordan Blum 978-1-78952-016-3
J. Geils Band – James Romag 978-1-78952-332-4
Elton John in the 1970s – Peter Kearns 978-1-78952-034-7
Billy Joel – Lisa Torem 978-1-78952-183-2
Journey – Doug Thornton 978-1-78952-337-9
Judas Priest – John Tucker 978-1-78952-018-7
Kansas – Kevin Cummings 978-1-78952-057-6
Killing Joke – Nic Ransome 978-1-78952-273-0
The Kinks – Martin Hutchinson 978-1-78952-172-6
Korn – Matt Karpe 978-1-78952-153-5
Led Zeppelin – Steve Pilkington 978-1-78952-151-1
Level 42 – Matt Philips 978-1-78952-102-3
Little Feat – Georg Purvis – 978-1-78952-168-9
Magnum – Matthew Taylor – 978-1-78952-286-0

Aimee Mann – Jez Rowden 978-1-78952-036-1
Ralph McTell – Paul O. Jenkins 978-1-78952-294-5
Metallica – Barry Wood 978-1-78952-269-3
Joni Mitchell – Peter Kearns 978-1-78952-081-1
The Moody Blues – Geoffrey Feakes 978-1-78952-042-2
Motorhead – Duncan Harris 978-1-78952-173-3
Nektar – Scott Meze – 978-1-78952-257-0
New Order – Dennis Remmer – 978-1-78952-249-5
Nightwish – Simon McMurdo – 978-1-78952-270-9
Nirvana – William E. Spevack 978-1-78952-318-8
Laura Nyro – Philip Ward 978-1-78952-182-5
Oasis – Andrew Rooney 978-1-78952-300-3
Phil Ochs – Opher Goodwin 978-1-78952-326-3
Mike Oldfield – Ryan Yard 978-1-78952-060-6
Opeth – Jordan Blum 978-1-78-952-166-5
Pearl Jam – Ben L. Connor 978-1-78952-188-7
Tom Petty – Richard James 978-1-78952-128-3
Pink Floyd – Richard Butterworth 978-1-78952-242-6
The Police – Pete Braidis 978-1-78952-158-0
Porcupine Tree (Revised Edition) – Nick Holmes 978-1-78952-346-1
Procol Harum – Scott Meze 978-1-78952-315-7
Queen – Andrew Wild 978-1-78952-003-3
Radiohead – William Allen 978-1-78952-149-8
Gerry Rafferty – John Van der Kiste 978-1-78952-349-2
Rancid – Paul Matts 978-1-78952-187-0
Lou Reed 1972-1986 – Ethan Roy 978-1-78952-283-9
Renaissance – David Detmer 978-1-78952-062-0
REO Speedwagon – Jim Romag 978-1-78952-262-4
The Rolling Stones 1963-80 – Steve Pilkington 978-1-78952-017-0
Linda Ronstadt 1969-1989 – Daryl O. Lawrence 987-1-78952-293-8
Roxy Music – Michael Kulikowski 978-1-78952-335-5
Rush 1973 to 1982 – Richard James 978-1-78952-338-6
Sensational Alex Harvey Band – Peter Gallagher 978-1-7952-289-1
The Small Faces and The Faces – Andrew Darlington 978-1-78952-316-4
The Smashing Pumpkins – Matt Karpe 978-1-7952-291-4
The Smiths and Morrissey – Tommy Gunnarsson 978-1-78952-140-5
Soft Machine – Scott Meze 978-1078952-271-6
Sparks 1969-1979 – Chris Sutton 978-1-78952-279-2
Spirit – Rev. Keith A. Gordon – 978-1-78952- 248-8
Stackridge – Alan Draper 978-1-78952-232-7
Status Quo the Frantic Four Years – Richard James 978-1-78952-160-3
Steely Dan – Jez Rowden 978-1-78952-043-9

The Stranglers – Martin Hutchinson 978-1-78952-323-2
Talk Talk – Gary Steel 978-1-78952-284-6
Talking Heads – David Starkey 978-178952-353-9
Tears For Fears – Paul Clark – 978-178952-238-9
Thin Lizzy – Graeme Stroud 978-1-78952-064-4
Tool – Matt Karpe 978-1-78952-234-1
Toto – Jacob Holm-Lupo 978-1-78952-019-4
U2 – Eoghan Lyng 978-1-78952-078-1
UFO – Richard James 978-1-78952-073-6
Ultravox – Brian J. Robb 978-1-78952-330-0
Van Der Graaf Generator – Dan Coffey 978-1-78952-031-6
Van Halen – Morgan Brown – 9781-78952-256-3
Suzanne Vega – Lisa Torem 978-1-78952-281-5
Jack White And The White Stripes – Ben L. Connor 978-1-78952-303-4
The Who – Geoffrey Feakes 978-1-78952-076-7
Roy Wood and the Move – James R Turner 978-1-78952-008-8
Yes (new edition) – Stephen Lambe 978-1-78952-282-2
Neil Young 1963 to 1970 – Opher Goodwin 978-1-78952-298-3
Frank Zappa 1966 to 1979 – Eric Benac 978-1-78952-033-0
Warren Zevon – Peter Gallagher 978-1-78952-170-2
The Zombies – Emma Stott 978-1-78952-297-6
10CC – Peter Kearns 978-1-78952-054-5

Decades Series

The Bee Gees in the 1960s – Andrew Mon Hughes et al 978-1-78952-148-1
The Bee Gees in the 1970s – Andrew Mon Hughes et al 978-1-78952-179-5
Black Sabbath in the 1970s – Chris Sutton 978-1-78952-171-9
Britpop – Peter Richard Adams and Matt Pooler 978-1-78952-169-6
Phil Collins in the 1980s – Andrew Wild 978-1-78952-185-6
Alice CoOpher in the 1970s – Chris Sutton 978-1-78952-104-7
Alice CoOpher in the 1980s – Chris Sutton 978-1-78952-259-4
Curved Air in the 1970s – Laura Shenton 978-1-78952-069-9
Donovan in the 1960s – Jeff Fitzgerald 978-1-78952-233-4
Bob Dylan in the 1980s – Don Klees 978-1-78952-157-3
Brian Eno in the 1970s – Gary Parsons 978-1-78952-239-6
Faith No More in the 1990s – Matt Karpe 978-1-78952-250-1
Fleetwood Mac in the 1970s – Andrew Wild 978-1-78952-105-4
Fleetwood Mac in the 1980s – Don Klees 978-178952-254-9
Focus in the 1970s – Stephen Lambe 978-1-78952-079-8
Free and Bad Company in the 1970s – John Van der Kiste 978-1-78952-178-8
Genesis in the 1970s – Bill Thomas 978178952-146-7
George Harrison in the 1970s – Eoghan Lyng 978-1-78952-174-0

Kiss in the 1970s – Peter Gallagher 978-1-78952-246-4
Manfred Mann's Earth Band in the 1970s – John Van der Kiste 978178952-243-3
Marillion in the 1980s – Nathaniel Webb 978-1-78952-065-1
Van Morrison in the 1970s – Peter Childs – 978-1-78952-241-9
Mott the Hoople & Ian Hunter in the 1970s – John Van der Kiste 978-1-78-952-162-7
Pink Floyd In The 1970s – Georg Purvis 978-1-78952-072-9
Suzi Quatro in the 1970s – Darren Johnson 978-1-78952-236-5
Queen in the 1970s – James Griffiths 978-1-78952-265-5
Roxy Music in the 1970s – Dave Thompson 978-1-78952-180-1
Slade in the 1970s – Darren Johnson 978-1-78952-268-6
Status Quo in the 1980s – Greg Harper 978-1-78952-244-0
Tangerine Dream in the 1970s – Stephen Palmer 978-1-78952-161-0
The Sweet in the 1970s – Darren Johnson 978-1-78952-139-9
Uriah Heep in the 1970s – Steve Pilkington 978-1-78952-103-0
Van der Graaf Generator in the 1970s – Steve Pilkington 978-1-78952-245-7
Rick Wakeman in the 1970s – Geoffrey Feakes 978-1-78952-264-8
Yes in the 1980s – Stephen Lambe with David Watkinson 978-1-78952-125-2

Rock Classics Series

90125 by Yes – Stephen Lambe 978-1-78952-329-4
Bat Out Of Hell by Meatloaf – Geoffrey Feakes 978-1-78952-320-1
Bringing It All Back Home by Bob Dylan – Opher Goodwin 978-1-78952-314-0
Californication by Red Hot Chili Peppers - Matt Karpe 978-1-78952-348-5
Crime Of The Century by Supertramp – Steve Pilkington 978-1-78952-327-0
The Dreaming by Kate Bush – Peter Kearns 978-1-78952-341-6
Let It Bleed by The Rolling Stones – John Van der Kiste 978-1-78952-309-6
Pawn Hearts by Van Der Graaf Generator – Paolo Carnelli 978-1-78952-357-7
Purple Rain by Prince – Matt Karpe 978-1-78952-322-5
The White Album by The Beatles – Opher Goodwin 978-1-78952-333-1

On Screen Series

Carry On… – Stephen Lambe 978-1-78952-004-0
David Cronenberg – Patrick Chapman 978-1-78952-071-2
Doctor Who: The David Tennant Years – Jamie Hailstone 978-1-78952-066-8
James Bond – Andrew Wild 978-1-78952-010-1
Monty Python – Steve Pilkington 978-1-78952-047-7
Seinfeld Seasons 1 to 5 – Stephen Lambe 978-1-78952-012-5

Other Books

1967: A Year In Psychedelic Rock 978-1-78952-155-9
1970: A Year In Rock – John Van der Kiste 978-1-78952-147-4
1972: The Year Progressive Rock Ruled The World – Kevan Furbank 978-1-78952-288-4
1973: The Golden Year of Progressive Rock 978-1-78952-165-8

Eric Clapton Sessions – Andrew Wild 978-1-78952-177-1

Dark Horse Records – Aaron Badgley 978-1-78952-287-7

Derek Taylor: For Your Radioactive Children – Andrew Darlington 978-1-78952-038-5

Ghosts – Journeys To Post-Pop – Matthew Restall 978-1-78952-334-8

The Golden Age of Easy Listening – Derek Taylor 978-1-78952-285-3

The Golden Road: The Recording History of The Grateful Dead – John Kilbride 978-1-78952-156-6

Hoggin' The Page – Groudhogs The Classic Years – Martyn Hanson 978-1-78952-343-0

Iggy and The Stooges On Stage 1967-1974 – Per Nilsen 978-1-78952-101-6

Jon Anderson and the Warriors – the Road to Yes – David Watkinson 978-1-78952-059-0

Magic: The David Paton Story – David Paton 978-1-78952-266-2

Misty: The Music of Johnny Mathis – Jakob Baekgaard 978-1-78952-247-1

Musical Guide To Red By King Crimson – Andrew Keeling 978-1-78952-321-8

Nu Metal: A Definitive Guide – Matt Karpe 978-1-78952-063-7

Philip Lynott – Renegade – Alan Byrne 978-1-78952-339-3

Remembering Live Aid – Andrew Wild 978-1-78952-328-7

Thank You For The Days - Fans Of The Kinks Share 60 Years of Stories – Ed. Chris Kocher 978-1-78952-342-3

The Sonicbond On Track Sampler – 978-1-78952-190-0

The Sonicbond Progressive Rock Sampler (Ebook only) – 978-1-78952-056-9

Tommy Bolin: In and Out of Deep Purple – Laura Shenton 978-1-78952-070-5

Maximum Darkness – Deke Leonard 978-1-78952-048-4

The Twang Dynasty – Deke Leonard 978-1-78952-049-1

... and many more to come!

Would you like to write for Sonicbond Publishing?

At Sonicbond Publishing we are always on the look-out for authors, particularly for our two main series:

On Track. Mixing fact with in depth analysis, the On Track series examines the work of a particular musical artist or group. All genres are considered from easy listening and jazz to 60s soul to 90s pop, via rock and metal.

On Screen. This series looks at the world of film and television. Subjects considered include directors, actors and writers, as well as entire television and film series. As with the On Track series, we balance fact with analysis.

While professional writing experience would, of course, be an advantage the most important qualification is to have real enthusiasm and knowledge of your subject. First-time authors are welcomed, but the ability to write well in English is essential.

Sonicbond Publishing has distribution throughout Europe and North America, and all books are also published in E-book form. Authors will be paid a royalty based on sales of their book.

Further details are available from www.sonicbondpublishing.co.uk. To contact us, complete the contact form there or email info@sonicbondpublishing.co.uk